Rewriting modernity

Once again for Joan and Kate,

this time also for James,

and in memory of Arthur and Peggy Attwell.

Rewriting Modernity

Studies in black South African literary history

David Attwell

Ohio University Press Athens

University of KwaZulu-Natal Press

Ohio University Press, Athens, Ohio 45701
www.ohio.edu/oupress

First published in South Africa in 2005 by
University of KwaZulu-Natal Press
Private Bag X01, Scottsville, 3209
South Africa
Email: books@ukzn.ac.za
Website: www.ukznpress.co.za

First published in the United States of America in 2006 by
Ohio University Press
The Ridges
Athens, Ohio 45701

ISBN 0-8214-1711-8 (hc)
EAN 978-8214-1711-9 (hc)
ISBN 0-8214-1712-6 (pb)
EAN 978-0-8214-1712-6 (pb)

Printed in the United States of America

Ohio University Press books are printed on acid-free paper ∞ ™

15 14 13 12 11 10 09 08 07 06 5 4 3 2 1

Editor: Andrea Nattrass
Cover image: *Young Boy Reading* by Gerard Sekoto. Courtesy of the Gerard Sekoto Foundation.
Typesetter: Patricia Comrie
Indexer: Cynthia Harvey-Williams

Library of Congress Cataloging-in-Publication Data available

Contents

Acknowledgements

There are too many influential conversations to enumerate here fully, but certain rites of passage deserve mention. Homi Bhabha's 1993 seminar on 'Modernity and its Discontents' at the School of Criticism and Theory proved to be crucial in providing a seed-bed for many of the obsessions that would develop into this book. Then, I must acknowledge my colleagues at the University of Natal in Pietermaritzburg, particularly Anton van der Hoven and Jill Arnott, who shared with me the precipitous launch of a postgraduate programme in postcolonial studies long before the appearance of any of the primers. Let's allow ourselves the observation that judging by the field's subsequent ascendancy, history has borne us out; furthermore, we were right to try to give it a local habitation, relevance, and language. I hope I have done some justice to that early, nervous commitment and its inspiration. A number of friends, former colleagues and students in Pietermaritzburg shared in these conversations, notably Colin Gardner and Catherine Woeber. Liz Gunner has been a fine friend and intellectual companion since her return to South Africa; to her I owe a great deal.

I would also like to acknowledge friends and hosts in several quarters who have given me food, lodgings, comradeship and inspiration in exchange for a few ideas: Barbara Harlow and my friend and mentor at the University of Texas at Austin, Bernth Lindfors; Tim Cribb and Ato Quayson in the African Studies Centre and the seminar on Commonwealth and international literature in Cambridge; Robert Young and Elleke Boehmer at their postcolonial seminar in Oxford; Rita Barnard and the Latitudes interest group at the University of Pennsylvania; the English department at the University of Natal in Durban and the 'Postcolonialism/South Africa' research group of the National Research Foundation led by Michael Chapman. My thanks also go to Gunilla Lindberg-Wada and the symposium on studying transnational literary history held at the University of Stockholm, in November 2004, under the auspices of the project on Literature and Literary History in Global Contexts, funded by the Swedish Research Council.

The following people generously read parts of the manuscript and shared their insights with me: Michelle Adler, David Alvarez, Don Beale, Margaret Daymond, Pier Paolo Frassinelli, Gerald Gaylard, Lucy Graham, Stephen Gray, Stefan Helgesson, Isabel Hofmeyr, Rosemary Jolly, Adrian Koopman, David Maughan Brown, Es'kia Mphahlele, Phiwe Mkhize, Sarah Nuttall, Mark Sanders, Cheryl Stobie, Michael Titlestad, and David Watson. Derek Attridge, Duncan Brown, John Coetzee, Kai Easton, and Zakes Mda did me the immense honour of responding to the entire manuscript. Phaswane Mpe had begun to do so shortly before his untimely passing. Carol Saccaggi assisted in the preparation of the bibliography. Of course, all the usual caveats apply: not even the combined acumen of these formidable readers could save me entirely from my failures of observation or judgement.

It was a particular pleasure to work with the whole team at the UKZN Press: Glenn Cowley, Andrea Nattrass, Trish Comrie, Sally Hines, Adele Branch, and Leslie Goddard.

I am grateful to the Research Office of the University of Natal, the Faculty of Humanities at the University of the Witwatersrand, and the Ernest Oppenheimer Memorial Trust for material support at various stages in the completion of this project.

EARLIER VERSIONS OF a number of chapters have appeared in various publications. The editors and publishers are gratefully acknowledged for their permission to reprint this material here. Chapter 1: *Critical Inquiry* 23, 3 (Spring 1997): 557–77 © University of Chicago; Chapter 2: *Journal of Southern African Studies* 25, 2 (June 1999): 267–85 © *Journal of Southern African Studies*, http://www.tandf.co.uk; Chapter 3: *Research in African Literatures* 33, 1 (Spring 2002): 94–119 © Indiana University Press; Chapter 4: *African Writers and Their Readers: Essays*

Preface

The interregnum years in South Africa, together with the rise of Black Consciousness, no doubt represent the point of origin of this book, for that is when it dawned on white students of my generation that we had to immerse ourselves in the literature of the continent of our birth. Thus began a journey into African literatures which is as compelling now as it was when it began for me in the 1970s, even as the years of postcolonialism and globalisation continue to unfold.

More recently there have been other provocations. By the early 1990s the debate over the place of postcolonial studies in South Africa was firmly under way: should we reject this foreign, homogenising, ahistoricising, 'poststructuralist' import, or should we reinvent it on our own terms and thereby re-enter an international conversation in which we could not fully participate during apartheid? I took the latter view, believing that in any event, there is no single position that defines the field and that its very incoherence is enabling. This book is an attempt to give substance to that position by connecting international currents in postcolonial studies with local literature. I do so, in part, by borrowing and adapting the idea of transculturation that comes into postcolonial studies from Cuba where it was developed by Fernando Ortiz. This is not 'high theory', by any means, but perhaps it is sufficient theory – theory sufficient to the purpose of signposting a particular kind of engagement with the cultural archive.

The prominent forms of postcolonial theory have all devolved from particular historical situations: the chemistry between metropolitan French philosophy and the Algerian war of liberation (perhaps most prominently); Australasian and Canadian settler-colonialism; the South Asian response to British imperialism; the Black Atlantic; African cultural nationalism. South Africa and its expressive culture have seldom been raised to the level of theory on anything like a comparable basis. This book is not wholly an attempt to address this lacuna, but the problem is certainly part of its *raison d'être.* If I am cautious on this point, the reason is that my overriding concern is not to fuel the academic polemic around postcolonial theory but to engage with the record of South Africa's literary-intellectual and cultural life.

The relationship between theory and empirical interpretation is surely a reciprocal one. Thus far, however, postcolonial theory has not sat comfortably with South African realities. The proposal I offer in *Rewriting modernity* is that we might begin again at the inductive end, in order to gauge what new emphases within theory might be developed from studying the cultural transactions of the past. In time, South Africa might come to be recognised as a particular theoretical space with its own genealogy amongst the formations of postcolonial theory.

Introduction

Your cattle are gone, my countrymen!
Go rescue them! Go rescue them!
Leave the breechloader alone
And turn to the pen.
Take paper and ink,
For that is your shield.
Your rights are going!
So pick up your pen.
Load it, load it with ink.
Sit on a chair.
Repair not to Hoho.
But fire with your pen.[1]
I.W.W. Citashe (1882)

The African people's cultural struggle is as important as the political because both aim at establishing the African as a free citizen.[2]
H.I.E. Dhlomo (1944)

Two general historical conditions mark South Africa's post-colonial history. The first is its textured postcoloniality, by which I mean that it combines the histories of settler-colonial and migrant communities with that of indigenous societies. In a sense, it combines in one country the histories of Australia and Nigeria (if I may be allowed to simplify their histories for a moment). In other words, in South Africa the heirs of settler and autochthonous cultures have gone together down the road of finding a common basis for their political, economic, and cultural life, following the departure of the colonial and later the imperial powers – first the Dutch, then the British – which so decisively shaped the region.

Further layers of complexity need to be added to this picture. Within settler-colonialism, South Africa went through a phase of racist republicanism that all but severed the country's tenuous connections to Europe. Everyone has been marked by this process, some more brutally than others, but even English-speaking South Africans were taken further away from their English apron-strings by Afrikaner republicanism than their anglophone cousins in other countries of the British Commonwealth. Indeed, for much of apartheid, South Africa defined itself outside of traditional colonial ties altogether, seeking dubious alliances almost randomly, that is, with similarly totalitarian regimes wherever it could find them. Then, within the traditions of anti-colonial resistance, the struggle for self-government and democracy was defined, predominantly, as secular and non-racial, a situation that still puzzles sympathisers familiar with the more ethnically driven movements for decolonisation around the world.

We can pass over these and other discriminations, however, in order to capture the general state of affairs: in a formal sense, South Africa became postcolonial in 1910 with the Act of Union, which brought about a coalition of Boer and Briton in a white colonial state; a bleaker kind of postcoloniality emerged with the triumph of Afrikaner republicanism after the National Party's electoral victory in 1948; then, mercifully, in 1994, a constitutionally-defined, non-racial democracy was established, representing the point at which these various postcolonial histories have begun to coalesce, at least in the legal sense.

The second general historical condition governing South Africa's postcoloniality is its experience of an aggressive modernisation, a situation that began with the industrialisation of the mining industry in the 1880s. Industrialisation, together with administrative centralisation (based on models of colonial control over frontier conditions earlier in the century) created the conditions for the emergence of a pan-ethnic, non-racial movement for decolonisation (in the discourse of the African National Congress [ANC], the 'national democratic revolution') in predominantly urban and polylingual environments. Far from being the natural expression of residual, primordial ethnic loyalties, apartheid itself was a quixotic attempt by the National Party to put this process of social confluence into reverse, essentially an attempt to police intimacy (nowhere was this more apparent than in its absurd laws attempting to regulate sexual contact between the races). In the long run, the ANC was able to capitalise on this aggressive modernity, by harnessing its centripetal forces and using them against the white minority rule that had tried unsuccessfully to balkanise the country. Even in its most gentlemanly phase, when it was ruled by a patrician group of missionary converts, the ANC was always in possession of a code of modernity that would eventually be triumphant. It always held the right cards.

Rewriting modernity tells a part of that story, the part that can be traced in black literature, beginning with the foundations of an indigenised local print culture in the nineteenth century, then continuing down to the experimentation with modernism by contemporary authors. It is a study of key episodes in South Africa's literary and cultural history which argues, essentially, that the use by black intellectuals of print culture has been crucial to their establishing themselves as modern subjects, in direct opposition to the identities ascribed to them in colonial and apartheid ideology.

MODERNITY IS, of course, a notoriously baggy concept that resists narrow definition. In the chapters that follow, the writers themselves guide me as they articulate their experience of modernity. We will find that the writers of each generation encounter it in a slightly different guise. If a simple philosophical definition were available, it might be that modernity is the currently governing concept of what it means to be a subject of history. It refers not only to technology and the emergence of an administered and industrialised society, but also to that fluid but powerful system of ideas that we inherit from the bourgeois revolutions of Europe in the late eighteenth century – ideas such as autonomy, personhood, rights, and citizenship.

These concepts, or their equivalents, could be found in many cultures, of both the past and the present, where they exist independently of the Western paradigm. Nevertheless, the *force* with which the post-Enlightenment ideoscape has been imposed on the world over the last 300 years or so has ensured that most societies have now come to define themselves in relation to it. In South Africa, modernity is inextricably linked to colonialism. Its promises were offered selectively to settler-colonials and their heirs and to a handful of indigenous people trained as an élite. Under apartheid, this history was exacerbated, with masses of people being proletarianised and (in a contradictory move) confined to pre-modern, and less than fully human, forms of social life and identity. For most black South Africans, therefore, modernity's promises have been fraudulent and inherently contradictory.

And yet it would seem that those promises, at least in their ideal forms, are so desirable that people cannot do without them. Following Gayatri Spivak, who speaks of this as *catachresis*, Robert Young points to 'a space that the postcolonial does not want, but has no option, to inhabit'. It is the space, says Young, of 'history itself' (2001, 418). There is no escape clause from the encounter with modernity, unless one is to accept isolation or eccentricity. In practice, however, people facing this situation make a continual effort to translate modernity's promises into their own situations and histories, indeed to de-Europeanise them wherever possible. Intellectuals play an important role in this enterprise, and it is one of the key historical functions of black South African writing culture to translate modernity into South African terms, to wrest its promises away from corruption and give them new meaning. This process, I argue, entails acts of *transculturation*, the end-products of which can be seen in the vibrant syncretism of the country's post-apartheid democracy.

SOME READERS WILL ask, why emphasise writing and print at the expense of orality, which is so much a feature of South African expressive culture? I do not ignore the oral. Indeed, the oral and the written are often in a symbiosis, notably where writers who move easily between the two seek to develop the resources of oral culture into a written literature. Nevertheless, I make no apology for concentrating on writing, because whilst oral culture is a renewable and living reality, writing's relationship with modernity is peculiarly intimate. Citashe's famous poem, quoted in the epigraph at the start of this Introduction, illustrates this. By the latter half of the nineteenth century, Citashe could say that what we have come to call the 'primary resistance' of the battlefield had to give way to the 'secondary resistance' of the pen – the 'pen' representing several aspects of colonial modernity such as education, Christianity, journalism, and political organisation. The poem, together with H.I.E. Dhlomo's remark, defines the parameters of this study: black South African writing has from its inception sought to appropriate intrusive technologies and ideas, displace their corrupted imaginaries, and create spaces in which intellectuals and their communities can reconstruct themselves as 'free citizens'.

This approach to the literary-intellectual history of South Africa is the product of several considerations, some historiographical, some theoretical, and some personal. The personal ones I touched on in the Preface; here, I will refer to the other, perhaps more important ones. The historiographical argument, stated simply, is that the post-apartheid situation requires a fresh approach to the cultural archive (using this term loosely, to refer to the accumulated expressive culture of the past). Some might disagree. In fact, in the Preface to his recently re-issued *Southern African Literatures* Michael Chapman argues that the end of apartheid does not have to entail a change in the way we relate to the cultural past, given the persistence of inequality both locally and on a global scale (2003, xii). Although I would share this political vision, I am not sure that it translates into the kind of reading that is most useful to the present – or particularly, that it answers to the hunger of current students, who seem more than ever to want to locate themselves as global citizens. Chapter 1, on what I have called 'the transculturation of enlightenment', was originally written in 1994, in the months preceding and following South Africa's first democratic elections.[3] It was an attempt to understand the historical-cultural roots of what I was witnessing in those remarkable events. The rest of the chapters, written at various times during the past ten years, were conceived in the wake of that first chapter, each of them an attempt to explore a particular episode in the same intellectual history.

TO STRAY BRIEFLY into the context: to be sure, constitutional democracy has not produced economic and social emancipation for the majority of the country's people. I could speak of the ways in which the country's celebrated pluralism masks the racist legacies of the past; of a deepening or a 'normalisation' of class division as the middle class becomes more black than white; of official corruption; of faltering public institutions – in education, and in the health sector in the context of an HIV/AIDS pandemic; of capital being directed to arms procurement rather than social development, and so on. Despite all this, the basic *script* of the present, both in constitutional and moral terms, has fundamentally changed. It is a script that could be described broadly as an attempt to re-enter the world of global modernity. The historical moment in which this re-entry is being attempted gives it an air of promise but also of danger. The prevailing paradigm, in the sense of a dominant political economy, is obviously liberal or transnational capitalism. The question for South Africa, then, is how to translate the terms of this current version of modernity in ways that are appropriate to our history and the country's political, social and cultural priorities. The nature of that 'translation' is the key, since the challenge is whether the country will repeat liberal capitalism's manifest failures or whether it will translate its underlying promises appropriately.

Such is the game that the post-apartheid settlement is playing. The fact that *South Africa*, with its particular history, is playing it means that the project involves more than simply another exercise in making liberal capitalism work. It also involves attempts to reconstruct modernity's longer history, beginning with the Enlightenment and some of its humanitarian if rather disabled discourses, into a vision for the future that involves, amongst other things, re-connecting the nation-state with a culture of rights and a truly participatory democracy. It means, in other words, localising and actualising what have become compromised universal principles.

What we call this vision is not especially important, but terms such as 'critical humanism', and a 'new cosmopolitanism', have been proposed.[4] I am conscious in writing such phrases how naïve, hubristic, even how anachronistic they seem. Nevertheless, the South African experiment continues to interest and give hope to many who see little grounds for optimism in the current geopolitical scene. John Comaroff puts this well in a recent interview:

> . . . the reason that South Africa grabbed so much world attention in the mid-1990s is because it represented a heroic, hopeful effort to build a modernist nation-state under postmodern postmortem conditions; at just the time, that is, when the contradictions of modernity were becoming inescapable. As Eric Hobsbawm said then, the African National Congress was perhaps the last great Euronationalist movement. He was not altogether wrong. (Bhabha and Comaroff 2002, 32)

In different terms, Homi Bhabha speaks of a 'time-lag' in postcolonial forms of modernity, a being-out-of-step with 'world' history that operates, paradoxically, as a source of potential renewal (1994, 239–41). Such may be the South African case at present. But to return to the purposes of this book: they do *not* involve attempts to sell or celebrate the country's cause nor its currently dominant political culture. Rather, I seek to take the discourse of the times into the field of literary and cultural studies, and literary history in particular. The task is to explore the cultural history of the present.

THERE HAS BEEN a lively literary-historiographical debate in the last ten years in South Africa, but it is one that has been conducted in other terms than these. Predominantly (perhaps predictably) the main issue has been how to cope with difference, how to write a properly comparative and integrated literary history that takes into account the multiplicity of languages, traditions, and social spaces in the country, the kind of literary history which could overcome the cultural balkanisation that was apartheid's peculiar *forte.* In fact, long before 1994, literary historians such as Albert Gérard looked forward to a time when such a history would be possible (for example, Gérard 1986, 172). Despite several bold developments, however, most notably Michael Chapman's encyclopaedic achievement, there has been surprisingly little consensus as to what a national-cultural literary history *should* look like, and even less about whether such a history would actually be desirable.[5] If the desire for an integrated literary history was a result, or perhaps a reflex, of pressures to overcome the divisive legacy of colonialism and apartheid, then it is already apparent from the sheer irresolution of the debate that the post-apartheid order is exercising our imaginations in ways that fall outside of the previously dominant paradigm. The axis has been shifting, I would suggest, from an emphasis on how to write about sameness and difference, to writing about *temporality*, which is to say, writing about one's place in history or one's place in the present and future.

Another reflex of the past has been the tendency to assume that there is really only one story to be told about black literary and cultural history: that of the growth of political consciousness. That narrative runs something like this: from a phase of mission-educated intellectual colonisation from around the mid-nineteenth century to 1912 (when the Congress movement was established), through the compromised civility of the 'New African' generation in the 1930s and 40s, to the lively, avowedly urban *Drum* era, to the period of exile in the 1960s, to the resurgent militancy of Black Consciousness in the 1970s, and then the trade union poetry of the 1980s (which seemed to bring together racial and class mobilisation), the narrative is one of a developing and finally triumphant political confidence. To be sure, this is not a story that I would want to treat lightly. Indeed, to suggest anything other than that writers have always seen their roles as being about promoting the liberation of their people would be to traduce some of the most important claims of the literature. There are, however, problems with this narrative. Firstly, it is uni-dimensional. The literary history shows writers engaged at a number of different levels, not only the obviously political. There are debates about religion, especially the place of black people in Christianity, about the value of written narrative as a way of claiming historical continuity and identity, about art and aesthetics, about gender, about the value of tradition, about the meaning of selfhood, about the social imagination. The chapters in this book will show that what we might be tempted to call the 'civil turn' in post-apartheid society, has actually been with us all along – what is different is simply our capacity to recognise what has always been part of a complex picture.

Secondly, the stringent narrative produces condescension about all but the most recent of texts. In fact, *all* texts, in this account, but especially those of the early years, are allegorised as representing particular phases or periods, like coloured pins on a battle-map. And yet this is supposed to be an intellectual history: the qualities of these texts, their construction, the journeys inscribed in them, have been obscured in the teleology. It is time to get beyond the survey to a more heuristic mode of reading, one that takes the literature's ideas more seriously. If we attend closely to the writing, I suggest we will find that resistance is a many-faceted thing, that it has been with us from the beginning, though sometimes at sub-textual levels that require careful excavation. This approach requires some adjustment to traditional forms of criticism; it certainly requires a suspension of strong evaluations, whether aesthetic or political, until something like an adequate contextualisation has been achieved.

Zakes Mda, arguably the most innovative of writers on the post-apartheid scene, has also suggested (albeit in the language of fiction) that the present demands a fresh approach to the cultural archive. In his recent novel, *The Heart of Redness* (2000), Mda shifts the emphasis away from the question of resistance to apartheid, narrowly conceived, and gives his fiction a wholly new orientation: the relationships that black humanity in South Africa has forged with modernity at various points in its history. Mda does this by de-privileging the struggle years as those of 'the middle generations', foregrounding instead two moments of seminal importance, indeed of crisis: namely, 1857, the year of the Cattle-Killing Movement in the Eastern Cape, and 1994, the year in which formal democracy was achieved. The significance of these dates is that they are moments of choice. As such, they represent high water marks in the definition of agency in black historical and cultural identity. In the Cattle Killing, the argument had to do with the efficacy of local knowledge-systems as they try to come to terms with the challenge of settler-colonialism. In 1994, the argument is related, circling around the choice in post-apartheid national development between isolationism or a version of indigenised modernity. Mda presents two historical narratives, each with its own cast of characters, in parallel, with continuities being suggested between the events and characters. In Mda's novel, therefore, what I have called the axis of temporality has moved to the centre of attention, the result being that it enables both a clearer dramatisation of choice and agency within each generation, and a richer and wider canvas for the work of the post-apartheid interpretative artist. It is that perspective that I wish to carry over into literary-cultural criticism.

FROM THE HISTORIOGRAPHICAL issues, let me turn to questions of theory, by which I mean transnational currents in reading and their relationship to South African literature. The international field most relevant to South African writing, the one enjoying extraordinary, if rather problematic, prominence at present, is postcolonial studies. In the last decade, one of globalisation's effects on academic life has been to bring together, under the sign of the 'postcolonial', developments in literary and cultural studies that had been emerging fairly contentedly in their own spheres for several decades.

Postcolonial theory in the form of colonial discourse analysis has been at work in what we might conveniently call the First World, emphasising the discourses of Empire at first, but gradually (and belatedly) discovering writing from outside the United Kingdom and the United States (to use the Modern Languages Association's compromised description). The legacy of the hermeneutics of suspicion, which was the dominant mode in relation to imperial discourses led, however, to an unsteady treatment of non-metropolitan writing, with suspicions of a new hegemony emanating from cultures positioned on the so-called 'periphery'. Edward Said's *Orientalism* (1978) was obviously one of the founding texts of this tradition, although his later *Culture and Imperialism* (1993) avoided the dangers I have mentioned.

Emanating from a different sphere altogether, though sometimes confused with colonial discourse analysis, is the brand of what I would call comparative literary history that grew out of 'the new E/english literatures' and then Commonwealth literary studies. Canadians and especially Australians have led the way in theorising this version of postcolonial studies (rather than postcolonial theory, now) for reasons we might speculate about. From the South African corner of the world, it sometimes seems that a largely white anglophone comparative-literary-historical practice has developed as an expression of the confident maturation of settler-colonial cultures, emphasising themes of displacement and the creation of new identities. South African historical conditions, however, have rendered that project suspect. *The Empire Writes Back* (Ashcroft, Griffiths and Tiffin 1989) is obviously the ur-text in this tradition, followed by a substantial literature complicating and enriching the positions taken in it. Behind this brand of postcolonial studies, I should also mention, lies the work of generations of postcolonial writers in whose work many later developments in postcolonial studies were anticipated.

Then, to continue with the southern African perspective, the 'postcolonial' could also be linked to a loose tradition of nation-based studies, developing initially on an axis between the United Kingdom and various African universities, then increasingly involving scholars in the United States, very much as the critical apparatus that accompanied the Heinemann African Writers Series. The contiguous presence of this critical literature as a paradigm of a new version of 'English studies' was strong in South Africa for several decades, so much so that it exercised a stronger influence than any version of 'Commonwealth Literature' more broadly might have done. The reason for this was no doubt the fascination of South Africans living under apartheid for the literary culture of a continent that had already passed through a political decolonisation. However, the distribution of 'theory' across these contexts has been uneven and incongruous. Given the literary-intellectual feuding in this country in the years of late apartheid, predominantly between liberalism and Marxism (and to a lesser extent also between liberalism and feminism and poststructuralism), postcolonial African criticism, at least until the 1980s, seemed remarkably orthodox and peculiarly 'metropolitan' in its assumptions. It found various kinds of organicism, empiricism and formalism taken over from British and American new criticism to be extremely congenial in the dominant ethos of cultural nationalism.[6]

These communities of reading – and there were others, but I have mentioned the most visible ones – were, and are, by no means hermetic, and my description is reductive. The underlying point, however, is that the 'postcolonial' has brought together critical lineages and the intuitions that accompany them in relationships that are bound to be fractious. Given the various contexts and histories involved, what is surprising is that so many participants seem to expect the field to deliver consensus. For how else can we explain such a welter of rebarbative accusations and counter-accusations over whose political card remains cleanest, a situation that detracts from the empirical work that needs to be done? Over the last few years, resistance to early assumptions that descriptions emanating from one kind of expressive culture can be generalised to others seems to have produced a general retreat, so that if there is consensus now, it is that the exigencies of the local and the historically specific need to be respected. There is no longer the chimera of a 'postcolonial position', nor even a common theoretical tradition.[7] However, while there may not be consensus, the globalisation of academic culture has seen to it that resources and ideas are being more widely distributed, with the result that what the 'postcolonial' does do is name those institutional spaces in which people from widely different backgrounds and situations can at least talk to one another. In the globalised spaces of postcolonial studies, it seems possible to begin the comparative mapping rather more carefully now, given the increasing agreement on the need to respect local specificity.

It is in this light, then, that I come back to the question of the place of South African writing on the postcolonial scene. We must acknowledge straight away that white writing of the stature of J.M. Coetzee's and Nadine Gordimer's – the country's two Nobel laureates in literature – does receive far more attention than any other writing, whether by black writers or in other languages than English. This is, of course, a pattern that has prevailed in surreptitiously anglocentric versions of postcolonial studies for some time. We have to note that despite a few exceptions – the lively interest in Bessie Head, for example – there is a general pattern involving the isolation of black writing from international communities of readers, and when we consider the full range of black writing culture, which goes beyond the strictly literary, not to mention the proximity of writing and oral culture, the isolation looks even deeper.

There are reasons other than the failings of anglocentrism for this isolation. Historical pressures have produced an image of South Africa's black writing as a literature *in extremis*. The common view is that a uniquely troubled history has brought out a literature whose necessarily *restricted* function has been to support political liberation.[8] This is a reductive reading but an inescapable one, for in some of its moments, black writing has indeed been produced out of the experience of brutality – torture, massacre, assassination, lifelong confinement. To the extent that this is indeed its provenance, we might note Achille Mbembe's astute comment when he says, from 'Martin Luther King to Nelson Mandela, [the] absolute authority granted to death or the possibility of death, this *otherworldliness of freedom*, is a fundamental aspect of modern black narratives of redemption' (Mbembe 2004, 5).

Inescapable it may be, but the 'otherworldliness of freedom' of which Mbembe speaks is tragically isolating. Etymologically, being *in extremis* is to be near death; therefore, writing which is *in extremis* issues from a sacred circle, and the polite response from those who cannot enter might be to turn quietly away, to close the book and be silent. Reflecting on the post-apartheid situation and its challenges, Mbembe also says, 'there comes a time when freedom has to be disentangled from the histories of spilled blood and sacrificial cruelty' (2004, 5). The practice of freedom, in other words, requires a suspension of otherworldliness, difficult though this may be. My hope, then, is that the time is right for a more heterogeneous and cosmopolitan dialogue, although I recognise that many may still disagree.

LET ME PROPOSE a way forward by referring to a contiguous tradition in South African writing, in particular to J.M. Coetzee's work on white settler-colonial literature. In 1988, Coetzee published a collection of essays called *White Writing: On the Culture of Letters in South Africa*, in which he was concerned with 'the ideas, the great intellectual schemas, through which South Africa has been thought by Europe; and with the land itself, South Africa as landscape and landed property' (Coetzee 1988, 10). The phrase 'white writing', he was careful to add, did not 'imply the existence of a body of writing different in nature from black writing. White writing is white only insofar as it is generated by the concerns of people no longer European, not yet African' (11). White writing is writing about the self and its relationship to Africa; it is writing in search of a language in which the self and Africa can enter into a fulfilled, reciprocal relationship. Needless to say, the hard realities of the colonial encounter preclude an easy passage into this reciprocity. Indeed, Coetzee is astute in showing the impossible longings, delusions and evasions in white writing in English-language South African literature of the colonial and early apartheid periods, so much so that it is disquietingly evident that we can hardly speak of a living tradition in 'white writing', certainly not one that, in the best sense, and with a few exceptions, nourishes writers of Coetzee's own and subsequent generations.

A question left unexplored in *White Writing* is whether it is true that we can really speak of a writing that is not 'different in nature from black writing', but that is distinguished 'only insofar as it is generated by the concerns of people no longer European, not yet African' (Coetzee 1988, 11). To speak pragmatically, the concerns that generate white writing are not likely to be those of most black writers. The question then becomes whether we can reverse Coetzee's terms, so that we inquire about the existence of a discourse representing the concerns of people who might be 'no longer African, but not yet European'? Such a question, though intriguing, fails to hit the mark. 'Yet' would imply a European teleology for black writing, an inappropriate implication given that the whole orientation of such writing would be towards cultural decolonisation, possibly African nationalism, however inclusive such a nationalism might be. Then, the phrase Coetzee uses in relation to white writing, 'no longer European, not yet African', purposefully shifts the emphasis away from the historical, bodily realities of race towards a more abstract concept of discourse. Such a move in the context of black expressive culture strikes me as inappropriate, since it is frequently about race and the historical body and their place in language and relations of power.

Coetzee's terms, then, are not easily transferable to black writing, which shows that it is not (yet) possible to avoid differentiations arising from the legacy of the past. In one respect, however, what

Coetzee says of white writing opens a question that could be applicable to South Africa's writing culture as a whole: if white writing emerges from a place of *instability*, *tension*, and *negotiation* – in this instance, between the self and Africa – is there an equivalently unstable place in black discourse? The answer is yes. While the vectors may point in other directions – in white writing, the self is 'here' while Africa is 'there' – tension and instability are nevertheless inherent in the relationships with modernity that black writers have carved out for themselves. The chapters that follow will give historical content to this assertion, but at this point, let me encapsulate things by saying that black intellectual life in South Africa often seems to have the character of a Faustian wager. This is true of the mission-educated intellectual toying with Christian liberalism; of the poet who experiments with European forms while writing in an indigenous language; of the modernist who uses fragmented prose forms to convey the precariousness of life in a township; even of the Black Consciousness activist who takes over liberal ideas of individualism, personhood, and autonomy, in an act of self-empowerment.[9]

We might extend Coetzee's lead, then, and suggest that tension, instability, and negotiation across a historical and cross-cultural divide permeate South African writing; they may even be the most characteristic features of all the country's literature. Homi Bhabha's Third Space is, in a sense, the culture's *sine qua non*. This observation is scarcely new. In fact, the historiographers I alluded to earlier, notably Stephen Gray and Leon de Kock, have agreed that South African literature is characterised by writing that, no matter from which community it comes, is forced into self-consciousness about difference – by the very pervasiveness of difference, or at least, by the presence and persistence of other, contiguous and powerful, voices. De Kock refers to this as an obsession with the 'seam', the site of repeated efforts to join what is separate, to 'suture the incommensurate', the result being a process that only 'bears the mark of its own crisis' (2001, 276).

I have spoken of tensions across historical divides and of the consciousness of difference not so as to conflate various degrees and forms of resistance and sites of enunciation within a common national-cultural framework.[10] Rather, I have done so in order to suggest that colonialism in South Africa has had the effect of disallowing everyone from remaining unchanged, and therefore has kept histories, traditions and identities radically in flux. The aggressiveness of modernity in South Africa has seen to this, although attempts to order patterns of settlement systematically and on a wide scale, to facilitate settler-colonial agriculture and political control, go back to the 1820s. This observation, first stated in the opening paragraphs of this Introduction, informs the overarching theoretical position that I wish to offer in this Introduction: the term transculturation is an apt description of the conditions governing the formation of black writing culture in South Africa. As such, it also represents a useful point of connection between international postcolonial studies and local black writing. In Chapter 1, I describe more fully the socio-historical basis of this position by revisiting nineteenth-century colonial relations, but let me develop the basic idea here.

The origin of the notion of transculturation lies in the work of Fernando Ortiz, the great Cuban anthropologist of the 1940s and 50s. It has received surprisingly little attention in English-language scholarship, although Mary Louise Pratt refers to it in *Imperial Eyes* (1992) in the context of Latin American culture. Before Pratt, the Uruguayan critic Angel Rama also applied Ortiz's theory, in *Transculturatión Narrativa en América Latina* (Coronil 1995, xxxvi), a work that remains unavailable in English translation. Pratt defines transculturation as the process whereby 'subordinated or marginalised groups select or invent from materials transmitted to them by a dominant or metropolitan culture' (1992, 6). This appears to be the only definition circulating in anglophone theory (Bartolovich 2002, 13), and while it is accurate as far as it goes, it does not capture the extent of Ortiz's intervention.

Ortiz offers the term in dialogue with Bronislaw Malinowski, as an alternative to the latter's notion of *acculturation* as a general condition of postcolonial societies, a term that implies a degree of passivity on the part of 'recipient' cultures. Transculturation, by contrast, suggests multiple processes, a dialogue in both directions and, most importantly, processes of cultural destruction followed by reconstruction on entirely new terms. Transculturation goes further than the weaker concept of cultural translation, which would be the translation of material from one culture into the terms of another. This is a possible limitation in Pratt's definition. Ortiz intended transculturation as a general description of the historical condition of Cuba throughout history:

> The real history of Cuba is the history of its intermeshed transculturations. First came the transculturation of the paleolithic Indian to the neolithic, and the disappearance of the latter because of his inability to adjust himself to the culture brought by the Spaniards. Then the transculturation of an unbroken stream of white immigrants. They were Spaniards, but representatives of different cultures and themselves torn loose, to use the phrase of the time, from the Iberian Peninsula groups and transplanted to a New World, where everything was new to them, nature and people, and where they had to adjust themselves to a new syncretism of cultures. At the same time there was going on the transculturation of a steady human stream of African Negroes coming from all the coastal regions of Africa along the Atlantic, from Senegal, Guinea, the Congo, and Angola and as far away as Mozambique on the opposite shore of that continent. All of them snatched from their original social groups, their own cultures destroyed and crushed under the weight of the cultures in existence here, like sugar cane ground in the rollers of the mill. And still other immigrant cultures of the most varying origins arrived, either in sporadic waves or a continuous flow, always exerting an influence and being influenced in turn: Indians from the mainland, Jews, Portuguese, Anglo-Saxons, French, North Americans, even yellow Mongoloids from Macao, Canton, and other regions of the sometime Celestial Kingdom. And each of them torn from his

> native moorings, faced with the problem of disadjustment and readjustment, of deculturation and acculturation – in a word, of transculturation. (Ortiz 1995, 98)

The 'counterpoint' provided by such a world stands in direct opposition to myths of essentialism and uniformity in both colonial and nativist forms of self-representation. 'Counterpoint' also suggests the way in which Cuba's history represents an alternative form of modernity, a peripheral modernity that provides its own guarantee of centredness. The philosophical basis of this point of view (as Fernando Coronil, who introduces the 1995 English translation of *Cuban Counterpoint* explains it) is that Ortiz's particular historicism came not from Hegelian idealism but from Spengler: *The Decline of the West* (1918) was translated into Spanish in 1923. Its 'depiction of multiple paths leading toward historical development encouraged many Latin American intellectuals during the inter-war period to view their societies as occupying not a lower stage in the unilinear development of Western civilization, but a unique position in a different historical pattern, one informed by its greater spiritual qualities and by the revitalizing mixture of races' (Coronil 1995, xvii–xix). The theory of alternative or multiple modernities – which is increasingly popular in postcolonial theory as well as cultural anthropology – has seldom received so clear a philosophical underpinning, although it has been around for more than a generation in this form.

The question for our purposes must be, then: does Ortiz's theory apply to South Africa? An honest assessment would acknowledge immediately that the theory does not fit entirely, for the simple reason that in Cuba, in Ortiz's terms, being a foreigner is a common condition, so much so that it almost defines the whole national culture, whereas in South Africa that is manifestly not the case. The autochthonous is not as strained a concept in South Africa as it might be in Cuba. In South Africa, however, the historical conditions I mentioned earlier – a highly textured postcoloniality and an aggressive modernity – do imply that there have been thoroughgoing processes of transculturation, with far-reaching consequences. To take just one, admittedly controversial example, it is not without an historical basis that the Black Consciousness (BC) movement developed such strong ties with diasporic ideas of racial identity, for the invasive effects of racial capitalism were such that intellectuals such as Steve Biko and his followers were, to a degree, culturally disenfranchised *at home*. Whilst I make this assertion about the BC movement, I would also agree that the concept of transculturation would not account for every aspect of South Africa's cultural history, nor for the countless ways in which South Africans might negotiate questions of identity. There would be some modes of oral culture, for example, that would be less transculturated than others, given the stronger links within oral culture to the autochthonous presence (although that presence could not be found in an entirely unmediated form either). Nevertheless, as a description of the conditions governing the development of writing by black South Africans it remains apt, because this literature has developed from exogenous sources and has ever since been through innumerable processes of adaptation and indigenisation.

It needs to be made explicit that nowhere does the theory of transculturation, as defined by Ortiz, suggest that it occurs in an equal or reciprocal exchange of cultures, despite recent materialist critiques of 'transactional' or 'negotiatory' analyses of colonialism (Parry 2004, 8–9). The transcultural relationship can and often does involve violence of every kind, both structural and direct. Indeed, my contention would be that it is precisely when the colonial relationship is violent, that transcultural formations are likely to emerge. Violence itself could be a mode of transculturation. The critique is directed at a straw target, a residue of a rather shallow and hermetic debate between materialists and poststructuralists, thankfully one that is now receding in pertinence. Interestingly, the apparent opposition between the material and the linguistic is never part of Ortiz's scheme. Indeed, his study foregrounds the role of material commodities in shaping Cuban history (tobacco and sugar) but only in order to narrativise the play of human interaction between and around them. So concerned is Ortiz with narrative, and especially with allegory, that despite the emphasis on commodities his text has remained an example of inspired *literariness* in anthropological research to subsequent generations of Cuban intellectuals (Coronil 1995, xxxv).

This book seeks to demonstrate that transculturation is an historical and archival reality of black print culture in South Africa. The niche into which this position fits within postcolonial theory lies somewhere between Marxism and what has been called 'culturalism' (Young 2001, 7–9). That is to say, it refuses the opposition between these positions, arguing that understanding local processes, and recognising material contexts, are indispensable to any responsible account of postcolonial cultural production. In fact, the archival emphasis of the chapters that follow (together with the emphasis on narrative and thick description) participates in the critique and correction of early developments in postcolonial theory, when there may have been a tendency to homogenise and globalise the description of colonial and postcolonial cultures. These chapters also decline the temptation to programmatic materialism, however, partly because it seems to me that the politics of such a position have been thoroughly compromised, not least by Marxist states in Africa, and partly because such an emphasis could de-privilege the subject-construction of intellectuals negotiating their way out of colonial marginalisation. In this regard, I share Robert Young's view that postcolonial theory, far from representing a radical departure from Marxism, 'is distinguished from orthodox European Marxism by combining its critique of objective material conditions with detailed analysis of their subjective effects' (2001, 7).[11] The chapters in this book, while remaining uncompromisingly local as well as attentive to material situations, will seek to track in detail the extremely varied projects and aspirations, whether ideological or aesthetic, of the texts being read. This will necessitate an eclectic methodology that combines historical narration, textual description and analysis, comparative literary studies, and theory. I am hopeful that the approach I am proposing negotiates a way through some of the inherent difficulties of postcolonial theory over the last decade or so, of which I will mention two in particular: the inadequacy of centre-periphery binarism, and the related, demeaning notion of authority being disposed exclusively from the metropolis in a linear vector, which carries with it the corollary that 'writing back' is the only possible kind of response – a kind of reversed linearity. The theory of transculturation, combined with the idea of alternative modernities, seems to me to overcome these difficulties. To speak more specifically of the project at hand: my intention is to negotiate a position somewhere between the idea of a colonialism that dictates terms, and blithe concepts such as appropriation and transformation. The middle ground of rewriting interests me, ground to which the historical record attests: a rescripting in and through transculturated discourses of modernity.

IN A RECENT issue of *Public Culture*, Charles Taylor says, 'perhaps the most important task of social sciences in our day is understanding the full gamut of alternative modernities which are in the making in different parts of the world' (1999, 153). If we are to understand modernity's multiple and alternative forms, we need to move away from what Taylor calls an 'acultural' notion of what it means – that it is essentially development driven, linear, and diachronic, the same for everyone – and move instead towards accepting that it has a certain cultural aetiology in the West, tied as it is to Protestantism, the Enlightenment, the scientific outlook, and liberal individualism. This 'cultural' view of modernity leads logically to a recognition of alternative modernities, especially in the context of local intellectual cultures.[12]

The reason for my emphasis on the role of intellectual cultures in producing alternative modernities is that this is obviously the provenance of a writing culture. Taylor argues, in fact, that alternative modernities are most likely to develop amongst élites, who engage with modernity most closely whilst seeking to adapt from traditional cultures: 'a call to difference [is] felt by modernising elites that corresponds to something objective in their situation', writes Taylor (1999, 163). This may be an overemphasis, since I am not convinced that it is *only* the élites who experience modernity this closely, especially in aggressive forms, nor am I sure that it is only the élites who are engaged in producing alternative modernities. Modernity is experienced 'objectively' as much by the migrant labourer as the writer-artist, and the chemistry of alternative modernity would be found in their own terms in many contexts – in oral popular genres and in the African independent churches, for example. It is true, nevertheless, that élites are, indeed, deeply involved in such work of interpretation and re-inscription.

An interesting question here would be how these élites are constituted, not so much in terms of race and class, which seem self-evident, but in terms of gender. Rosemary Jolly has put it to me that *Rewriting modernity* deals with the 'boys' game', an observation that I find as consoling as it is critical. The project of recasting modernity as I describe it may well be inherently masculine. While I would hope that my readings of the texts illustrating this process are reasonably gender-sensitive, it does strike me as inevitable that my efforts to describe and theorise some of the relationships between race and modernity in South African intellectual life will be limited in their scope, and that the relationships between *gender*, race, and modernity require a different and distinctive kind of treatment. I am also conscious of the scholarship that has already gone into such a project, in *Women Writing Africa: The Southern Region* (Daymond, et al. 2003), where the distinctiveness of women's experience under colonialism in southern Africa and of feminine discourses in contexts of transculturation have been documented and discussed.

In early versions of the approach developed here, I suggested that the investment in modernity on the part of South Africa's black writers had a 'fugitive' quality, that it produced something like 'fugitive modernities'. By this I meant that such investment was never complete or unguarded. It always involved an element of counter-humanism; it always sought, in other words, to define itself outside of received, colonial versions of authority. Fugitiveness, in this sense, has less to do with flight – as in, for example, the fugitive slave culture of nineteenth-century African-American experience – than with the fugitiveness of being in-and-out simultaneously, a condition that is evoked by the musical implications of fugitiveness: glimpses, intimations, aperçus, night-pieces, which take us beyond the cold realities of the present. In case I am construed as being too lyrical, this fugitiveness has a basis in social reality: as Es'kia Mphahlele once put it, 'we are digging our feet into an urban culture on impossible terms . . . . Ours is a fugitive culture: borrowing here, incorporating there, retaining this, rejecting that' (1960, 346).

Homi Bhabha, in conversation with John Comaroff, and searching for whatever it is that constitutes the postcolonial optic, offers several propositions that chime with the main emphases of this book: the re-inscription of modernity, transculturation, modernity's multiple nature under postcolonial conditions, the possibility of a 'fugitive' relation to modernity. Here is Bhabha's version of these themes:

> [The postcolonial] is the conviction that being colonial or post-colonial is a way of 'becoming modern', of surviving modernity, without the myth of individual or cultural 'sovereignty' that is so central a tenet of liberal individualism and its sense of serial progress or cultural evolution. The disciplinary and temporal orders of Progress, Rule, Rationality, and the State become corrupted in the colonial and postcolonial conditions where they play a double, aporetic role: as norms of value they make emancipatory claims, crucial to the definition of modern citizenship; however, as part of the power practices of the colonial state they create inequality, injustice, and indignity. It is from the interstices of this paradoxical situation that the postcolonial perspective emerges. It unsettles the ubiquity, the ordinariness of those orders of common sense, those polarities of perception, that modernisation has bequeathed to the rest of the world. So, for instance, postcoloniality is open to the contingent and hybrid articulations of the sacred-in-the-secular,

> psychic fantasy as part of social rationality, the archaic within the contemporaneous. (Bhabha and Comaroff 2002, 24)

LET ME DRAW this Introduction to a close by mentioning, in brief, what the forms of South African alternative and fugitive modernity are that will be explored in the chapters that follow. I have already mentioned the first, the 'transculturation of enlightenment' that occurs in the journal of Tiyo Soga, where discourses of reason, and Christian emancipation and freedom, which Soga took over from his missionary brethren, are disarticulated from colonial racism and applied in what is arguably the first sustained expression of modern black or Afrocentric consciousness in South Africa.

I proceed in Chapter 2 to a discussion of written narratives – biographical, historical and fictional – in the work of a generation of mission converts and African nationalists: John Knox Bokwe, John Langalibalele Dube, Solomon T. Plaatje, Thomas Mofolo, and others. Their writing establishes ideas of collective continuity and alternative teleology in a situation in which they had been schooled to imagine the cultural death of the African.

In Chapter 3, I examine a twenty-year dispute between close allies, B.W. Vilakazi and H.I.E. Dhlomo, who sought to construct what they saw as a 'modern' written literature from the resources of Zulu oral culture. From similar backgrounds, and comparable perspectives, they could not agree on how this passage should be achieved, though both were immersed in the post-Romantic aestheticism of the 1930s.

I then move to the 1950s and 60s, to the apartheid era, passing over the *Drum* period in South African writing (only because it has been so thoroughly examined already) to look at one of its major representatives, Es'kia Mphahlele, and his encounters with the Black Atlantic over the period of his exile. Here, the sense of alternative modernity is doubly removed from the Western paradigm. With his distinctively urban, transcultural background, Mphahlele had difficulty in locating himself in the counter-cultural myths around

Africanity that circulated in the diaspora; over time, he reconciled himself to them and on his return, integrated them into a more encompassing 'African humanism'.

In Chapter 5, I move into the 1970s, to Black Consciousness, where the discourses of anti-colonial liberation and civil rights introduce a radical revisionism into the anti-apartheid struggle and simultaneously into notions of selfhood. The attention falls in this chapter on the poetic genres of lyric and epic, how these forms became transculturated by Black Consciousness, and how and why the changing rhetorical formation necessitated a shift from the one to the other.

Finally, I examine the debate around literary experimentalism, arguing that contemporary black fiction in South Africa does have an 'experimental turn' in which modernist and postmodernist influences have been felt. This is contrary to the way the writing is often perceived, as comprised exclusively of flat, uninventive forms of documentary realism. Such experimentalism needs to be properly understood as the product of a complex web of local history and international, travelling modernism.

From enlightenment discourse, then, through nineteenth-century discourses of collective progress, to post-Romantic aestheticism, to diasporic consciousness, to the influence of anti-colonial discourse on local constructions of self and expressive culture and, finally, to the reception of modernist and postmodernist aesthetic practices: these are some of the 'fugitive modernities' of South African writing culture. They are not meant to be wholly representative, and indeed there are a number of major figures who are not represented here, including Peter Abrahams, Mazisi Kunene, Bessie Head, and others. Such significant omissions indicate the degree to which this book ought *not* to be taken as a representative survey of South African literature. It is not a survey, but a study of significant transitions and transactions in a history that is more variegated and complex than I am able to describe here.

1

The transculturation of enlightenment

The *Journal* of Tiyo Soga

Subsequent to a skirmish during the last of what came to be called the frontier wars in the Cape Colony early in 1878, a company of colonial troops was preparing a mass grave for seventeen of their Xhosa enemy when they came across a copy of John Bunyan's *The Pilgrim's Progress* on one of the bodies. The flyleaf bore the following inscription:

> Lovedale Missionary Institution. First Prize in English Reading, Junior Division, First Year, awarded to Paul Nkupiso. [Signed] James Macdonald, Lovedale, Dec, 1875. (Shepherd 1940, 210)

Soon afterwards, the discovery was reported in the settler newspaper, the *Tarkastad Chronicle*, together with the sarcastic remark: 'it is unnecessary to make any comment on the subject. The book will be kept as a standing advertisement of missionary labour' (in Shepherd 1940, 210).

Always wary of settler opinion, and arguably the pre-eminent centre of missionary education on the African subcontinent, the Lovedale mission was immediately put on the defensive. The report was false, it said, because no Lovedale boy could possibly have died fighting the Colony. Paul Nkupiso was a loyal 'Fingo', the very people whom the British were trying to protect. The principal, James Stewart, boldly stated that 'sooner or later they would be able to produce Paul Nkupiso in bodily form as the best proof that the whole story was a fabrication – and one of a numerous class of the same order' (Shepherd 1940, 211). His bravado did pay off, for the mission newspaper, *The Christian Express*, later reported:

> Paul Nkupiso is still in the flesh. About a month ago, he walked into Lovedale, having spent the interval since his last visit in work of various kinds, with the view of earning a little money . . . [to obtain] a teacher's certificate. He is here now . . . and can be seen any day by those who are incredulous. (Shepherd 1940, 211)

The incident passed into history but Stewart began compiling a register of his graduates in case it should prove necessary to protect the school's reputation again.

After the affair had blown over the question remaining in the air was this: if it were not Nkupiso, who *did* carry that copy of *The Pilgrim's Progress* into the Battle of Quanti, as the amaXhosa later called it? More pertinently, *why* did this young fighter do so? There are, of course, several possibilities. If he were not a product of Lovedale, as Stewart insisted, nor another mission, and if the book had fallen into his hands by chance, he would probably not have been literate. If so, did he hope that if the British could protect the rival Mfengu (whom the missionaries and settlers called Fingo) with guns, perhaps this other sign of British power – what the amaXhosa, mimicking the language of the pulpit, called 'the Word' – might protect him?[1] Tiyo Soga (whom I shall introduce more fully shortly) is said to have remarked:

> The prevalent opinion [amongst the amaXhosa] . . . is, that missionaries are the emissaries of Government, to act upon the minds and feelings of the people, with an Instrument which they call 'the Word'; and those who become afflicted by the Word, and exchange Kafir customs for those of the white men, become subjects of the English Government. (Chalmers 1877, 327)

Soga is referring to a functional linkage between colonial words and colonial force, a linkage that was not entirely the product of the pre-modern imagination. It was made by both sides, as is famously illustrated in the War of the Axe, just a generation earlier, when colonial troops had melted down the printer's type of the

Lovedale Press to make bullets (Shepherd 1940, 400; De Kock 1996, 31). It is possible too, that the young fighter *had* been through Lovedale's doors (though he may not have been Nkupiso) and that Stewart was reluctant to identify him properly; perhaps that he came from another mission, such as Healdtown. After all, there would later be generations of young men, nationalists who from their position of knowledge of what the mission had to offer, *would* become the antagonists of the Colony. Whatever his circumstances, and whatever thoughts the young fighter may have had, the military power of the Colony was not placated, although the symbolic power of the book he carried was, indeed, turned for a moment against the missionaries, thanks to the *Tarkastad Chronicle*.

TIYO SOGA WAS the first ordained African minister in South Africa. He was also the first to be trained abroad (in Glasgow) and, in effect, was the country's first black missionary. His father, 'Old Soga', as he was known in mission circles, had been an adviser to the Ngqika chief, Sandile. Old Soga and Sandile died in the same war that saw the end of the young man who carried that copy of *The Pilgrim's Progress* into battle. According to Lovedale's records, when it became clear that the war was lost, Old Soga went to ground with a few weapons in a cave – where he was found and summarily executed (Shepherd 1940, 191). By the time the father was killed in this way, he had lived for six years with the grief of his son Tiyo's death. Tiyo was buried in an orchard of fruit trees near his mission house at Tutura, in Xhosaland proper, across the Kei River, where tuberculosis had taken him at the age of 42. The church where he had preached was burned down in the same conflict that killed the father. It is a story of bitter ironies and, seemingly, of failure.

One of Tiyo's greatest achievements near the end of his life, however, was to have produced *Uhambo lo Mhambi*, the Xhosa translation of the first part of *The Pilgrim's Progress*, published by the Lovedale Press. In different ways, both the unnamed Xhosa soldier and Tiyo Soga seem to have revered Bunyan's story. For the young fighter the appeal might have been the materiality of the book as magical icon; for Soga it was, as the author had intended it, a devotional narrative worthy of the kind of heroic intellectual labour it took to translate it into what was still an unstable orthography. These responses are related in their attempt, as John and Jean Comaroff put it, to 'recast . . . European forms in their own terms' (1992, 235). This is our first instance of transculturation, arising from what the Comaroffs also call the country's 'long history of symbolic struggle', a history in which the consciousness of coloniser and colonised – as well as those falling somewhere in between – is fashioned and refashioned through generations of interaction, from the most mundane to the most violent (1992, 235).

These patterns were first established in the Eastern Cape, but by 1910, following the Act of Union that brought together the Boer republics and the English colonies, South Africa's symbolic struggle had produced a colonial state that was both 'an institutional order of political regulation *and* a condition of being, a structure *and* a predicament' (Comaroffs 1992, 236). Both the structure and the predicament were to harden after 1961, when the Union became a Republic under the National Party. That event, which signalled in its time the complete ascendancy of the Afrikaner, enabled a kind of amnesia to develop amongst the heirs of the British settlement in South Africa, a settlement that began in 1820. From 1961, indeed, English-speaking South Africans, together with their cousins in the former British Dominions, became more reluctant to acknowledge their historical responsibility for bringing about the oppression that arose from the process leading to the formation of the colonial state. This responsibility is emphasised in a strand of argument amongst historians of the Eastern Cape, which holds that it was in the years 1820–57, from the arrival of the first British settlers to the year of the disastrous, millenarian Cattle-Killing Movement, that the legal, administrative, and even epistemological basis for what Sol Plaatje in *Mhudi* (1984 [1930]) called 'the settled system', was first laid down.

By the mid-nineteenth century, a new order in the Cape Colony had come about that entailed a shift from a largely patriarchal mode of authority vested in the person of the Dutch pastoralist, to a diffused, administrative, emerging statutory form of power that limited the authority of the chiefs, defined the conditions of movement and labour for Africans, and consolidated a regulatory language predicated on the otherness of the native (Crais 1992, 92–95).[2] The systemic quality of these developments implies that the search for the historical roots of apartheid must, to some degree, be conducted in the effects of the British settlement of 1820, rather than exclusively in the seventeenth- and eighteenth-century histories of Dutch agrarianism and slavery. The 'stabilising presence' of the settlers was to make use of 'civilised free labour' rather than slavery, but the settlers' prosperity came increasingly to depend on other, as effective, forms of coercion. Indeed, as Martin Legassick puts it, 'the basis of "civilisation" – the aspiration of the Enlightenment – lay in the practice of "barbarism"' (1993, 334; see Crais 1992, 95).

It was under these conditions that the English language assumed the position it still holds, that of being what J.M. Coetzee aptly calls 'a deeply entrenched foreign language' (1993, 7). With the end of apartheid, the expansion of the black middle class will bring with it a more complete indigenisation of English, another reason to contemplate the ironies of history. The entrenchment of English beyond its usage by the settlers themselves was initially the task of the missionaries, who undertook what Michael Chapman has called a 'vast "literacy" project' in both English and the indigenous languages. In the case of the latter, this involved creating what were less-than-perfect phonetic orthographies to record what the missionaries could grasp of the oral languages (Chapman 1993, 36).

In the fields of literacy and book production, the missionary enterprise was hugely consequential. As Leon de Kock has demonstrated in *Civilising Barbarians*, the ethos and representational forms of mission literacy defined the terms on which a black South African written literature was to emerge (1996, 64–104). The missions also governed access to African social empowerment, a process in which literacy and a literate education were important ingredients. 'Africans aspiring to social elevation in colonial society,' says De Kock, 'had little choice but to embrace Protestant values which were embedded in the exalted medium of English and promoted in missionary education' (1996, 30). Sol Plaatje would bear this out: 'The key of knowledge is the English Language. Without such a mastery of it as will give the scholar a taste for reading, the great English literature is a sealed book, and he remains one of the uneducated, living in the miserably small world of Boer ideals, or those of the untaught natives' (in Willan 1984, 36).[3] As Plaatje's tone suggests, a rather stiff and constricting Victorian ethos became the *sine qua non* of African self-expression among the educated intelligentsia until at least the 1940s. Inevitably, the entrenchment of English – the language, its ethos, and its literary genres – was marked by the same ambivalence that was evident in the legacy of the British settlement itself.

However, the constraints also represented grounds of opportunity. It is commonplace nowadays to observe that the ideals associated with nineteenth-century evangelical liberalism were corrupted by hypocrisy, and it is certainly true that for many settlers, administrators, and missionaries, the cross was indistinguishable from the flag. This argument was memorably made in 1952 by Dora Taylor, writing under the pseudonym of Nosipho Majeke, in *The Role of the Missionaries in Conquest* (1953).[4] However, we can now see that this point of view is too blunt an instrument: it obscures just how consequential missionary institutions and discourse have been in the history and development of African nationalism itself. Some of the questions that beg asking are therefore the following: how are the ideals associated with evangelical liberalism taken up and acted upon by those who fall under their influence? Indeed, what is the agency of black Christianity?

Tiyo Soga shared the mission ethos almost as deeply as any child of a white missionary family. When we unravel the events from what is, as we shall see, a rather tangled archival record, what we will discover is that, in Soga's case, the adoption of mission discourse in the English language would entail a transculturation into African terms of the aims and instruments of colonialism's civilising mission. It was in this context that Soga would lay claim to one of the key instruments of the European Enlightenment, what Immanuel Kant called 'the public use of reason', although, rather tellingly, Soga would have to enter the public domain through the use of a pseudonym.

Some readers will find it easier to associate the Enlightenment with eighteenth-century Europe than the nineteenth-century Cape Colony, but we should remember that the so-called civilising mission was, among other things, the historical form in which the earlier Enlightenment would reach the colonies. That is to say, for people such as Soga, and for the succeeding two or three generations of black intellectuals, the principle of human perfectibility projected through the mission enterprise represented the grounds on which autonomy and social emancipation would be sought – the local equivalent of the Whiggish or bourgeois emergence of the eighteenth century. The kind of emancipation that could be envisaged under colonial conditions, however, would have to be salvaged from economic and political instrumentalism, imperialism, and racism, and pressed into the service of all humanity. To effect this salvaging operation was Soga's task, indeed his generational destiny and that of the two or three generations that succeeded him. It was to bring into being the transculturation of enlightenment.[5]

WHY SHOULD WE be so concerned with this particular turn in our cultural and political history? The answer is two-fold: firstly, this is the moment and these are the terms in which a black literary culture first develops in South Africa (a writing culture that draws on, though is distinct from, an oral tradition). Secondly (and here I will risk some speculative hindsight), the transculturated enlightenment resurfaces in the political culture of the transition in the early 1990s. Having been forced into the half-life of exile or incarceration, and then having given way to the more politically instrumental rhetoric of revolutionary struggle, enlightenment discourse returns with the end of apartheid as the recovery of human rights. With the democratic transition, in other words, South Africa makes peace with the eighteenth century. It is this reinvented tradition that the novelist Dan Jacobson was noticing when he remarked, after a visit to the Mary Moffat Museum near Kimberley, that 'occasionally, what seems truly amazing about the subcontinent is not the ferocity generated by the divisions manifest wherever you turn; it is the regard for order that many people of all races somehow still manage to preserve' (1994, 3). Jacobson was speaking in the wake of the 1994 elections, and about attitudes that were to find their way into the Constitution:

> there is a need to create a new order in which all South Africans will be entitled to a common South African citizenship in a sovereign and democratic constitutional state, in which there is equality between men and women and people of all races so that all citizens shall be able to enjoy and exercise their fundamental rights and freedoms. ('Preamble', 1–3)

This is surely the profoundest legacy of the transculturated enlightenment.[6] Apart from its philosophical centrality, there was also, at the time of the transition, a way in which it made its mark on the political style of the Mandela presidency: the much-remarked dignity, the Edwardian air, the charming of the wives of former opponents over a cup of tea, were all traces of an ethos that had been forgotten through the steely years of apartheid.

Tiyo Soga's moment would be the appropriate place to begin to trace the historical origins of this ethos. In what follows, then, I will explore his example by looking into the archival record of his life, both as he lived it and as his biographers told it. What we need to understand is how he became such a paradox: how his first biographer, John Aitken Chalmers, could in 1877 appropriate him to the colonial cause as 'the Model Kafir', and how the second biographer, Donovan Williams, writing a century later, could in *Umfundisi: A Biography of Tiyo Soga* construct him as the progenitor of Afrocentric nationalism (1978, 97). The point will be to understand how the man could play such apparently diametrically opposed roles at the same time.

UNLIKE HIS AGE-MATES, Tiyo Soga was never sent for initiation. His father, Old Soga, had heard Ntsikana, the first Christian Xhosa prophet, preach, and he and his Christian wife, Nosutu, sent Tiyo to Lovedale under the patronage of the first principal, William Govan Bennie. Thereafter, whenever war broke out between Xhosa and British – in 1846 and again in 1850 – Tiyo was taken into the missionary fold and twice travelled to Scotland with missionary families. He had most of his formal education in Glasgow. When he was ordained in the John Street United Presbyterian Church in December 1856, his mentor, the Revd Dr Anderson, with his Scottish hand on Soga's head, produced a 'tirade against the colonial policy of England' and offered 'supplications for the noble Kafir chieftain, Sandilli' (Chalmers 1877, 89). With his Scottish wife, Janet Burnside, Soga sailed for Kaffraria as a missionary on the *Lady of the Lake* in April 1857. In that year, while David Livingstone was being mobbed by admirers in London's streets and churches for his work in southern Africa (although by all accounts his success as a healer of souls, as opposed to an explorer, was not as successful as was generally accepted), Xhosaland was experiencing serious trouble: people were dying by the tens of thousands in the Cattle Killing. If Livingstone's presence in London had fired Soga's imagination at all in Scotland, the reality he was to encounter on his return would be disheartening.

Of all his writing – translations, hymns, speeches, letters, notebooks, and newspaper columns – Soga's historical significance emerges most clearly in his private journal, which he kept from 1857 to 1870, shortly before his death. The narrative begins with the embarkation, with the ship lying at anchor off Gravesend, when

Soga goes ashore to buy a remedy because he is expecting sea-sickness. That the journal opens this way is interesting: narration begins with the voyage 'out' to the Colony, even though Soga had, in fact, already made several voyages, both cultural and literal.[7] 'Home', in other words, is Glasgow – Soga is writing himself into the script of the outbound missionary. He anticipates the first Sunday on board because he has had the assurance that the John Street congregation will be praying for him and his party (Soga 1983, 12). As the journal progresses, notably after the arrival in the mission field, the writing becomes a record of divine revelation with God's purposes being revealed in day-to-day hardships and accomplishments:

> Glenthorn S. Africa – Octr 17th 1857. A new era in my ministerial and missionary history – This Lord's day I admitted into the church by the rite of holy Baptism *ten* individuals – the fruits of an abundant harvest . . . in this part of the Lord's Vineyard. (Soga 1983, 15)

The private journal was supposed to be the precursor to a more official journal and regular reports submitted to church headquarters in Edinburgh. This partly explains its teleological emphasis and the connection it makes between journal writing and Providence. The official journal has not survived (Williams 1978, xviii), but in any event the private journal is probably the more interesting document, since the providential aspect of the narrative and its official overtones are interrupted with anecdotes, confessions, candid social observations, and, most significantly for our purposes, polemic. Soga's situation in the Colony was fraught with difficulty. At his mission station at Mgwali in the Stutterheim district, progress was slow, even though mission work was generally made easier by the Cattle Killing. Among other things, Soga had to contend periodically with what he saw as the demoralising resurgence of traditionalism, with white-painted initiates (*abakweta*), some of whom were sons of elders in his own church, appearing at the door of the mission house in open mockery of the uncircumcised black missionary (Williams 1978, 84–85).

The year 1865 was a time of crisis. In March, the colonial government proposed to remove Soga's people, the Ngqika, from their home near the Amatole Mountains to a stretch of land across the Kei River that had been taken from the Gcaleka chief Sarhili. Soga drafted a strongly worded memorandum that set out why this was both unjust and unsafe (1983, 4). He was, however, driven into public statement by what amounted to an act of betrayal by his fellow missionary at Mgwali. Ironically and cruelly, this was the man who was to write Soga's biography – John Chalmers. Soga and Chalmers had virtually grown up together. It was Chalmers's father, William, who had secured Tiyo's place at Lovedale and urged him to further his studies in Glasgow. Eight years younger than Soga, John Chalmers followed him to Scotland for ministerial training and ordination and then joined him at Mgwali. Chalmers had none of Soga's patience and he held orthodox settler views of the Xhosa (Williams 1978, 94).[8] By November 1864, Chalmers was complaining in the *Missionary Record of the United Presbyterian Church* that 'sometimes I have felt almost brokenhearted at the small signs of spiritual life around me. Sabbath after Sabbath do I gather the heathen, and repeat to them the old story of redeeming love, and still the same obduracy, still the same deadness' (Chalmers 1864, 199). By February 1865, he was exasperated. He sent an article to the Lovedale newspaper, the *Indaba*, entitled 'What is the destiny of the Kaffir Race?', which was republished in the *King Williamstown Gazette and Kaffrarian Banner* (as 'Recreations of a missionary'). In an accompanying note to the editor Chalmers writes, 'if you have any objections to it you can let me know. I have written it *simply*, so that some of our Kaffirs who read the Indaba may have something to think over' (1865a).

Chalmers argued in his article that Africans were doomed to extinction, for three reasons: indolence, an antipathy to education, and an addiction to European vices, especially drink. These weaknesses were anything but trivial; they pointed to a fatal malady of indifference to change: 'there is nothing so deadening, nothing which keeps down a nation, nothing so unnatural as to keep things fixed when all the world is by the very law of its creation in eternal progress' (1865b). Chalmers was, in some ways, what the nineteenth century would have called a progressive: he had imbibed the Victorian scientific spirit. In the same article he advocated industrial training – years before Lovedale and other institutions actually implemented it. If Soga was a transitional figure, so was Chalmers: as imperialism unfolded, he lived out the decline of liberal humanitarianism and the consolidation of racism; the transition, in a sense, from Rousseau to Darwin. But one statement in particular would have offended Soga: 'when a Kaffir youth has got a smattering of knowledge . . . he wishes nothing more. His ambition then is to be a gentleman, a sort of peacock bedizened with ornaments of the gaudiest hue' (1865b).

Chalmers had not counted on Soga seeing this article, nor on Soga's seeing himself positioned in it. In the journal, Soga began a reply:

> One of our missionaries – wiser than his predecessors, has pronounced in an article in the native periodical – . . . Indaba – on the doom of my Race – Without disputing his superior Sagacity and foresight, I should like to know for myself – Whether in this doom is included – the Kaffir races of – Tambookies – Mapondo's – Napondomisi – Mabomvana – Galekas – Zulu's – MaSwazi – These races are all pure, Kaffir races – one in language – & manners – with but slight differences – If in this doom is included all these races – I venture to say the process of destruction will take a very long time to accomplish its work. (1983, 38–39)

This restraint is carried over to the text of his anonymously published reply in the *King Williamstown Gazette* of 11 May 1865. Soga gains a foothold in the discourse by appealing to an Englishman's sense of 'fair play'; he draws attention to the missionary efforts of the previous 50 years, wondering why Chalmers, a missionary himself, belittles them; he asks whether anything can be measured on the scale of 'civilisation' in 50 years, and provides counterfactual evidence. 'Permit me, Sir,' he then proposes, 'before I close to make some general observations':

> Africa was of God given to the race of Ham. I find the Negro from the days of the old Assyrians downwards, keeping his 'individuality' and his 'distinctiveness', amid the wreck of empires, and the revolution of ages. I find him keeping his place among the nations, and keeping his home and country. I find him opposed by nation after nation and driven from his home. I find him enslaved – exposed to the vices and the brandy of the white man. I find him in this condition for many a day – in the West Indian Islands, in Northern and Southern America, and in the South American colonies of Spain and Portugal. I find him exposed to all these disasters, and yet living – multiplying 'and never extinct'. Yea, I find him now as the prevalence of christian and philanthropic opinions on the rights of man obtains among civilised nations, returning unmanacled to the land of his forefathers, taking back with him the civilisation and the christianity of those nations. (See the Negro Republic of Liberia.) I find the Negro in the present struggle in America looking forward – though still with chains in his hands and with chains on his feet – yet looking forward to the dawn of a better day for himself and all his sable brethren in Africa. Until the Negro is doomed against all history and experience – until his God-given inheritance of Africa be taken finally from him, I shall never believe in the total extinction of his brethren along the southern limits of the land of Ham. The fact that the dark races of this vast continent, amid intestine wars and revolutions, and notwithstanding external spoliation, have remained 'unextinct', have retained their individuality, has baffled historians, and challenges the author of the doom of the Kaffir race in a satisfactory explanation. There has been observed among these races the operation of a singular law, by which events have readjusted

> themselves when they threatened their destruction. I believe firmly that among the Negro races of South Africa events will follow the same law, and therefore neither the indolence of the Kaffirs, nor their aversion to change, nor the vices of civilisation, all of which barriers the gospel must overthrow, shall suffice to exterminate them as a people. (Soga 1865a)

Despite appearances, Soga's use of biblical metaphor was forward-looking, for nineteenth-century Protestantism produced a revaluation of the curse of Ham – which the Vatican eventually came to accept – in order that 'the interior of Africa may participate in the solemn coming joy of the Church's triumph' (in Mudimbe 1988, 46).[9] Soga capitalises on this revision, using the curse of Ham to claim access to God's grace and to envision the full participation of Africans in human progress. He attaches a pseudonym to the essay, 'Defensor', from *defensor fidei*, defender of the faith, positioning himself anonymously as a spiritual guardian on the model provided most obviously by the monarch and head of the Church of England. His first rhetorical gesture, therefore, is to produce incorporation into a Christian sense of history. But this is not incorporation at any price: if Africans play a part in the divine purpose, they do so in their 'distinctiveness'. This emphasis is among the earliest examples of race-conscious and diasporic thinking in South African intellectual life, linking the trials of the ordinary Xhosa homesteader to a global and redemptive history emerging from the end of slavery. On the strength of this, Donovan Williams links Soga with the rise of pan-African thought in West Africa and credits him with being the first spokesperson of black- and 'Africa-consciousness' in South Africa (Williams 1978, 97). Soga repeats his affirmation of distinctiveness elsewhere, notably in a book of homilies that he gave to his sons on their departure for higher education in Scotland:

> I want you, for your future comfort, to be very careful on this point. You will ever cherish the memory of your mother as that

> of an upright, conscientious, thrifty, Christian Scotchwoman. You will ever be thankful for your connection by this tie to the white race. But if you wish to gain credit for yourselves – if you do not wish to feel the taunt of men, which you sometimes may be made to feel – take your place in the world as coloured, not as white men; as Kafirs, not as Englishmen. You will be more thought of for this by all good and wise people, than for the other. . . . I consider it the height of ingratitude and impiety, for any person to be discontented with the complexion which God has given him. (in Chalmers 1877, 430)

Let's return to 'Defensor's' argument against Chalmers's accusation of indifference to change; Soga observes the operation of a 'singular law' of adaptability in African cultures that has ensured and will continue to ensure the survival of the race. In this manner, in the language of natural science and ethnography, Soga repudiates the racism of Darwinian determinism. All told, Soga's argument is about incorporation into a global and teleological history, the retention of racial distinctiveness, and adaptability. These positions are Soga's currency. They have no precedent before him, which may explain his use of an iterated present tense which has the effect of confirming an irruption into history: 'I find the Negro . . . I find him keeping his place among the nations . . . I find him opposed by nation after nation . . . I find him enslaved. . . . Yea, I find him now . . . returning unmanacled to the land of his forefathers'.

I have mentioned the irony that Soga's legacy had to come to us via Chalmers, but not how cruel that irony could be. Chalmers expunged his clash with Soga from the biography. He certainly would have discovered who the author was of the magisterial reply to his outburst, for he had access to Soga's papers after his death, including the journal where it was first drafted. Chalmers's labour of love was therefore also a labour of expiation: 'From channels least expected,' he writes, 'and from men who were well able to strengthen his hands, there came during the last years of [Soga's] life the very bitterest wounds that can be inflicted on a pious earnest soul'

(Chalmers 1877, 487). Indeed, some of those wounds came from Chalmers himself. Soga acknowledges his pain – and a desire to make his response known to certain colleagues – in a letter he wrote to another missionary, J.F. Cumming, shortly after the controversy: 'did you see an article in the last "Indaba" by Chalmers on the Destiny of the Kafir Race? – Will send you the Kingwilliamstown Gazette with a long article, in answer to that of Chalmers – by *Defensor* – alias your correspondent – great talk about them both – the first has caused a great deal of pain to some' (1865b).

Chalmers's apparent sympathy after the fact did not prevent him from committing further acts of betrayal as the biographer, by attributing words to Soga that he never actually uttered. His tendency to take liberties with Soga's writing is neatly illustrated in an episode in which Soga recounts the dying moments of a woman called Notasi, the wife of Dukwana, Ntsikana's son and a church elder:

> she said, with an audible loud whisper, which produced the stillness of death among all present – 'Tell me who that person is that is speaking – ?' – 'The Teacher' – was replied – 'Who – Tiyo?' – she enquired again – 'Come and let me bid you farewell . . . my dear Teacher – I was waiting for you hitherto' – She never uttered another word after this – & in half an hour or so she calmly and peacefully fell a sleep in Jesus. (Soga 1983, 21)

Chalmers transcribes this as follows:

> 'Tell me who that person is that is speaking.' 'The teacher,' was the reply. 'Who? Tiyo?' she enquired again; 'come and let me salute you, my teacher; I was hitherto waiting for you.' She never uttered a syllable more on earth. *I pressed her cold hand in mine.* In half an hour after she calmly and peacefully fell asleep. (Chalmers 1877, 176; emphasis added)

Other interpolations are less amusing than this, though equally melodramatic. When Soga was at Tutura in 1870, some of the tensions from the days of the Cattle Killing resurfaced with a new outbreak of lungsickness among Sarhili's herd. A counsellor named Maki, who was a Christian and close to Soga, was accused of bewitching the cattle and came to seek Soga's advice because it seemed his life was in danger:

> I found him in great dejection of spirits, & meditating a serious removal from this country. The meshes of Galeka jealousy of his reputation & commanding powers, are compassing his Ruin, and as he does not belong to the old killing party – that say the customs of our Fathers are good enough for us – but to the liberal party that hails light – improvement, good & orderly Govt from the whiteman, all, from the chief downwards, seek his Ruin! (Soga 1983, 42)

Soga's interpretation of Maki's predicament relates the problem back to the Cattle Killing, in which a 'killing party' – which slaughtered cattle and burnt crops in expectation of the destruction of white rule – was opposed by a 'liberal party', which did not. While Soga's dislike of sorcery is implicit, as is his acceptance of white rule, Chalmers ignores Soga's contextualisation, turning the entry into an occasion to attack Xhosa custom and giving a quite different meaning to the phrase 'killing party'. The animus against the Xhosa is a severe misrepresentation of Soga's sympathies:

> This land of the Galekas is being ruined by the baneful influence of the witch doctors. Human beings, yearly, and in no small numbers, are secretly put to death. . . . there is no security for the most precious life amongst this people. They are all sheep for the slaughter. The butcher of a witch doctor has only to point out his victim, where and when he likes. (Chalmers 1877, 396)

Most puzzling of all, however, are Chalmers's lengthy transcriptions (nine pages in all; 1877, 271–79) of confessional passages purporting to come from the journal, which present Soga in a state of alarming spiritual turmoil. While there are moments in the journal when Soga acknowledges doubt, notably about his vocation – interestingly, such passages are written in Xhosa (Soga 1983, 22, 35) – they certainly do not occur on the scale presented by Chalmers. In addition, the contrast between Soga's spontaneity and Chalmers's didactic transcription and editing is striking:

> [Soga:] Into elusizi bubume beyam intliziyo. Idinga no ntywila ngokuntycoila ehomini-kndakwenzayo ngokuzinikela ebufundisini ndingazifumanelanga inkululeko ngokwenganiso. [Trans. I am concerned about the spiritual condition of my heart. I wish that you would embrace the new life – I fear that I decided to be a preacher while I was yet aware of not being fully converted.] (1983, 35)

> [Chalmers:] Sunday, 11th November. – Since my last entry I have passed through various frames; but I am sure the prominent blemishes of my character have been indifference, indolence, unbelief, and faithlessness. What is it that will save me? Father, let me experience the enormity of my guilt, and the greatness of Thy mercy. The Gospel has all that time been preached by me in hypocrisy. I cannot take credit to myself for anything; yet I live. Lord, Thou has saved many thousands from hypocrisy and indifference. To whom shall I go? Thou alone canst save me! (1877, 277)

The words attributed to Soga are not in the journal, as Chalmers claims. They are either invented or transcribed from letters that have been lost (Williams 1983, 11). This raises the question of the purposes of the biography: why does Chalmers construct such formidable evidence of a soul in anguish? The answer that suggests itself is that Chalmers wants to show that the Protestant spirit could be found alive and well in an African, and the more hand-wringing there seemed to be, the better for his tendentious narrative. Soga's crises of faith could be read into a pattern of heroic, self-chastening individualism that would provide ample justification for the missionary enterprise. He was an example of all that could be achieved if the civilising mission were to be allowed to restructure the African's symbolic universe. Add to this Chalmers's Calvinism: Soga's intimations of doubt could be assumed merely to confirm the workings of a higher Providence – a Providence for which Chalmers is, of course, the privileged interpreter. Chalmers always doubted the success of the missionary endeavour, but the life of Soga held the promise of its ultimate fulfilment. The biography is subtitled *A Page of South African Mission Work*: the 'page' is Soga's own contribution to that work, but Soga himself is also a page in that work, the work's subject, rather than its agent, the work itself being larger and more encompassing than the life being described.

At the time the biography was published, Chalmers expressed some uncompromising views about frontier policy. The Colony was shamefully negligent in failing to achieve complete subjugation in the war of 1877–78: 'here was an opportunity granted to us to explain clearly to [the Ngqika] the system of our rule, and to tell them that for their own peace and prosperity it was needful to conform to our laws, and to abandon their national practices and be industrious and obedient' (Chalmers 1878, 11). He also returned to his old theme, the future of the African, arguing that now that the chiefs were vanquished, 'this part of Ethiopia will stretch out her hands unto God' (Chalmers 1879, 7). Chalmers would surely not have regarded his version of Soga's life as being in conflict with these views.

CHALMERS ERASED HIS encounter with 'Defensor' from the biography and, as we have seen, ruthlessly re-inscribed Soga's life and words into Chalmers's own narrative. Perhaps this is what Homi Bhabha would call the untranslatable element, when cultural translation meets a certain resistance (1994, 215–16). If so, can we take it that the anomaly is resolved, clarified, and restored to articulacy now, through the rediscovery of Soga himself, and through the words we know he penned in his private diary? To some extent, this must be true, but the effects of that original moment of untranslatability linger on, even becoming part of the further transculturated discourse of Soga's heirs.

For instance, the 'Tiyo Soga' who appears as a character in H.I.E. Dhlomo's play of 1936 about the Cattle Killing, *The Girl Who Killed to Save*, does not speak at all (Dhlomo's play will be discussed more fully in Chapter 2, but I will make a few remarks here). He is introduced in the final scene as 'the new African missionary from Scotland' who 'has come to work among you, his kinsmen' (Dhlomo 1985, 28). This silent and enigmatic presence turns Soga into a larger-than-life figure, a legend rather than an historical being. Indeed, Dhlomo's Soga is simply a living embodiment of the cultural shift Dhlomo himself seeks to recognise: in the terms of the play he represents a transition from superstition and ignorance to Christianity and light (Dhlomo 1985, 29). This may be difficult to comprehend today, but Dhlomo, as a prominent cultural nationalist of the 1930s, interpreted the Cattle Killing as an episode in the unfolding of a historical destiny in which Africans would embrace modernity while preserving their distinctive memory. Dhlomo sees Soga as a pathfinder in this destiny. Dhlomo's interpretation of the Cattle Killing probably came from Chalmers's biography, which was the sole repository of Soga's legacy for subsequent intellectuals and which quotes Soga as saying soon after his arrival in Kaffraria in 1857, 'it is by terrible things that God sometimes accomplishes His purposes. In the present calamities I think I see the future salvation of my countrymen, both in a physical and in a moral point of view' (Chalmers 1877, 140). Of course, if Dhlomo did read Chalmers, he also relocated Soga in a teleology of liberation that Chalmers sought actively to undermine.

Soga was indeed a 'man of two worlds', but he was also a transitional figure *within* Xhosa history, marking a choice that subsequent generations would have to remake for themselves. The choice Soga did not make, indeed could not have made, is represented in the person who was possibly his most powerful contemporary in the sphere of culture: Mhlakaza, the orchestrator-in-chief, it would seem, of the Cattle Killing. Mhlakaza began his career in the same way that Soga did, in the patronage of a missionary family. The historian J.B. Peires, in his account of the Cattle Killing, describes Mhlakaza as the first African to be baptised in the Anglican Church, after he became a retainer to Archdeacon N.J. Merriman of Grahamstown, in settler circles going by the name of Wilhelm Goliath. Merriman walked the Eastern Cape with Goliath at his side; they taught one another their languages, read scripture together around campfires and, occasionally, Goliath would preach (Peires 1989, 309–10; also Merriman 1957, 65, 123). Goliath built a house in Merriman's garden but declined becoming a houseboy – he wanted to be a 'Gospel Man' (Peires 1989, 309). He had his day: on the insistence of Mrs Merriman, he left the Merrimans' service to become a teacher, only to resurface as Mhlakaza – uncle, protector, and priest to the prophetess Nongqawuse (Merriman 1957, 127). It was Mhlakaza who interpreted and disseminated Nongqawuse's prophecies to the chiefs, and renewed them when they aroused scepticism, thus helping to precipitate the greatest disaster of nineteenth-century Xhosa history.

If Soga and Mhlakaza represent a critical choice within Xhosa culture and society in the mid-1850s, that choice is not strictly between tradition and modernity. For, like Soga, Mhlakaza was at one time positioned *within* the world of the mission. Indeed, as far as the whole movement was concerned, Peires shows that far from being a 'pagan reaction', as earlier historians called it, the Cattle Killing was in fact a wholly syncretic project, influenced by the Xhosa reception and revision of Christianity (Peires 1989, 122–38). The choice was not whether to choose tradition or modernity in a straightforward way, but whether to turn one's back on the Enlightenment and modernity, thus repudiating these things – having experienced them closely enough to know their ambivalence – or to embrace them in qualified terms. Mhlakaza and Soga together show how volatile is the condition of what Ashis Nandy calls intimate enmity that we associate with settler-colonialism. Unlike Mhlakaza, however, Soga embraced the civilising mission but sought to establish a new point of departure within it, one that placed an

African consciousness and identity within the larger framework of modern history.

Was Soga successful? How do we measure this? Towards the end of his life he agreed to minister to Sarhili's people, the Gcaleka, in the heart of Xhosaland. Sarhili was paramount chief of all the amaXhosa. Soga spent only three years at Tutura before his death. The move from Mgwali to Tutura across the Kei River, near the present-day town of Butterworth, was a deeply symbolic one, for it drew Soga closer to traditional society, as if he were trying to heal one of the contradictions of his life. He could not, however, sustain himself for long. Understandably, the obituaries all speak of his isolation from both Xhosa and settler society and the burden this was to him. Apart from his tuberculosis, anxiety no doubt also took its toll. Although nothing remains of Soga's church, his grave is still there, and it is a scene of pathos: grasses and pine trees have grown up through the orchard. One of these trees, seemingly felled by lightning, has crumbled the stone wall surrounding the grave, and the heavy Victorian ironwork on which his name is now illegible has been augmented by a makeshift headstone that has also succumbed to the weather. It is as if Africa were trying to reclaim the son it lost to Empire.

On a larger historical canvas, Soga's life raises the question asked by Partha Chatterjee, of whether nationalism can ever break the historical link between the civilising mission and racism, between reason and callous instrumentalism, between the Enlightenment and oppression (1986, 169). Perhaps this link is never broken once and for all and, given the power of capitalism in its global dimensions, perhaps each generation of postcolonial subjects is obliged to attempt it. Following the transition to democracy in 1994, South Africans are living in a time and place where another attempt to do this is being made. I suggested earlier that one of the reasons Soga's example ought to hold our attention today is that what he represents is relevant, historically and philosophically, to the situation which contemporary South Africans are having to negotiate. Indeed, in *The Heart of Redness* (2000), Zakes Mda makes this connection, seeing the conflict over the interpretation of modernity in the mid-nineteenth century as having strong parallels with the choices that current South Africans are facing. In Chapter 6 I will read Mda's account of this situation, but suffice it to say at this stage that Mda's solution is to suggest the importance of an Africanised modernity. It is not too fanciful to see Mda's leading protagonist, Camagu, as a contemporary version of Tiyo Soga, standing at a similar crossroads.

Finally, Jacques Derrida's discussion of the critical choices facing Nelson Mandela is instructive in the light of Soga's example. In an essay written in 1987, shortly after Mandela's refusal of conditional release from prison in exchange for a renunciation of violence, Derrida examines the implications of Mandela's declared admiration in *The Struggle Is My Life* for the tradition of political liberalism – an unholy tradition, in the context of postcolonial liberation struggles – represented by the Magna Carta, the Universal Declaration of Human Rights, parliamentary democracy, the doctrine of the separation of powers, and the independence of the judiciary. 'But if he admires this tradition,' Derrida asks,

> does it mean that he is its inheritor, its simple inheritor? Yes and no, depending on what is meant here by inheritance. You can recognise an authentic inheritor in the one who conserves and reproduces, but also in the one who respects the logic of the legacy enough to turn it upon occasion against those who claim to be its guardians, enough to reveal, despite and against the usurpers, what has never yet been seen in the inheritance: enough to give birth, by the unheard-of act of reflection, to what had never seen the light of day. (1987, 17)

By 'reflection' Derrida means reflecting the traditions of the European Enlightenment back to those who claim to own them, and repossessing them in a new context. When Mandela speaks to his judges at his trial, he makes them represent a 'virtually universal' instance; he 'speak[s] to them . . . while speaking over their heads'

(Derrida 1987, 36). The judges' claim to represent an abstract principle of law is used to produce a new species of authority, one in which the hollowness of their claim stands revealed.

What Mandela does with the principle of law, Soga did nearly a century and a half earlier, but with biblical metaphor. In Soga's hands, even the unpromising theory of the curse of Ham is used to imagine the full participation of Africans in modern history. Soga resisted the nineteenth century's decline into instrumentalism and racism, and although the task might have been too great for him in the end, we are able now to read his life as helping to instantiate a tradition of nationalism in which the European version of reason is made to confront racial difference, its irrational doppelgänger.

If Soga represents a tradition, however, there is no easy continuity between past and present. Soga's legacy was buried in Chalmers's biography before his second biographer, Donovan Williams, revisited it. There is no ready-made continuity between Soga and intellectuals such as Dhlomo or leaders such as Mandela who follow him. That tradition has had to reconstruct itself through intellectual work. Alternatively, each time the crisis of how to engage with the current version of modernity presents itself, the underlying roots of the response most likely to ensure survival have to be recovered.

As John Bunyan's character Ignorance discovers at the threshold of the Celestial City, there is a path leading directly to Hell (1974 [1678]). In the language of this chapter, the cords that hold universality and difference, modernity and identity, in creative tension are always in danger of being broken. In the event that they are severed, we spin off either into the pseudo-universalism of pure rationality, a world of colour-blindness that has proved itself to be oppressive, or into the pseudo-gratifications of the parochial, a temptation that may offer a homely comfort zone but that would leave us outside of history altogether.

2

Time and narrative

Writing at the mission

What of the Night, watchman? – The Dawn cometh!

*(*Ilanga Lase Natal *18 May 1906)*

Early in 1904, Rudyard Kipling earned a laconic editorial in the Zulu-language newspaper *Ilanga Lase Natal* for the following pronouncement, seemingly a piece of propaganda for British post-Anglo-Boer War reconstruction. South Africa, says Kipling, will one day become

> [a] vast country revelling in prosperity. All the land not devoted to fruitful fields will be cultivated gardens. Sanatoria will be found on every hillside, and hotels in every valley. Corn will be so plentiful that not only will there be enough to feed the British Empire, but also to supply the United States when they run short. Huge herds of cattle of the finest quality will be bred. The rising sun of prosperity will never set. All the poor will become rich, and for every poor man planted in South Africa there will be reaped a crop of millionaires. Victoria Falls will be the rendesvouz [*sic*] of the rich, and its parks will be the playground of the world. The falls with their 35,000,000 horse-power will furnish electricity to make the Dark Continent a blaze of glory which will illuminate the earth. (*Ilanga* 26 February 1904, 4)

Ilanga's response was to say that, like poets before him, Kipling had 'gone off his head', that this 'glorious vision' was merely the product of 'snatched intervals' of residence in the country. South Africa had been scourged repeatedly by rinderpest, locusts and drought, and in any event, 'prosperity will dawn to reign for ever when the insatiable greed of capitalists has unreservedly declared equal rights for all in the struggle for gold' – even then, 'the poor will still remain'. Curiously, *Ilanga*'s counter-vision to Kipling's – authored, no doubt, by the newspaper's founding editor, John Langalibalele Dube – was anchored in biblical morality. He cites Revelation, specifically the passage where the prophet John on the island of Patmos foresees a time of famine, imaged as a marketplace where a day's labour buys little more than a meal (Revelation 6, 5–8). Dube, the Congregationalist (and Calvinist), was also offended by what he saw as Kipling's sheer hubris: the apparent miracle of a crop of millionaires reaped for every poor man placed on the land was a 'moral impossibility' (*Ilanga* 26 February 1904, 4).

Whilst Dube is sceptical, therefore, of the version of progress to which Kipling subscribes, in some respects he and Kipling were allies. Kipling's industrialising imperialism and Dube's implicit faith in the terms of the civilising mission shared the legacy of Victorian liberalism. In what has been called the 'comedic' vision of missionary education, notions of scientific progress and Christian eschatology were easily combined.[1] Dube carried these ideas into the founding of the Zulu Christian Industrial School at Ohlange, where they were part of the mix that included the doctrine of self-reliance that he had learned from Booker T. Washington. (The African-American connection should not be underestimated since, amongst other things, it would have strengthened Dube's use of the Bible as a form of counter-modernity.) So while Dube might have been dubious about hydro-electric power from the Victoria Falls turning the Dark Continent into a 'blaze of glory', he could still name his newspaper 'Ilanga', 'light', after Romans 13, 12: 'The night is far spent, the day is at hand: let us therefore cast off the works of darkness, and let us put on the armour of light.'

The question raised by Dube's response to Kipling is whether the intellectuals of Dube's class – the *kholwa*, or converted – merely accepted the metaphorics of the civilising mission, or whether they appropriated them to serve their own interests. In all probability, the answer cannot simply be either-or: as products of the mission system they had absorbed its language, values, and ethos, but at the receiving end of colonial racism and the limitations it imposed on their social, political and economic ambitions, they were aggrieved by the contradictions between their ideals and actual experience. As Shula Marks and Paul la Hausse have both demonstrated for Zulu-speaking Natal politicians of the 1920s and 30s, ambiguity was a keynote that sounded in almost every project they undertook (Marks 1986; La Hausse 1992).[2]

This kind of ambiguity is an endemic feature of the written literature of the earliest generations of black writers. In an essay by a pupil at Zonnebloem College in Cape Town in the 1860s – the college started by Governor George Grey to prepare the sons of the traditional Xhosa élite for a Christian future – Africa is described as 'remarkable for its vast deserts of burning sand, the ignorance and barbarism of its inhabitants, and the number and ferocity of its animals', and so on. Nevertheless, in the same essay, Maqomo, who had been prominent in Anglo-Xhosa conflict, was described as a 'brave and clever man', comparable to 'Napoleon or Duke Wellington' (Hodgson 1984, 18). From Zonnebloem's windows, the pupil who wrote this could look out over Table Bay towards Robben Island, where Maqomo at that very time was imprisoned. A generation later, in 1898, the poet A.K. Soga could write of Portuguese explorer Bartholomew Diaz's cross off Algoa Bay, that

> It speaks of Freedom's flag unfurled
> For Christianity;
> A beacon light, in this dark world,
> To God and liberty. (in Couzens 1984, 73)

'Freedom' here is both religious and secular; 'darkness' is ignorance of Christianity but also oppression, and 'liberty' leads directly from salvation to social justice.[3]

The debate between Kipling and Dube is essentially about contested teleologies. In this chapter, I take this debate into written narratives (biographical, historical, and fictional) by Dube and others, narratives that revisit and reprise colonial versions of progress. Discussion is organised around the two most prominent themes of this writing: firstly, the emergence of Christianity in indigenous communities, and secondly, auto-ethnographic representations of the traditional past (Scheub 1985, 493). The former theme traces the formation of the Christianised present, often on the understanding that Christianity also represents the future; the latter theme seeks to establish continuity with a traditional past that is judged to be disappearing but that is still highly prized.

Before proceeding, let me make a few remarks about the literary character of this writing. I am concerned, in part, with the ambiguities, pitfalls, and achievements of writing that takes on the task of 'modernisation'. Leon de Kock speaks of the need for attention to be given to the 'prior representational processes' that eventuated in the emergence of local written literatures, his own work focusing on the nineteenth-century Eastern Cape. (His reading of the structural difficulties confronted by John Tengo Jabavu in his journalism for the newspaper *Imvo Zabantsundu* is especially instructive [De Kock 1996, 105–40].) De Kock suggests that the 'dislocations' that are a feature of the writing's transculturated forms ought to be the subject of study in their own right (1996, 190). Two forms of such dislocation, I suggest, would be *belletrism*, meaning displays of gentility, often in a code that is Shakespearean, Romantic or Victorian, and *bricolage*, or an eclectic experimentalism. Both tendencies, for example, are illustrated in an anonymous poem printed in *Ilanga* celebrating the spirit of the rebel Mehlokazulu in the Bambatha uprising of 1906, which is clearly composed with 'The Charge of the Light Brigade' in mind:

> The crash of the rifle, the whizzing of spears;
> No longer I hear their sweet sound in my ears!
> The war cry, 'Usuthu' my warriors yelled
> Like hounds, as they leapt from the leash where I
> held

> Them straining and eager, to fly at the foe;
> All now is hushed in this Valley of Woe! (*Ilanga* 29
> June 1906)

The Tennysonian elevation of the poem grants to Mehlokazulu's memory a certain abstraction and monumentality, and this mode recommends itself to anyone wishing to construct a national-cultural discourse within modernity.[4]

The drive to modernise is also clearly expressed in D.D.T. Jabavu's papers on the subject of 'Bantu belles lettres'. He published two authoritative essays, one in 1921, a largely bibliographic exercise in which he responded to the chestnut that 'the Bantu had no literature', and the other in 1943, in which he updated the earlier compilation and discussed the relationship between indigenous-language literatures and the English canon (Jabavu 1921, 1943). Jabavu's emphasis on a 'race' towards a culture of 'Letters' amongst the indigenous languages was not unlike R.H.W. Shepherd's belief – he was the director of the Lovedale Press at the time Jabavu was writing – that written African literature was in its 'adolescent' phase (Shepherd 1945, 75). Doubtless it was this kind of thinking that went into the formation of the Bantu Treasury Series, which was presided over by Clement Doke and his colleagues in Bantu Studies at the University of the Witwatersrand. The Bantu Treasury Series was an attempt to establish an archive of modern literature in the vernacular. That the Series long outlasted the generation of 'New Africans' who inaugurated it shows how powerful the notion of literariness can be as a signifier of national achievement.

JABAVU'S IDEA OF a 'race' towards a modern literature suggests that what we might call *kholwa* writers were working under a sense of *accelerated time*. Their narratives foreground temporality in various ways – as emergence, continuity, memory, and survival – suggesting that temporality was spinning out of control and needed to be contained. Paul Ricoeur shows in *Time and Narrative* that it is of the essence of narrative to manage perceptions of time (1984, 3); but in this context, the project is much more difficult and critical than the generic observation would suggest. We cannot escape noticing the connections between *writing*, as a medium lending itself to abstraction, and one not bound by immediate communicative contexts; *narrative*, as an attempt to capture and re-order the movement of time; and the attempt to engage with and *manage* the threatening metanarrative of 'civilisation' that had been imposed through mission teaching. (The power of 'the Book' could also leak into oral culture, incidentally; for example, in the religious performances of women amongst the *amaNazaretha*, where special symbolic powers are ascribed to the bible-as-object [Muller 1997, 4].)

In the 'Exhortations' that preface *Abantu Abamnyama* ('The Black People', 1922), the first written historical narrative in isiZulu, Magema Fuze encourages future generations to devote themselves to their own *written history*, reminding them of the fable of the 'chameleon' and the 'salamander' (or lizard) (Fuze 1979 [1922], viii). At the Creation, the chameleon was sent to tell people that they were immortal; the salamander was sent to tell them they were only mortal. On the way, the chameleon dawdled, and the salamander arrived first. When the chameleon arrived the people said, 'sobamba elentulo' ('we will stick to the word of the salamander') (Fuze 1979 [1922], 151). The implication is that writing provided for immortality, both religious and secular, an immortality that people in their ordinary gullibility and foolishness had surrendered.

In still other terms, writing for Fuze was a kind of Ariadne's thread, without which the future meant cultural death: 'It does not mean to say that because you see civilised people and wish to become like them, that you should discard your own which is good. It may happen that in seeking to do so, you may suddenly find yourselves being cast into a bottomless pit' (Fuze 1979 [1922], viii). The 'chasm' into which Fuze was staring was, of course, simply the effect of the post-Darwinism that encouraged missionaries and administrators alike to talk about the 'future of the native races'. Nevertheless, the representational gloom of mission discourse about Africans was perceived by men such as Fuze as an ontological *fiat*, forcing them into chronicle-writing as a mode of survival – not unlike the castaways of European literary history.

In a 1992 essay, Peter Osborne argues that while periodisations of history have been common since the Renaissance, during the Enlightenment a significant shift occurs that emphasises the *newness* of the present. That is to say, by the late eighteenth century the present comes to be seen in terms of a *qualitative* transcendence of the past. Citing Reinhart Kosseleck's notion of 'Neuzeit', where Kosseleck speaks of time in modernity as acquiring 'a dynamic and historical force in its own right', Osborne sees modernity as a transformation in the experience of historical time. In this transformation the present is exclusively valorised over the past and, furthermore, the present becomes open towards an indeterminate future, the effect being that the present becomes a 'vanishing point' that can never fully be grasped. The key historical development underlying this shift, says Osborne, is not only the triumph of the bourgeoisie (under the pressure of which, in Marx's celebrated phrase from the *Communist Manifesto*, 'all that's solid melts into air') but more particularly, colonialism, which brings the awareness for the first time of 'noncontemporaneousness of geographically diverse but chronologically simultaneous times'. In other terms, the abstraction into perpetual newness of what would otherwise be a normal process of change occurs because colonialism enables 'certain people's presents [to be perceived] as other people's futures' (Osborne 1992, 32–33).

In its desperate work of bringing its charges into the present and securing their future, nineteenth-century mission discourse participated in this production of newness. It is not surprising that those who came to see themselves through this lens found the heady atmosphere irresistible. William W. Gqoba, one of the earliest of the Xhosa literary poets (born 1840), writing under the influence of Tiyo Soga's translation of *Pilgrim's Progress*, staged the debate between non-Christians and Christians ('red' and 'school' people) in the characters 'Present-world', and 'World-to-come' (Jordan 1973, 64).[5] In the early twentieth century, the force of 'the new' can still be registered by the 'old man' in H.I.E. Dhlomo's play *Ntsikana*, who reflects on its power as follows:

> . . . the age of the earth weighs heavily on men these days, casting its senile shadow even on youth, on thought and life. Thus it is that our young people, fresh and full, are enveloped in the boredom and weariness of the shadow of Age and Time. Yes, Time ages, and will pass into Timelessness where there will be the endless Now. (Dhlomo 1985, 32)

In certain contexts, Christianity itself was judged to be malleable and manipulable, but not this headlong rush into new time, which it seemed to imply. In *Ilanga*'s poem 'Amagunyana's Soliloquy' (*amagunyana* – 'the young chiefs'), for instance, printed in 1906 (again, a poem informed by the Bambatha uprising), the anonymous poet adopts the voice of a pre-literate traditional chief who interprets the current erosion of his freedom and authority. The poem's resolution endorses the possibility of a transculturated Christianity in the spirit of the independent churches, together with an assertion of the speaker's right to fashion the future for himself:

> 'Tis true the Whiteman brings a Book which tells
> Of many a vision yet unknown to mine.
> I may not read the hazey mazes of
> His much curved ink, but I read earth and sky
> And men; and should it all prove true in hours
> Not yet arrived, that his Eternal one
> Is Great, or greater than our own Great-Great,
> Then will I do Him homage and serve Him,
> And in the manner He had fashioned me,
> But not in theirs. (*Ilanga* 18 May 1906)[6]

Alaine Touraine, in *The Critique of Modernity*, says that the passage into modernity is not a transition to a 'bloodless rationality', but an adaptation to a world that is continually changing, from 'reason that discovers eternal ideas to the action which, by rationalising the world, liberates and recomposes the subject' (1995, 230). 'Amagunyana's Soliloquy' is a case in point. While modernity as a technological and industrial project had already begun, by this stage, to affect the lives of large numbers of black South Africans, it was not a prominent feature of the culture by which the educated class was interpellated. Consequently, Touraine's point concerning modernity's capacity to provide scope for creative self-fashioning has a particular relevance.

ONE OF THE first written narratives dealing with the emergence of Christianity in traditional society was John Knox Bokwe's biography of the Xhosa prophet, *Ntsikana*. Published in 1904, parts of it had appeared in the Lovedale newspaper the *Christian Express* as early as 1878. The outlines of Ntsikana's story will need brief recounting: having heard as a child the preaching of J.T. van der Kemp of the London Missionary Society in 1799–1801 (and intermittently thereafter that of James Read and Joseph Williams) Ntsikana had a vision in which he saw an unusual light striking the side of one of his cattle, named Hulushe, an event that would come to be read as the equivalent of the conversion of Saul. There followed other signs of providential awakening; Ntsikana declared himself converted and began summoning his people with song for prayers and preaching. His influence was significant as he was an hereditary counsellor to Ngqika, chief of the Rharhabe Xhosa, and his emergence coincided with intra-clan rivalry between Ngqika and Ndlambe, who had been regent but refused to cede power when Ngqika came of age. In this conflict Ngqika sought the aid of the Cape Colony, so that the Ngqika/Ntsikana position of accommodation came to be contrasted with the resistance of Ndlambe, who was supported in turn by the traditionalist prophet Nxele, Ntsikana's natural rival. Matters came to a head in 1818 at the Battle of Amalinde, where Ngqika was defeated. Thereafter, Ntsikana and his followers seem to have lived a rather persecuted existence amongst the depleted Ngqika clan until Ntsikana's early death (Hodgson 1984, 24–27).

Ntsikana's legendary stature grew with the subsequent Christianisation of the Ngqika Xhosa in the Tyhume valley, the story surviving both in oral history (a history to which Bokwe had direct access – his grandparents had been amongst Ntsikana's followers) and in the writing culture that followed the establishment of the Lovedale mission and its press. Bokwe's narrative is therefore an important link in the early years of Xhosa literature, and more especially in a tradition within the Ngqika-Xhosa memory, which constructs Ntsikana's role as that of founding-father to a line of indigenised Christianity. As A.C. Jordan puts it, 'through [Ntsikana's] influence, a few young disciples were introduced to the arts of reading and writing, and . . . inspired by his exemplary life and teaching, these men became the harbingers of the dawn of literacy amongst the indigenous peoples of Southern Africa' (Jordan 1973, 51).

The story that Bokwe tells is providential: the child Ntsikana, sitting amongst a group of boys in karosses, 'their black bodies rendered grey by the scratches of the thorny thickets', is described as receiving the 'precious seed' from Van der Kemp where 'it lay in his heart as it were barren, but it was destined one day to take root, to spring up and bear abundant fruit, to the glory of its ever-careful Husbandman' (Bokwe 1914 [1904], 5–6). The biography is driven by this obvious desire to enter the prevailing Christian metanarrative. The opening chapter begins by establishing a racial typology for the Ngqika-Xhosa, continues with manners-and-customs descriptive ethnography, and concludes, 'the story of Ntsikana forms a connecting link between that period of utter darkness . . . and the now dawning epoch of civilisation' (Bokwe 1914 [1904], 4). Subsequent chapters dealing with clan rivalry and the Battle of Amalinde subordinate the historical issues entirely to illustrating Ntsikana's powers of prophetic prediction. In this respect, therefore, Bokwe's narrative is foreclosed and circular, substantiating its assumptions in the arrangement of its plot.

However, Bokwe's purposes involve more than a linear demonstration of the workings of providence, as is evident from the fact that the text is interleaved at suitable moments with Ntsikana's hymns, transcribed in 'tonic sol-fa', with English translations. The text is therefore a repository – the most complete one available – of a much-revered tradition of Africanised hymnology (Ntsikana's 'Great Hymn' is still widely sung), which speaks of a lyrical subjectivity not bound by, or into, the civilisational rhetoric. In a sense, the narrative has two axes: a vertical, Christian axis, and a horizontal, or communal and subjective, axis. In the horizontal axis, Christianity is adapted into a hybrid textuality, with clear links to a form of orality that connects the past to, and affirms, the subject's speech community in the present. There are moments when Bokwe has difficulty in reconciling these lines of force – when he is describing the clapping and singing at a traditional festival, for instance, his enthusiasm for oral memory dominates. However, the fact that the 'heart' of the narrative lies in its Africanised subjectivity (the horizontal axis) is clear from the conclusion, where Bokwe cites a description of Ntsikana's physical stature and voice from oral sources, and then exhorts his readers to follow the prophet's example (1914 [1904], 31). In other words, it is the reputed stature and personality, as much as the story, of his subject that inspires Bokwe. We might argue that matters come together in the conclusion where, for the first time, Bokwe explicitly draws attention to the hymnology, speaking of it as the precious legacy of his narrative's hero – here the argument and the charisma of the subject are at last fused.

What I have called the two 'axes' of Bokwe's text illustrate Touraine's contention that modernity is a 'twofold affirmation', a 'dialogue between reason and the subject, and it can never be broken off or brought to an end because it keeps open the road to freedom' (1995, 375). Touraine's is indeed a normative view of modernity, which argues that it has always been an inherently bipolar structure, accommodating both instrumental reason and subjectivity. If this is correct, we might conclude that it is obviously the 'soft', subject-oriented pole of modernity that is most amenable to reconstruction and hybridisation in terms of non-Western experience, and it is here that we would locate Bokwe's celebration of Ntsikana.

If Bokwe reprises modernity, the word 'reprisal', with its roots in the military raid, can suggest the capture of flawed or damaged goods. This is the case with another reconstruction of the Ntsikana legend, an epic poem by the Xhosa writer of the 1930s, J.J.R. Jolobe. 'Thuthula' is an ambitious work originally written in isiXhosa in 1936 but translated by the author into English blank verse, though the original, presumably under the influence of the kind of English Letters taught at Lovedale, was also written in pentameters (or, at least, ten syllables to the line) – the English 'national dress' of blank verse being put to analogous use. Whilst the pentameter is masked by Xhosa intonation – 'Ewe siyawuvula umlomo,/Sivuma ngabantwana begazi' – in the English translation the gap between verse form and intonation narrows, so that the line reproduces blank verse's familiar effects: 'Oh yes, in sooth I open now my mouth/To sing and tell of men of royal blood' (Jolobe 1974 [1936], 85, 1946, 9). (Curiously, the translation is closer to the formal model the poem is following than the original isiXhosa itself!)

The poem is based on an episode of 1807, when Ngqika abducted one of Ndlambe's young wives, with the effect that large numbers of Ngqika's followers and several subsidiary chiefs deserted him in the belief that it was tantamount to incest, though there was also some resentment over Ngqika's proprietary attitude towards the property of deceased members of his clan (Peires 1981, 59; Moodie 1959, 15–16). In his reconstruction of these events, Jolobe avoids the subject of incest as well as the argument over death-duties, and conflates Thuthula's abduction with the rivalry between Ntsikana and Nxele described by Bokwe, which actually took place a decade later. This alteration enables Jolobe to reflect on the emergence of Christianity amongst the amaXhosa, using the figure of Thuthula as the representative, or victim, of an epochal cultural shift.

Thuthula is the plaything of historical forces raging around her. Some of Ngqika's counsellors, unsympathetic to Ntsikana, plot to rid the clan of the white man's religion by provoking an attack by Ndlambe, which is accomplished by suggesting Thuthula's abduction to Ngqika. Jolobe's handling of Thuthula in this is equivocal. On the one hand, she is treated sympathetically: she and Ngqika had exchanged youthful professions of love but Ndlambe had won her by the payment of *lobola* (bride-price), which means that she is caught in a loveless situation as Ndlambe's eleventh wife. On the other hand, when Ngqika's clandestine agents offer her the choice to stay at Ndlambe's homestead or return, and she decides to return, Jolobe unleashes a bitter interpolation on adultery:

> Alas! Thuthula, thou didst bring disgrace
> And shame on marriage vows. Thy conscience, too,
> Did witness to the violation made.
> In man's association wedlock's pure.
> Thou now didst lose the crown of womanhood,
> And see the charm and beauty's dignity
> Seem to depart from thee, and there is left
> Thine outward glitter, dazzling still to eye,
> But now a husk without a character. (Jolobe 1946,
> 25)

The implications are that whilst Thuthula's autonomy and subjectivity – constructed through romantic love and the pathos of her marriage – are highly prized, that freedom is also curtailed through a Christian insistence on monogamous wifehood and the need to keep a pure conscience. Liberated into autonomy by love, she is immediately recaptured by a puritan and decidedly patriarchal ideal. The implication is also that only when the currently imperfect historical adjustment to Christianity is complete – a process Jolobe presents as inevitable, despite the setback represented by Ngqika's defeat – will the unhappy Thuthulas of the world be relieved, because by then monogamy will be the norm. Jolobe's poem is one of the more vivid illustrations of the patriarchy that surfaces regularly in the writing under discussion.

After Ntsikana's story, the most fertile episode in nineteenth-century history for telling the story of Christian emergence was the Cattle Killing. The consequences of this episode – widespread famine, tighter colonial administration, greater numbers of converts at the missions, and destitute people moving south in thousands to become labourers or vagrants in the Colony – came to be interpreted providentially in missionary narratives, notably in Chalmers's biography of Soga, as we have seen (Chalmers 1877). From one of the earliest written accounts of the disaster, by Gqoba (who was sixteen when it started) we learn that popular memory tended from the outset to regard the event as literally incredible: 'Thus it was that whenever thereafter a person said an unbelievable thing, those who heard him, said: "You are telling a Nongqawuse tale"' (Jordan 1973, 75).[7] The providential interpretation exploited this anomaly, and reached its height in H.I.E. Dhlomo's play, *The Girl who Killed to Save*. The play rather ruthlessly represents the event as beneficial, effecting the passage into Christianity.

On closer inspection, Dhlomo was less concerned with consolidating the missionary viewpoint than with establishing a nationalist narrative. In the debate between the missionary Brownlee and his brother-in-law Hugh Thompson, history's 'scavenging process of accident' is emphasised (hardly a providential formulation), which requires an 'enlightened scepticism' to understand (Dhlomo 1985, 19). The event will prepare the 'national soil – soul' for 'new intellectual and moral structures', not just the message of the missionary, but also scientific medicine, law, and literacy – in short, modernity (Dhlomo 1985, 19). What passes for providence here is in fact nationalist re-narrativisation watched over by calculating reason.

In Dhlomo's hands, Nongqawuse herself is a fairly complex figure. Far from being the innocent dupe of Mhlakaza, the traditional patriarch, she is racked with doubt about her own prophecies and tempted by a lover to elope into a monogamous marriage. As was the case with Bokwe, we find that a work that is overtly acquiescent turns out, in fact, to encode an excess ideological freight that tilts the argument in the direction of national reconstruction. The interpretation that the early, 'Christian' Dhlomo's acquiescence is replaced by a later, 'nationalist' Dhlomo's independence (the view of Dhlomo's editors) proves to be too simplistic.

It is characteristic of this period that 'modernity' is represented by the church and the school – and possibly also the justice system. From the 1930s onwards the paradigm will be supplied increasingly by the *city* – certainly, by the 1950s, city styles and virtues will be the norm (glamourised by their association with America, the glittering metropolis), and literary belletrism will be replaced (though not entirely) by the culture of jazz.[8] The rural context that was ruled by the mission station would become tainted with apartheid policy, which was designed to tie people to traditional identities. *An African Tragedy*, by R.R.R. Dhlomo (the brother of H.I.E.) – what the publisher, the Lovedale Press, called 'the first novel in English by a Zulu writer' – might be considered a transitional narrative between these paradigms. It is transitional in the sense that it carries the mission ethos into the urban context, producing contradictions that the formal possibilities of tragedy are brought in to resolve.

R.R.R. Dhlomo's narrative is this: Robert Zulu (the name is clearly allegorical) leaves his betrothed in semi-rural Edendale (in Pietermaritzburg) and travels to Johannesburg, partly to make enough money to pay *lobola* and partly to sow his wild oats. There, with biblical predictability, he falls among thieves and prostitutes, from one of whom he contracts syphilis. After narrowly escaping arrest following a skirmish in a shebeen, he returns to Edendale to the loving embrace of his family and fiancée, Jane Nhlauzeko. The marriage is followed by efforts to bear a child. Eventually the couple is successful but inevitably he has passed the disease on to both Jane and the offspring. Robert is then poisoned by the jealous male lovers of a mistress, a situation that produces a dramatic deathbed peroration (accompanied by a Shakespearean storm) in which he confesses that he has brought corruption to the family, and through the local minister he begs forgiveness and salvation. The novella ends with Robert receiving the assurance that pardon is granted to those who are sincere.

In this story, the novelist represents modernity as an ambiguous zone demanding judgement and choice: Robert Zulu must negotiate the corruption of urban life and embrace the bourgeois modernity of a prosperous marriage. The achievement of the latter is inseparable from Christian salvation, a point that the text's most dramatic moments are eager to emphasise. The structure also connects personal salvation and family life with tradition, through the ties that are secured by the bride-price, although Dhlomo insists that loveless marriages secured only by *lobola* are doomed. In every way, these connections establish Dhlomo as the modern nationalist.

However, the narrative's awkwardness reveals that Dhlomo achieves his purposes – and those of the Lovedale Press, for whom this cautionary tale was obviously worth the investment – with some difficulty. For one thing, he cannot sustain the impersonality of the narrative voice, and he interpolates into his already parable-like tale (in part, too, the story of the prodigal son) comments such as the following: 'Many marriages are still arranged and conducted by many modern Christians without consulting the contracting parties. How far this error is responsible for some of the misunderstandings between parents and their otherwise praiseworthy sons and daughter it is not my intention to probe here' (R.R.R. Dhlomo 1930, 25). As is clear from this example, Dhlomo abandons his realism, partly because it leads to an explicitness that he seems to find embarrassing: 'it is not necessary to dwell on how Robert was received by his country people in general; and by his people-in-law in particular; and by Jane in private. These things are better imagined than described' (R.R.R. Dhlomo 1930, 26). In other words, whilst striving for objectivity and the 'sovereign subject' of realism, Dhlomo repeatedly falls back on didacticism and allegory. Although certain attributes of modernity are available to him, Dhlomo finds the *novel* – as one of modernity's great epistemological achievements – just beyond his grasp.

Narratives of Christian emergence in early black South African literature involve, then, far more than a mere recapitulation of missionary imperatives. Often a distinctly secular sub-text underpins an overtly Christian text. These works entail attempts to resituate African experience on the 'world's stage' of modernity, as the place where some of the formal and ideological resources that buttressed colonial conquest could be re-coded and appropriated. Given the scale of the project, it is not surprising that the results were sometimes mixed.

THE STORY OF Christian emergence has its counterpart in acts of remembering; in other words, in narratives about traditional society, or traditional society in its earliest encounters with colonial intrusion. If the sub-text of the previous theme entailed the elaboration of modern ideas, this latter theme serves, amongst other things, to reconnect the writing subject with the traditional past. The two most respected works of the period fall into this category: Thomas Mofolo's *Chaka*, written in 1908–09 but published in 1925, and Sol Plaatje's *Mhudi*, written in 1920 but published in 1930.

In both cases, as with any historical fiction, the dates of composition are significant to the version of the past being constructed. Mofolo's novel was written shortly after the Bambatha rebellion, during the trial for high treason of the incumbent Zulu king, Dinuzulu, and it appears that Mofolo undertook a journey to Natal from Lesotho to gather oral sources for his tale (Attwell 1987, 52–55). Since Bambatha mobilised his followers on the basis of recalling pre-colonial Shakan independence (Marks 1970, xix), and given the topicality of Dinuzulu's trial, the status and memory of the Zulu monarchy would have been an especially live issue.

However, whilst critics frequently turn to *Chaka* as one of the earliest texts of a nationalist canon, it hardly sustains this role – or rather, it has not been established exactly how it might do so, for it is filled with the kind of ambiguity already discussed. As Es'kia Mphahlele puts it in *The African Image*, 'the manner of telling is in the tradition of oral literature', but Mofolo 'tells his story as a Christian' (Mphahlele 1962, 210). To this we might add, following Gérard, that Mofolo also tells the story from a Sotho perspective, or at least, from that of a relative outsider (Gérard 1971, 125–26). The equivocation in Mofolo's narrative has been persuasively analysed by Kwame Ayivor, who shows that in several respects, Mofolo follows closely the structure of a traditional oral epic and makes use of *izibongo*. However, epic and panegyric are also inverted to produce an anti-hero and a critique of his single-minded commitment to power and gratuitous violence. That the nation is born through the moral catharsis of these acts raises serious questions. Whereas the epic bard, says Ayivor (following Scholes and Kellog), 'must confine himself to one version of the story', 'the *histor* can present conflicting versions in his search for the truth, or fact' (1997, 54). Mofolo's own account of his intentions is very much that of the *histor*, for in a letter in 1928 to the Morija mission's newspaper *Leselinyana*, he said:

> I believe that [historical] errors . . . are very many in the book *Chaka*; but I am not very concerned about them because I am not writing history, I am writing a tale, or should I rather say I am writing what actually happened, but to which a great deal has been added, and from which a great deal has been removed, so that much has been left out, and much has been written that did not happen, with the aim solely of fulfilling my purpose in writing this book. (in Kunene 1981, xv)[9]

Not that Mofolo's purposes in *Chaka* are resolved or transparent. An example of the ambivalence would be the novel's imagery of snakes. In its early ethnographic descriptions of Nguni lore, we learn that snakes are divine or ancestral messengers (Mofolo 1981 [1925], 2); we also learn that Chaka's royal destiny is marked by his initiation with the bile of a snake (Mofolo 1981 [1925], 8), and that destiny is later sealed by a visitation of the King of the Deep Pool, which 'coiled itself around his entire body, and . . . unwound its tongues and started licking him from the head right down to the soles of his feet' (Mofolo 1981 [1925], 23). Mofolo's materials here are folkloric, but these events take place in a context in which we are also told that Chaka's illegitimate birth was sinful, and that his initiation produced sadistic urges, so much so that 'at the end of a fight he would feel a sense of happiness, . . . of relaxation, like a poisonous snake which, after biting a person, lies sick until that person dies' (Mofolo 1981 [1925], 15). There is little doubt that the King of the Deep Pool is a Serpent of another kind altogether, and that the moral universe of Chaka's birth and upbringing is, in fact, the book of Genesis.

The ambivalence surrounding the use of snakes is matched by a similar ambiguity in the figure of Isanusi, who is part sorcerer (as opposed to healer/herbalist) and part tempter, offering Chaka supernatural aid in the accumulation of power through violence (including, eventually, the murder of his lover, Noliwe) in exchange for loyalty and, finally, for Chaka's life. Part-traditional, a continuation of the notion of the serpent as messenger, and a figure who can shape destiny by prophetic power, Isanusi is also part-biblical and could, in some respects, have been created by John Bunyan. Gérard interprets Isanusi as follows: 'At every decisive point, the meaning and consequences of contemplated actions are fully described by Isanusi, and Chaka always makes up his mind in complete awareness of what he is doing. Few African works exhibit such a profoundly integrated sense of the meaning of freedom and guilt in Christian ethics' (Gérard 1971, 125). The prism of judgement through which Mofolo constructs his Zulu history is this emphasis on Chaka's pilgrimage to damnation, and it casts a strange light over the depiction of the Zulu past. Even if it is the case, as Mphahlele surmises, that the novel represents a strongly centralised and pre-Christian state that would have alarmed some of his missionary patrons (Mphahlele 1962, 210), Mofolo's own position in relation to Shaka seems to have been a mixture of fascination and recoil.

It should be remembered that as a 'Progressive' (which meant being a member of the Basutoland Progress Association) Mofolo emphasised the values of education, Christianity, and social mobility. If he was a nationalist as well, his brand of nationalism was early enough to predate the resacralisation of the traditional past that occurs only when a diasporic or perhaps pan-Africanist ideology filters into southern African cultural politics. To make this point is to measure the distance between Mofolo's 'Chaka' and Leopold Senghor's, for example, a far more romantic character. Without the solace of a full-blown Africanism, Mofolo experiences the birth of secular national consciousness as a loss of moral anchorage, and his response is to demonise it while, at the same time, being engrossed in its urgency. However, Mofolo seems conscious of the fact that nationhood will be constructed agonistically through global forces impinging on African society. It is for this reason that the novel's final peroration has Chaka say to his brother-assassins: 'You are killing me in the hope that you will be kings when I am dead, whereas you are wrong, that is not the way it will be because *umlungu*, the white man, is coming, and it is he who will rule you, and you will be his servants' (Mofolo 1981 [1925], 167). Chaka was wrong, to some extent, since Dingane did rule in a fair degree of independence after his death, as did his successor Mpande, but the prediction expresses the unarguable intuition that nationhood will in future have to be wrested from within the terms of an exogenous grand narrative. As it turns out, the nationalist reading of the novel, though it ignores the text's ambivalence and Christian emphases, is actually correct, albeit in terms it has not adequately assessed.

If Mofolo is in awe of the secular, generative agency of nationalism, Sol Plaatje, like Tiyo Soga, is more confident of his position. Plaatje's relationship with the eighteenth century was explicit. A.E. Voss has shown the range of Plaatje's references to eighteenth-century sources in *Native Life in South Africa*, his polemic on the Native Land Act of 1913, prominent among which is *The*

Deserted Village (Voss 1994, 68–72; Plaatje 1991 [1916]). Plaatje would soon become disillusioned, however, with the capacity of colonial governments to share the discourse of reason, because whilst *Native Life* documents the case of the South African Native National Congress (SANNC) in sending a deputation in 1914 to seek a British imperial veto against legislation emerging from the Union parliament, Plaatje's novel, *Mhudi*, seems to have been written in a mode of reflection informed by the failure of that deputation. Written in England between 1917 and 1920 (Willan 1984, 349), Plaatje's novel adopts a diagnostic view of history, in which he attempts to re-envision some of the historical processes that predate the formation of the colonial state. To this end, he turns to epic, representing the large-scale migrations of the late 1830s that played a significant role in shaping the fortunes not only of the Barolong Tswana (Plaatje's own ancestry) but other communities with whom they came into contact, mainly the Boers and the Matabele. The novel is a pan-ethnic epic, and expresses the emerging broad national vision of the SANNC.

However, epic is also overlaid with the more wistful discourses of fable and romance, through which Plaatje imagines the reconstruction of historical allegiances and identities. The novel's cyclic encoding of history, achieved through the use of prophecy and the periodic return of Halley's comet (elements Plaatje understood as both traditional and held in common with other cultures), certainly implies an optimism of the long term. I will dwell, however, on the importance of Plaatje's sense of irony. Through irony, he establishes contrasting perspectives between the claims of the various groups competing for land and sovereignty. Much of this is handled dramatically, showing the influence of Shakespeare. Some examples would be Gubuza's warning to his Matabele compatriots after the sacking of Kunana that the terror they inflict on the Barolong will be revenged, which it is; Chief Moroka of the Barolong questioning the Boer leader Siljay (Cilliers) on the meaning of Christianity and extracting from him the recognition that '[T]he point of view of the ruler is not always the point of view of the ruled' (Plaatje 1989 [1930], 88); and Mhudi witnessing the flogging of a 'Hottentot' servant in the Boer encampment and then questioning her future husband Ra-Thaga on his indiscriminate friendship with the Boers. Here the irony implies a certain detachment before which the regressive tendencies of chauvinistic cultures are played out. It then reaches a higher level of seriousness in the plot-construction, where Plaatje engineers several cross-cultural friendships: Ra-Thaga and the young Boer Phil-Jay (Barolong-Boer), and Mhudi and Mzilikazi's estranged wife, Umnandi (Barolong-Matabele). These relationships are cemented in the typically comic resolution of a triple marriage/ reconciliation, which includes that of Phil-Jay and Annetjie, who are nudged into marriage by Ra-Thaga playing a Barolong matchmaker to a Boer liaison. The purpose of these friendships is easy to find: they illustrate Plaatje's faith in human fraternity based on the possibility of individual change.

Nadine Gordimer observes that the Ra-Thaga/Phil-Jay relationship represents 'the literary wish fulfilment of what South African society could be if only the facts of the power struggle could conveniently be ignored'. To which Brian Willan replies, 'in Plaatje's view, it is also the means of actually attaining such a society, the means of altering these facts of power by peaceful means, the means of avoiding the violent but inevitable alternative' (Willan 1984, 357). This is why Plaatje has Phil-Jay articulate for the ears of his Boer friends the ethical principle on which the plot rests, making explicit reference to race (not in the New Testament original) when he says, 'What did Paulus mean, . . . when he said to the Galations "There is neither Greek nor Jew, bond nor free, male nor female, White nor Black, but all are one in Christ Jesus"' (Plaatje 1989 [1930], 197).

In epistemological terms, Plaatje's irony enables him to anchor an enlightened reasonableness that could provide the focal point from which a reconstructed social order might arise. Citing Benedict Anderson, Voss has remarked that enlightenment ideas do not in themselves enable us to imagine an alternative community; it was left to what Anderson calls the 'provincial creole functionary' and the 'provincial creole printman' to provide the 'framework of a new consciousness' to accomplish this purpose (Voss 1994, 72). Plaatje played these roles – as interpreter, editor, politician, diarist, and writer. From a position of marginal authority, like Soga again (though undoubtedly with more success) Plaatje fashioned a public life out of the transculturation of enlightenment. Though Voss is writing about *Native Life*, his thesis holds for *Mhudi* as well. In the novel, the (postcolonial) enlightenment subject is established through the perspective of ironic comedy.

There are, of course, good reasons for Gordimer's scepticism about the friendship between Ra-Thaga and Phil-Jay. Plaatje himself was not by any means starry-eyed about this, as is clear from Mzilikazi's Lear-like condemnation of the Boer-Barolong alliance, and his prophecy that the Barolong will live to regret it. Plaatje was conscious that the colonial state and racial capitalism, modernity's other face, had 'uncivilised' the 'civilised' values to which he held fast, but his comic romance (energised, it would seem, by temporary exile) projected forward to another time when, with the implied return of Halley's comet, the current situation would be transcended. It is certainly as if Plaatje were writing out of what Osborne calls the 'vanishing point' of the present, the hiatus between the corruption of the past and the swing forward into a future of hope.

As with Jolobe and Dhlomo, the gesture towards a reconstructed future is gendered and feminine: Mhudi is in possession of her covered wagon in the closing paragraph, going off into the sunset, laying claim to occupation of the landscape in the way the Afrikaner did. The difference between Plaatje and the other writers is that Mhudi is party to the irony – in fact, she is its highest embodiment.

As South Africa's forced march into segregation continued into the second and third decades of the twentieth century, the writing of the past – particularly by African-language writers – began to quarry into traditional society for principles around which a modern African state might develop. The poet and novelist S.E.K. Mqhayi, widely respected as the foremost of Xhosa *iimbongi* (praise poets) and writers, devoted his historical fiction to this project. *Ityala lamaWele* ('trial of the twins') deals with the subject of primogeniture in traditional society (taking off from Genesis 38, 28–29). It does so dramatically, recording the formality and due process of legal procedure during the reign of Hintsa a hundred years earlier. It then launches into historical narrative, recounting the divisions that arose between amaXhosa and Mfengu, and the two main Xhosa chieftaincies, divisions that are attributed to British interference (Jordan 1973, 107–08).

In his next novel *UDon Jadu*, the *amaRunaga* (Westernised), under the educated and influential Don Jadu's patronage, set up the province of Mnandi ('pleasant land', a utopia), which encourages immigration, non-racialism, gender equality (though the women do decline parliamentary representation, saying they are too busy at home), constitutionalism, and reconciliation between traditional religion and Christianity, and between the church and the legal system. A.C. Jordan feels that 'in constructing a "bridge" between our present South Africa and his Utopia, the author wishes away a few hard facts'; nevertheless, the work's 'soul is right' (Jordan 1973, 110–11). The novel could be described as an experiment in the construction of an Africanised civil society, in the recognition that its traditional equivalent that existed at the time of Hintsa had gone and that its foundations would have to be reconceptualised.

John Dube's *Insila kaShaka*, the first novel in isiZulu (1930), translated as *Jeqe, the Bodyservant of King Tshaka*, continues the project, though in this case the debate over social models is conducted through the hero's adventures in the tradition of the picaresque. Gérard suggests that the novel was written in a spirit of disillusioned retreat into the past after Dube found himself at odds with some of his more radical contemporaries (Gérard 1971, 212). This is possible, but the novel ought to complicate to some degree Dube's reputation as a traditionalist who turned his back on the national ANC and trade union movement, because what it does attempt is, in fact, to reconcile certain 'Progressive' leanings (faith in Christianity and education) with a respect for tradition.

The novel is set during the last phase of Shaka's rule, when he is supposed to have become arbitrarily and wearyingly violent. After a museumised, ethnographic description of Zulu custom, we are introduced to Jeqe who is appointed bodyservant when he excels in battle. But Jeqe becomes increasingly unhappy as his master tests him with a series of unpleasant missions: murdering an acquaintance, stealing cattle, slaughtering a pregnant woman out of curiosity about the foetus, etc. The last straw comes with the King's death, when it is expected that the bodyservant will be buried with him – Jeqe flees (quite unlike the equivalent figure in Soyinka's *Death and the King's Horseman*, incidentally, who embraces this tragic destiny). At this point, the picaresque takes off as we follow Jeqe, now disguised and having to reconstruct his social identity, through various encounters with new terrains and social contexts. In Tongaland he falls in love and learns the arts of magical healing from Sitela, 'queen of doctors and diviners' (Dube 1951 [1930], 55). He proceeds to Swaziland to procure cattle for *lobola* where, with a new identity, he gains notoriety as a healer in the court of King Sobhuza. After a dangerous visit home to Zululand, and after assisting Sobhuza to win a decisive struggle against Dingane, Jeqe returns to Swaziland to a contented polygamous life under the Swazi king's benign patronage. Jeqe's is certainly the story of the 'disembedded' autonomous subject (Giddens 1991), seeking anchorage in a world where traditions offer conflicting possibilities. The drunken authoritarianism of Shaka is spurned; the arts of traditional healing are rediscovered amongst the Tonga; these are linked, in turn, to Sobhuza's benign dictatorship, where autonomy and tradition are reconciled in Jeqe's new identity. The connections we are familiar with in Zulu nationalism, between modernity and neo-traditionalism, are given clear expression in Dube's text.

We can see in these several narratives of traditional society, then, a spectrum of views, ranging from Mofolo's, in which emerging nationhood is treated equivocally, to Dube's, in which traditional society is recast as a rational order in which the modernised subject may feel at home. In conclusion, it would be too bold to claim that the texts discussed in this chapter introduced a wholly new and transformative potential over the missionary-civilisational discourses that informed them; but equally, it would be too dismissive to say that they were completely entangled in oppressive forms of thought. We may safely agree with Osborne that modernity 'embraces a conflicting plurality of projects, a conflicting plurality of possible futures'. 'Which of these projects will turn out to have been truly modern', he continues, 'only time (historical time) will tell' (Osborne 1992, 37). Who is to say that the struggles of the past were fundamentally different from the struggles of the present?

3

Modernising tradition

The Dhlomo-Vilakazi dispute

From June 1938 to July 1939, a dispute took place in the pages of the journals *Bantu Studies* and *South African Outlook* between H.I.E. Dhlomo and B. Wallet Vilakazi, arguably at the time the most eminent figures in the field of Zulu literature.[1] The vituperation seems at first to be disproportionate to the subject at hand: the place of rhyme in Zulu poetry. That the argument became over-heated was the result of the fact that the two figures involved were rivals, as interpreters of tradition and pathfinders in the development of modern Zulu literature. Apart from questions of temperament, which certainly played a role, the dispute was significant because it touched symptomatically on crucial questions for black writers of the day.[2]

The conflict had its origins in the MA thesis Vilakazi had submitted to the University of the Witwatersrand on 'The conception and development of poetry in Zulu', a portion of which was published in the same university's recently founded journal *Bantu Studies*. By this time (1938), Vilakazi's poetry was well known, since it had been published in *Ilanga Lase Natal* and the *Native Teacher's Journal*, followed by the collection, *Inkondlo kaZulu* ('Zulu Songs', 1935). In *Inkondlo*, Vilakazi's most striking project had been to experiment with rhyme, following a range of English models of versification – the couplet, rhyming quatrains, etc. For these efforts he earned sceptical notice, as he acknowledges in the article, 'Conception and development of Zulu poetry', three years later: 'By trying to adopt this rhyming I have found that there is a feeling among European critics that Zulu can achieve only a limited success with rhyming, since most of the words in Zulu end in [unstressed] vowels, and thus do not permit variety of sound that makes successful rhyming possible' (Vilakazi 1993 [1938], 78). By 'European critics' he meant J. Dexter Taylor, whose review of *Inkondlo* was entirely complimentary except for this one minor disagreeable note (Taylor 1935, 163–65).[3] Though Vilakazi may have been chastened, he remained defensive: he justifies the use of rhyme with reference to the abundance of alliterative derivatives in isiZulu; he draws on examples of existing successful rhymed compositions, notably hymns; and he clarifies his position by saying that it is not only the final syllable that should rhyme, but the penultimate one with its preceding consonant, *iphaba* with *ubaba* and *ukubaba*, *vela* with *fela*, *amatata* with *amathatha* and *amadada*, and so on. In laying out this theory, he is meticulous in drawing distinctions between successful and unsuccessful rhymes, paying attention to such elements as nasalisation, fricatives and clicks (Vilakazi 1993 [1938], 77–81).[4]

Herbert Dhlomo found this all too much. He published two responses, 'Nature and variety of tribal drama,' also in *Bantu Studies*, and 'African drama and poetry' in *The South African Outlook*. In the essay in *Bantu Studies* he offers a quite different theory, based on the idea – the details of which I will return to later – that much oral poetry, with the exception of certain *izibongo*, consists of incomplete records of communal performances. His scorn for his rival's efforts emerges in the second piece, in which he calls rhyme a 'cold tyrant' and Vilakazi's scheme 'rigid', 'inflexible' and 'crippling'. Particularly humiliating for Vilakazi, who was eager to preserve his academic reputation (let us not forget the pressures of being the first black appointment to the University of the Witwatersrand), is Dhlomo's citing of Sir Arthur Quiller-Couch:

> Those elders of you who have followed certain earlier lectures 'On the Art of Writing' may remember that they set very little store upon metre as a dividing line between poetry and prose, and no store at all upon rhyme. I am tempted today to go further, and to maintain that, the larger, the sublimer, your subject is, the more impertinent rhyme becomes to it: and that this impertinence

> increases in a sort of geometrical progression as you advance from monosyllabic to disyllabic and on to trisyllabic rhyme . . . (Dhlomo 1939, 88)

Dhlomo himself was attempting to develop what he called 'literary drama', which characteristically dealt with 'actions, passions, and furies that burst through the stagnant, dam-like banks of rhyme' to the 'wider, less defined sea-basin of blank and parallel verse' (1939, 89). His view – which looks for validation in biblical Hebrew and in Shakespeare – emphasises rhythm rather than rhyme: 'In fact, one may almost say that the greatest gift of Africa to the artistic world will be – and has been – Rhythm' (Dhlomo 1939, 90).[5]

Vilakazi was stung by Dhlomo's attack. His riposte was to insist that Dhlomo's understanding of these matters was superficial and unscholarly – he had no grounding in Zulu linguistics, let alone classical languages or Shakespeare. More tellingly, in a personal assault on Dhlomo's efforts in drama, Vilakazi said, 'I do not know of any Bantu dramatists and their works; but I know there are poets with published works of reputable hallmark in all our South African Bantu languages which are worthy of study' (1939, 166). Bearing in mind that Dhlomo was writing historical dramas on the Zulu kings in English, the full implications (which resonate down to later generations) emerge in Vilakazi's final paragraph:

> By Bantu drama, I mean a drama written by a Bantu, for the Bantu, in a Bantu language. I do not class English or Afrikaans dramas on Bantu themes, whether these are written by Black people, I do not call them contributions to Bantu Literature. . . . I have an unshaken belief in the possibilities of Bantu languages and their literature, provided the Bantu writers *themselves* can learn to love their languages and use them as vehicles for thought, feeling and will. After all, the belief, resulting in literature, is a demonstration of people's 'self' where they cry: '*Ego sum quod sum*'. That is our pride in being black, and we cannot change creation. (1939, 167)

It was an argument, then, about where one's deepest loyalties lay in the struggle for racial and national self-affirmation, and it was about the aesthetic consequences of these choices. What we witness in the dispute – in these polemics but also in the more sober essays and statements that surround them – is an acting-out of the dilemmas facing the nationalist writer-intellectual of the day; an enactment of the ideological and aesthetic difficulties confronting writers in what Bhekizizwe Peterson calls 'the poetics of the crossroads' (1997, 103).

EXACTLY HOW SERIOUSLY Vilakazi would take Taylor's review of *Inkondlo* in subsequent years emerges from his doctoral thesis, 'The oral and written literature in Nguni' – a substantial elaboration of the earlier work – submitted in 1946. Taylor also provides a starting point for assessing the climate Vilakazi found himself in. Vilakazi, he said, had the spirit of the *imbongi* but he himself was not the *imbongi*; he was a follower of J.E.K Aggrey rather than Shaka.[6]

> He is the human poet rather than the Zulu poet . . . in the attention he pays to his own emotions and those he observes in others. It is the *imbongi* come to consciousness of the abstract and of the inner self, through contact with the work of other poets and through the unconscious influence of education and European culture. (Taylor 1935, 164)

In a direct response in his thesis, Vilakazi contrasts the generation of S.E.K Mqhayi with that of the slightly later J.J.R. Jolobe in Xhosa literature, and argues that the greatness of the earlier generation lay in their 'combining and using the knowledge and craft of the dead *izimbongi*, while the greatness of Jolobe and his confrères lies in experimentation and innovation, backed by their knowledge of past history, and in the delicate culture of mind drilled in the study of European literature which generates true poetic poise'.

Vilakazi then cites Taylor's comments about himself (Vilakazi), making them represent his entire generation: 'A young African poet [who] composes "in the truly African flavor of his imagery and in the exuberant extravagance of some of his descriptions is a true descendent of the *imbongi*. But the background of his thought is not that of the *imbongi*. He is not much concerned with warlike prowess"' (Vilakazi 1946, 348).

Taylor's preference for the 'abstract' and 'inner self' reveals how far Romanticism had come to define the terms of judgement in the period. Vilakazi repeats this emphasis – the key marker being 'imagination' – as a *sine qua non* of present and future achievement in Nguni poetry: the younger 'African poet' has not 'neglected or despised the past, but drawn it into himself and compressed it, and then interpreted it through his own imagination' (1946, 348). In all Vilakazi's critical prose it is clear that he had picked up the garden variety Romanticism that had become institutionalised in English literary-critical writing by the 1930s. A poet's 'happiness' comes from a special ability to interpret life 'in emotive words' (1946, 25); this ability stands in opposition to the sterility of mass culture; technology and art occupy different spheres (1946, 26); the imagination of the poet is in touch with the ineffable, things 'which none of us can touch or handle' (1946, 321). Romanticism in this form is, in fact, an essential marker for Vilakazi, separating traditional from modern aesthetics: the contemporary poet's imagination, his special ability to use words as 'elusive agents seeking answers to the final problems of life and even immortality' is what distinguishes him from 'the old world of primitive life, where savages wondered at the appearance of a train or at a minister of the Gospel' (1946, 321). Such apparent self-alienation is painful and all the more puzzling because, as we shall see, Vilakazi's life's work entailed the justification of traditional Zulu expression – even if this is tradition reinvented.

Part of the explanation for Vilakazi's drawing a line between traditional and modern aesthetics lies in prevailing constructions of traditional expression. Journals such as *Bantu Studies* and *The Critic* (both read by Vilakazi and Dhlomo) were overwhelmingly ethnographic in their treatment of black expression with all the attendant problems of othering and 'fixing' representations in condescending and ahistorical terms. It is not surprising that black intellectuals would have wished to put as much distance as possible between themselves and such representations. However, what is not immediately clear from this explanation is why literature defined in terms of a reductive post-Romanticism should have provided the means for them to do so.[7]

There were, of course, general shifts of culture in Europe on which this development depended – broadly speaking, the conventionalisation of Romantic orthodoxy described by Raymond Williams in *Culture and Society* (1963 [1958], 48–64). Added to this, and relying on it, was literary criticism's emergence as a university discipline, following the success (though perhaps not the example) of I.A. Richards's *Principles of Literary Criticism*.[8] Local conditions also played their part: in the 1930s there was a good deal of public discussion about the social role of literature amongst black South Africans, a discussion that assumed a connection between race and literature as a marker of 'progress'.[9] The debate was joined by liberal intellectuals such as Rheinhallt Jones and C.M. Doke (on the staff of Bantu Studies at the University of the Witwatersrand), R.H.W. Shepherd (director of the Lovedale Press), and Ray Phillips (of the American Board mission) as well as black writers and intellectuals such as Peter Abrahams (who recalls these years in *Tell Freedom*), D.D.T. Jabavu (author of two brief but pioneering monographs on black literary history), Selope Thema, Benedict Vilakazi, Herbert Dhlomo and others associated with the Bantu Men's Social Centre (BMSC) in Johannesburg (Couzens 1985, 102–06).

The discussion – which Couzens refers to as 'moralising the leisure time' of urban Africans – led in 1932 to the BMSC becoming a book distribution centre for the Carnegie Corporation. This brought into being the Carnegie Non-European Library, which, by 1937, was run by Herbert Dhlomo (Couzens 1985, 110). The intervention of the Carnegie Corporation in 1932 also led to the founding of *The*

Critic, after a commissioned report found 'there is no English critical periodical in the Union and no belletristic periodical of any value' (Reyburn 1932, 1). By 1935 *The Critic* was carrying articles on black expression, including an essay by G.P. Lestrade, the government ethnographer, on praise poetry to which, as we shall see, both Dhlomo and Vilakazi would respond. In June and October 1936, two conferences of 'Bantu authors' were held – one in Bloemfontein and the other in Florida near Johannesburg – in Shepherd's words, to 'organise and promote' the production and distribution of literature, and 'to emphasise the value of the use of literature' in African upliftment (in Couzens 1985, 104).[10] With white and black referring to the example of African-American literary achievement, the participants in these conferences had different emphases: white philanthropists emphasised progress towards non-racialism and civility; black authors complained about the poor level of support from the presses (Couzens 1985, 105). Although the proposal was never implemented, Clement Doke's idea of starting a 'Bantu Academy' was widely supported (Vilakazi 1946, 364).

Occasionally, the tension in this period between belletristic aspiration and social reality is painful to rehearse. In 1929, Selope Thema approvingly cited W.E.B. du Bois on the apparent freedom and universality inherent in the culture of the book:

> Across the color line I move arm in arm with Balzac and Dumas, where smiling men and welcoming women glide in gilded halls. From out the caves of evening that swing between the strong-limbed earth and the tracery of the stars, I summon Aristotle and Aurelius and what soul I will, and they come all graciously with no scorn nor condescension. (in Couzens 1985, 198–99)

As if in cynical rebuke, by 1936 South Africa would see the refinement of segregationist ideology leading to the Hertzog Bills, which entrenched the racial franchise and exacerbated existing laws governing access to landed property. In the absence of strong leadership from the ANC at the time, the All-African Convention brought the élite together to protest. Couzens suggests that

Dhlomo's play of this period, *Cetshwayo* – which, in my view, contains his most trenchant political writing – provides a critique of segregationist thinking by tracing its genealogy back to the 'native administration' policies in place during the Anglo-Zulu conflict of 1879 (Couzens 1985, 125–34).

Indeed, Thema's generation would experience nothing but injury to its social and political aspirations, and the literate culture of the mission school would steadily become an anachronism. Except, perhaps, in one respect: in the experience of this group, Romanticism was not merely around as dead convention. It spoke powerfully to young, ambitious people adrift in a world scarcely imagined by their forebears. Then, as they faced exclusion, frustration, and disappointment, the 'wounded self' of Shelley and Keats could provide a relevant idiom. In Dhlomo's case, even when in his later, more militant phase of the 1940s he was writing about the disappointments he personally suffered at the hands of white liberals (in poems such as 'Frustration' and 'Fired!') or the general disappointment felt by Africans to whom it was clear that the victory celebrations at the end of the Second World War excluded them ('Our Country Dear', 'Not for Me', 'Royal Visit, 1947'), the appeal of Shelley's 'thorns of life' is all too evident: 'this betrayal wounds and sears my soul. I bleed' (Dhlomo 1985, 377).

It seems safe to assert that the linkage of literary culture – coloured by the legacy of Romanticism – and modernity was a significant feature of this generation's intellectual life. Or, to put it differently, we may say that one of the ways in which this intelligentsia encountered the culture of modernity was through the institutionalisation of literature and criticism – 'Literature' – first in the mission school, then later, in civil society, namely the press, philanthropic organisations, and the universities. Repeating in a few compressed decades, perhaps, a history familiar in Europe, these institutions began taking over the Enlightenment tradition that had been the sole preserve of the church (as-mission). But this is to speak of only half of the encounter; equally important is to consider what African intellectuals brought to it, the prevailing constructions of African culture they inhabited, whether by circumstance or explicit affiliation. Their 'recognition' – to borrow the term used by John and Jean Comaroff to cover the range of apprehensions whereby colonised people engage with the culture of modernity – of the power of 'Literature' would have been governed by their particular circumstances, which were decisive in determining the forms of 'experimental practice' they could improvise in response (Comaroffs 1991, 29–31). The decisive aspect of these circumstances and the practices to which they gave rise was that they were profoundly split.

By the 1930s, rural or traditional or indigenous life and culture – the source of what we can call Africanity – did not exist in a space free of the history of colonial rule. It had been subject, not just to encroachment but to administrative control – certainly in the case of Natal and Zululand – for nearly half a century. The general character of this control has again been the subject of lively debate recently, following Mahmood Mamdani's eloquent study of colonial modernity, *Citizen and Subject* (1996). Mamdani's thesis is that the British and, after 1910, the South African state with remarkable consistency over this entire period – from indirect rule to apartheid – constructed and maintained a bifurcated world, with the rights of citizens within the framework of civil society being distinguished from the rights of communities living under customary law and traditional authority. Mamdani does not position these modes of power in a linear, developmental relationship: both were part of the armoury of late-colonial modernity, which instituted racially exclusive democracy at the centre (largely for whites or settlers) and decentralised despotism at the periphery, largely for the peasantry. Between these groups fell 'urban-based natives, mainly middle- and working class persons, who were exempt from the lash of customary law but not from modern, racially discriminatory civil legislation. Neither subject to custom not exalted as rights-bearing citizens, they languished in a juridical limbo' (Mamdani 1996, 19).

For our purposes, the pressing question is whether this 'limbo' was only juridical. It seems to me that Mamdani's thesis is pushed too far with respect to the analysis of culture. He argues that the bifurcated world manifested itself relentlessly:

> This divided world is inhabited by subjects on one side and citizens on the other; their life is regulated by customary law on one side and modern law on the other; their beliefs are dismissed as pagan on this side but bear the status of religion on the other; the stylised moments of their day-to-day lives are considered ritual on this side and glorified as the arts on the other; their verbal communication is demeaned as vernacular chatter on this side but elevated as linguistic discourse on the other; in sum, the world of the 'savages' barricaded, in deed as in word, from the world of the 'civilised'. (Mamdani 1996, 61)

The potential confusion here is whether individuals of the middle zone – by definition, where intellectuals would belong – reside entirely within a single sphere, or whether they inhabit both, as 'citizens' *and* 'subjects'. Presumably, Mamdani is implying the latter, but if so, do the poles of their experience remain permanently sealed off from one another, 'barricaded', in Mamdani's terms? This would be a misguided view. In any version of the thesis – the term 'limbo' carries these unfortunate associations – it would lead directly to the 'men of two worlds' stereotype, the analysis of Joyce Cary's *Mister Johnson*, for instance, which suggests that if one were not 'authentically' located in either world, one was located nowhere, which is simply a *non sequitur*. It could also lead to such mystifications as the notion of 'oral man', against which Leroy Vail and Landeg White caution us in their persuasive study of historical representation in oral culture, *Power and the Praise Poem* (1991). 'Oral man' is an ahistorical being, his (or her) culture a static, and exotic reflection of modernity's childhood.

The fact is, the intellectuals of Mamdani's middle zone did negotiate the poles of urban and rural, literate and non-literate, traditional and modern, shuttling between them constantly. So much so, that it would be no exaggeration to say that for some of them –

including Dhlomo, Vilakazi and most of the New African intelligentsia – precisely to accomplish this negotiation comprised their life's work. It is true that these oppositions constituted an historical reality; the question is, how were they negotiated? It was a choice between modes of synthesis, for the question was not whether to choose tradition or modernity but how to put the two spheres together in a performance that best served one's interests. Dhlomo and Vilakazi, as intellectuals with roughly similar backgrounds, were united in confronting this dilemma. What divided them, as we shall see, was that they responded differently to the only choice that was really available to them: either to modernise tradition, or to traditionalise modernity, or at least, certain forms of modern literary culture. When in a poem such as 'Imfundo Ephakeme' ('Higher Education'), Vilakazi contemplates the co-presence of the 'white man's books' and the praises of the 'black poets', then 'Namhla zixaben'ekhanda lami' ('Today they quarrel in my mind') – the tension demands resolution. In Vilakazi's case, this takes the form of an injunction to write his books for the children of Zululand, but at the behest of the *amadlozi*, the spirits or shades, who irritate and badger him into action (Vilakazi 1945, 7–8).

'POETRY TODAY', wrote Vilakazi, in a passage that reveals much about his poetics,

> is still but a trumpet call to those who cherish, in the midst of disillusion and despair, the ideal of intellectual and spiritual liberty, for it enables man to cultivate the philosophic mind. In other words, poetry means knowledge of the human heart in its depths, and it interprets to the world by creating a new feeling in the full of imagery and a pleasant recognition. There must be some witchery of word arrangement and selection together with the incantation of the rhythm. The writer can never forget the thrill of joy with which he recalls to mind the old man dressed in his Zulu war attire, adorned with a shining headring, reciting to the family the

exploits of Zulu heroes in Shakan times, and in the midst of his narration, suddenly picking one Mvundlane ka Menziwa of the Biyela tribe and praising him. In the long praises he was always struck by one line: *uNdonga zeLungwe, ngiba ngiyazibize ziyesabela* – 'the echoing of the precipitous battle fields of Langwe [*sic*].' The line always brought home to my mind the echoing of the precipitous battlefields and the reverberation of the voices of herd boys I used to hear at sunset in the Valley of a Thousand Hills. The situation became real to me with the words: *Ziyesabela.* Later, as a college boy I was attracted by a very big church bell called 'Angelus' which rang with its mellow tone wafted over forests and mountains. I do not know why it became a habit that at 9 every Sunday we would listen to its voice with unsatisfied delight, for we could not express our feelings, until one day in a Latin class our lecturer who gloried in Classics, noticed the ringing of this bell. The sound threw him into ecstasy and he said it brought back to him his home in Germany, where, in the city cathedral, there hung a bell with this inscription: 'Vivos Voco, mortuos plango, fulgura frango.' My understanding of these lines brought me perpetual content, ever afterwards whenever I heard the toll of this Angelus. The quotation was at once connected in my mind with the old *Ngibengiyazibize, ziyasabela* [*sic*]. To my mind both these lines are great poetry. When I read them my mind is filled with pleasant recognition. I can hear the echoing broken cliffs, visualise thick forests and winding rivers. While on the other hand on hearing the tolling of the 'Angelus' for a funeral, or, on the approaching of the storm with heavy dark clouds, a feeling of safety and relief from fear is immediately engendered by the remembrance of the 'Angelus' tolling on a Sunday morning and the people streaming to church along different winding footpaths, up and down the echoing mountains. The swinging of the bell is felt in the rhythm of the Latin composition, while the Zulu line presents a queer scanning, imitating the wafted waves of a re-echoing voice: *donga zeLangwe, Ngibengiyazibize, ziyesabela.* (1946, 28–29)

Ndonga's praise-name merges in Vilakazi's mind with the memory of the Angelus bell calling across the hills around the Mariannhill mission.[11] Rhythm and place are reconstituted in such a way that a line of oral poetry and a Latin inscription reinforce one another in a collective set of associations. Vilakazi's Catholic teacher – in all probability, Mariannhill's principal, Fr. Bernard Huss – offers his students an impassioned memory that (almost literally) resonates with an idea drawn from oral poetry, and in that hybrid resonance, the associations acquire form and memorability. 'Aesthetic distance' – a term Vilakazi uses (1946, 30) – is achieved through transculturation, in a combination of oral culture, a cross-cultural encounter in a mission classroom, and the process of poetic recollection described in Wordsworth's Preface to the *Lyrical Ballads*. (In his poem 'Izinsimbi Zesonto' Vilakazi would ascribe a related meaning to the mission bells of his youth, in which, having once signalled conquest, they come to herald a 'bright new world' led by men such as Albert Luthuli, A.W.G. Champion, and John Dube.)

'Aesthetic pleasure', Vilakazi goes on to say, 'derived from content and remembrance, is a *psychic form*. I do not believe in *physical form*; I rely more on the *psychic* – the spirit of a poem' (1946, 29). Against his critics, Vilakazi asserts that he does not reduce everything to 'mechanical standards'; nevertheless, 'it is only when the genius who knows his work, plays with the *physical form* in interpreting the visions of his plastic soul, that we can have the *psychic form* revealed unspoilt in the art of poetry' (1946, 29). The important aspect here is the *reworking* that makes a statement oracular, beautiful and memorable, thus answerable to the 'plasticity' of the mind creating it. We can now see that Vilakazi's seemingly obsessive fondness for rhyme, together with his interest in prosody, were essentially means to an end, which was to enable Zulu writing to acquire abstraction, distance, monumentality, and perfection – broadly speaking, the qualities of modern aesthetics. Vilakazi's position is to modernise tradition: the project involves passing Zulu expressive forms through what he often calls a 'tempering' process, which gives them 'psychic form', thus making them recognisable contributions to modern world literature. Elsewhere he says, 'if we are to believe and teach other races of humanity to believe our tale, the poets must be truthful', and 'telling the truth' entails finding forms that can be *recognised*: 'Just as face answers to face, so does the heart of man to man' (Vilakazi 1993 [1938], 83). The latter sentiment would no doubt have been shared by Vilakazi's contemporary, Alan Paton.

Using the mechanics of Western poetry was therefore not mere imitation:

> If we imitate the form, the outward decoration which decks the charming poetry of our Western masters, that does not mean to say that we have incorporated into our poetry even their spirit. If we use Western stanza-forms and metrical system we employ them only as vehicles or receptacles for our poetic images, depicted as we see and conceive. (Vilakazi 1993 [1938], 77)

Similarly – to put it in the language of my argument – the accession of modernity's aesthetics is not inimical to the expression of nationalist aspirations. On the contrary, it is instrumental to it. Comparing the famous line of the spiritual, 'Nobody knows the trouble I see', to a line from a Zulu burial song that echoes a dying warrior culture, Vilakazi says:

> There is a dream in the song reflecting the Zulu mind's devastating experience, and the vanishing of his shadowy faith in war. The poet does not surrender his dream for he knows it has its counterpart when he lives by its enchantment. He has to make himself of a certain quality, to fashion himself to a certain temper. . . . His dream works upon his soul and never diminishes. Even though his military faiths are wrecked. There remains one thing in which he believes without fear of disillusion, and that is the beauty of his dream. (1993 [1938], 83–84)

While oral poetry reaches this state frequently, it does so unselfconsciously, and the 'modern poet' has to take it on as his particular *métier*:

> We have to use some form to embody or clothe the beautiful spirit of our poetry. We have no definite form so far, and our starting point will be at the standards given us by the Western education we have imbibed at college. We are beginning the work which may be given perfect form in generations to come. (Vilakazi 1993 [1938], 79)

G.P. LESTRADE'S ESSAY in *The Critic* on 'Bantu praise-poems' precipitated the Dhlomo-Vilakazi dispute. I shall turn to it in order to approach the essentials in Dhlomo's poetics. The key passage is the following, in which Lestrade reveals his bemusement when confronted with the transcribed text of oral poetry:

> With regard to the language in which [*izibongo*] are couched, very little can be said in an essay which is not meant for Bantu linguists. It may be sufficient to indicate here that the language is in general difficult and obscure, that a very large number of words and phrases occur the true meaning of which is no longer known, that many archaic forms present themselves; that the construction of sentences tends to be laconic and even staccato, and that the poems are all extremely rich in allusions whose significance has been lost in course of time, or whose meaning has been preserved only indifferently. These statements refer more particularly to the older poems, those that have come down to modern times from a past which must have been long enough ago for the names of their authors to have been completely lost, and for their meaning to have been preserved only imperfectly. But even quite modern poems are difficult enough in their language, since the poets imitate the old models, and employ expressions and constructions whose significance they themselves do not understand fully. (Lestrade 1935, 5–6)

These observations have some validity, because *izibongo* can be gnomic and arcane. Harold Scheub makes a similar observation, pointing out that details relevant to a particular historical episode are often presented elliptically. Scheub offers as an example an excerpt from the praise of Xhoko, the founder of the Biyela clan, as performed by Umhle Biyela (born 1930):

> Axe to those who took refuge at Qaphela-bazozela,
> Rope of the *umsenge* tree of Sikhakha's household,
> I fear it because it has an ear like that of an elephant,
> Ndaba's eagle was born, and immediately started
> walking,
> Saying it was going to Maziyane . . . (Scheub 1985,
> 514–15)

This is a problem, however, only for those who are not part of the culture, or who know nothing about the incident, as Scheub points out (1985, 514). The conclusion Lestrade draws from the obscurity is racist: he asserts that both oral and literate poets are content with such 'incoherence' because of the workings of the Bantu mind, which is essentially non-linear and unanalytical. With extraordinary composure in response, Dhlomo and Vilakazi in their respective *Bantu Studies* essays seek to supply the sense of coherence that eludes Lestrade. Vilakazi draws on gestalt psychology and his ideas on psychic form to establish that a certain mental set is required to grasp such poetry. He refers to its emotional aptness, but most of his reply consists of a demonstration of the rhythm and diction of oral poetry using a love poem, 'Umcayi kaVuma' ('Vuma's daughter') as an example. The rather technical elaboration of breath-units, stresses and prosody in this demonstration obviously irritated Dhlomo, who uses the same poem for his demonstration of its coherence, but with a quite different analysis. Dhlomo's thesis is that 'the tribal literary forms whose nature and construction have baffled many investigators, are in reality mutilated and distorted remains of primitive, tribal dramatic pieces' (Dhlomo 1993 [1939], 187). The oral poet was 'handicapped and fettered' by traditional methods of composition and was forced to present what was, in fact, dramatic dialogue, in quasi-linear, unsuccessful monologue. Excluded from this analysis are the *izibongo* of certain chiefs and kings, which are 'pure poetry'. Dhlomo's demonstration involves re-transcribing 'Umcayi' in English translation into a piece of drama, with the lines being assigned to four contending characters, with movements on- and off-stage. Vilakazi has the last word on 'Umcayi' when he later insists it is a simple love poem, accusing Dhlomo of the 'anthropologist's fallacy' (Vilakazi 1946, 94).

Vilakazi is surely correct, for it seems clear that Dhlomo sucks the quasi-historical analysis of the poem out of his thumb. More importantly, though, we should consider Dhlomo's underlying purposes. Clearly, he wishes to collectivise the creative impulse that he sees taking shape in a rather individualistic poetic voice in Vilakazi, overlaid with too many technical obsessions. The idea of collective creativity being intrinsic to traditional culture stands at the core of Dhlomo's theoretical interventions. He believes that the 'poems of amatory and general character are earlier and more genuine native stuff than the ordinary praise-poems of kings' (Dhlomo 1993 [1939], 190) because it is in these poems that this communal voice can be detected:

> Nothing in tribal society belonged to the individual. . . . art was no exception to this rule. The harmonic sense was so highly developed that it was enough for one individual to compose the melody of a tune and then introduce it to his companions, who would instantly learn the given melody, compose parts to it, sing the whole song there and then, and dance to it rhythmically. (Dhlomo 1993 [1939], 192–93)

Dhlomo's ideological interest in the collective creativity of traditional society was reinforced by his reading of the mythopoeic anthropology so favoured by literary critics of the period. His personal copy of Sir James Frazer's *The Golden Bough* was carefully annotated, from which he borrowed the idea that 'tribal drama' was based on sympathetic magic (Couzens 1985, 161, 190n). Africa thus shares with Europe a past in which religious ritual and festival – notably around the death of a king – provided the terms for the later development of the theatre (Dhlomo 1993 [1939], 195–202). Furthermore, the 'tribal dramatist' is poised to create great 'literary drama' that could model itself on the Greek and Elizabethan stages, partly because

> we live under conditions in many ways similar to those that produced great Greek dramatic literature and the immortal Elizabethan drama. . . . It is a time when an old indigenous culture clashes with a newer civilisation, when tradition faces powerful exotic influences. It is a time when men suddenly become conscious of the wealth of their threatened old culture, the glories of their forefathers, the richness of their tradition, the beauty of their art and song. (Dhlomo 1977a [1939], 41)

In these remarks Dhlomo's writing on traditional drama is seen to repeat the Janus-faced orientation of all cultural nationalism: the desire for participation in a global modernity, but on the basis of an intrinsic, distinctive character.[12] He moved between affirming the underlying unity of African and European forms (in the spirit of some contemporary anthropology), and affirming the unity of distinctively African traditions (an attractive political proposition). The universalism is apparent in statements such as these: 'And to those who hold that tribal man was incapable of intellectual work of this kind, let us say that by means of intuition and imaginative art, the Universal Mind can and does express itself actively through primitive men and humble' (Dhlomo 1993 [1939], 202). Similarly,

> great art or thought . . . is more than racial and national. It is universal, reflecting the image, the spirit, of the All-Creative Being

> who knows neither East nor West, Black nor White, Jew nor Gentile . . . The tragedy of a Job, an Oedipus, a Hamlet, a Joan, a Shaka, a Nongqawuse, is the tragedy of all countries, all times, all races. (Dhlomo 1977a [1939], 42)

Before being admitted to the universal feast, however, the dramatist had to practise 'literary necromancy', raiding tradition to

> gather sticks to fight our literary and cultural battles, timber to build our dramatic genius, wood to make our poetic fires, leaves to decorate our achievements. *Izibongelo* [traditional poems] are the essence of our being, the meaning of our name. . . . Above all they reveal the common origin, the spiritual unity, the essential Oneness, the single destiny of all Bantu tribes. (Dhlomo 1977a [1939], 37)

In the terms sketched out earlier, Dhlomo's position – the reverse of Vilakazi's – was to traditionalise modernity, not to pass traditional forms through a modern crucible but, as it were, to stamp modern literary self-consciousness with the seal of Africanity.[13]

The consequence of Dhlomo's stance, however, was that he was obliged to work in a *lingua franca*, which could only be English, despite his sensitivities as a dramatist. It is true that in the late 1930s he supported the idea of the development of 'Union' languages – Nguni, Sotho, Venda, Thonga – each of which would represent a cluster of related languages, an idea widely discussed by linguists, anthropologists, missionaries and administrators. For Dhlomo's own purposes, the advantages of such a scheme seemed clear: 'First, there would be the blend of the genius of each racial group resulting in the greater genius of the nation. Second, there would be a richer field of tradition, folk-lore and ideas. Third, African literature would enjoy a wider circle of readers. Fourth, it would lead to the establishment of a national school of African Drama' (Dhlomo 1977b [1939], 9). But the Union languages scheme had little practical chance of success, and since English would accomplish most of these goals more effectively than Union languages anyway, Dhlomo was to fall back on the use of English. By the 1940s, his commitment to it was aggressive: 'English [would be] the universal language of the future by force of commanding factors'; 'all this talk about bilingualism and Native languages in this country is futile'; the 'practical' solution was simply to come to terms with the language of power (in Peterson 1997, 84, 225).

Part of the irritation, I surmise, was because liberal segregationists (Doke, Rheinhallt Jones, Philips and, later, Hugh Tracey), with whom Dhlomo came increasingly into conflict – assuming the position of tutelage, they could not refrain from expressing opinions about the way he conducted his personal life – and whose authority in this matter stretched back to missionary attitudes to the use of English in African education, generally advocated the use of indigenous languages. It is also possible, however, that Dhlomo and Vilakazi's very different positions on this question go back to differences in the mission education they received, with the Congregationalists of the American Board in Dhlomo's experience being arguably more laissez-faire about the use of English than the Catholics at Mariannhill who contributed to Vilakazi's formation. Mariannhill was bilingual, but the language question was foregrounded there by several disputes over the translation into isiZulu of the catechism (Peterson 1997, 85–94). As the language assistant to Fr. Huss, Vilakazi was invested in this debate, an experience that would later contribute to his being appointed as the language adviser in Bantu Studies at the University of the Witwatersrand (Nyembezi 1973, xviii).

If Vilakazi's intimate relationship with isiZulu was sustained through his institutional position, Dhlomo's drift towards English would have been confirmed for ideological reasons. In this respect, it is interesting that his brother, Rolfes, wrote mainly in isiZulu, and remained on the other side of the language debate. In Herbert's judgement, the 'nation' would have to use English, whether this was to be interpreted as the 'essential Oneness' of Africans or the 'universalism' of a hybrid Euro-African culture (1977a [1939], 37).

WE CAN NOW distinguish clearly the two writer's positions. In *The South African Outlook* essay that annoyed Vilakazi so much, Dhlomo had proposed that the repetition and parallelism of oral poetry could be maintained in English as the basis of literary poetry; he also claimed that he had already achieved this in his own drama (Dhlomo 1939, 89).[14] Vilakazi disputed this, saying that it was one thing to apply 'such a purely primitive Bantu form of poetry as a criterion of a new English poetry by Bantu authors', but another to advocate 'the possibility of new Bantu forms being generated from the primitive material which is itself good poetry' (Vilakazi 1946, 276–77). This distinction, rather crisply, defines the dilemma that divided them. The first position – deriving a theoretical criterion from oral poetry by which to develop and judge poetry in English – was Dhlomo's. The second position was Vilakazi's: developing 'new [written] Bantu forms' based on the oral material. It is not enough to point to – much less to celebrate – a rather vaguely defined cultural 'synthesis' or 'hybridity' to characterise the choices that writers of this generation were required to make. Vilakazi himself was to wrestle with suitable metaphor in describing the historic project that lay before his and subsequent generations: the new literature would be 'something that has the elements of both, but which has its own Bantu life, and is yet new, harmonious, developing and integrally African':

> What future literature needs is not a compromise between the old and the new ideas, but a fusion, as it were; not a mixture but an amalgam. The virile elements of both African and Western cultures must fuse and give birth to a new life, expressed in a new literature. (Vilakazi 1946, 372)

To modernise tradition (Vilakazi) is to produce an 'amalgam' ('harmonious, developing, integrally African'); to traditionalise modernity (Dhlomo) is to produce a 'mixture'. Both strategies are neo-traditionalist, but while Vilakazi seeks to build from a sense of continuity within the language – since it is in the forms of the language that one hears the original speech community and imagines its survival – Dhlomo's relationship with tradition is retroactive, possibly even voluntarist, which is another way of reading the notion that we need to 'gather sticks to fight our literary and cultural battles, timber to build our dramatic genius, wood to make our poetic fires, leaves to decorate our achievements', etc. When Dhlomo writes, the 'African dramatist cannot delve into the Past unless he has grasped the Present' (1977b [1939], 40), he shows an astute understanding of tradition, but he also licenses a certain voluntarism. Instead of developing continuities within the language, Dhlomo assumes the position of the nation's genius, the pathfinder whose speech is uttered in conditions of relative isolation, to be understood by the people only when sufficient are able to follow his call. It is Dhlomo's strategy, perhaps, rather than Vilakazi's, which best exemplifies Benedict Anderson's thesis that nationhood comes to fill what Walter Benjamin called the 'homogenous, empty time' of a post-religious and post-dynastic age (Anderson 1991 [1983], 24), the reason being that Dhlomo intuitively apprehends that dizzying emptiness and tries to fill it with heroic ideas. The difficulty for writers is that the nation could only be imagined in conflicted terms, since the public sphere was divided. There were, to continue with Anderson's analysis, the instruments of 'print capitalism' – novels and newspapers – with which to construct the idea of community, but which 'novels', using what genres, which newspapers, printed in which languages? Dhlomo's route was that of post-enlightenment rationality, in order to reach the maximum degree of leverage on modernity's emancipatory promises. Vilakazi's, by contrast, was to preserve the voice, the speech, of his people, and to expand the forms available to them in a steady acquisition of modernity's cultural riches.

Was Dhlomo's position revolutionary and Vilakazi's evolutionary? This is the conclusion that Maria K. Mootry (1973) reaches in her assessment of the two poets: Vilakazi reached the stage of 'protest' in his development, but never went as far as Dhlomo in reaching the properly Fanonist stage of 'revolution'. This is true, to some degree, but is an over-simplification since both positions carried a price. In fact, as with many rivalries, each writer needed most what the other possessed. Lewis Nkosi comes close to making this observation when, recognising the failure of both poets 'to adapt lessons learned from English verse to their own native tradition', he argues that

> Vilakazi at least enjoyed the advantage of having written mostly in his mother tongue, with the result that however derivative his poetics it could not include the use of an exact European imagery and terminology as Dhlomo was sometimes compelled to do. Regrettably, . . . lyrical 'purity' is precisely what Dhlomo's poem [*Valley of a Thousand Hills*] fails to achieve. (Nkosi 1981, 115)

To this we must add the caveat that it is not simply an issue of Vilakazi's (or anyone else's) having written in the mother tongue, since the production of a literary aesthetics – in whatever language – entails an act of synthesis. Rather, it is a question of whether such synthesis that is achieved, recognisably echoes the voice of the community whose interests it seeks to reflect.

Tim Couzens concludes his biography of Dhlomo with a telling anecdote that captures an unforgiving aspect of his subject's legacy. One of his interviewees, a Mrs M. Sesedi of Kimberley, recalled an amusing incident in which a certain Mr Msomi was attempting to pay tribute to Dhlomo in a speech: 'So he wanted to quote the greatness of this man, Dhlomo. And one of the pieces that I remember well, *Valley of a Thousand Hills*, he just remembered the first line, then he stuck. One of the fellows in the audience said, "He doesn't know it", but he said it in Zulu, "He doesn't know it"'. As Couzens puts it: 'Dhlomo is like that – half in and half out of the collective memory' (1985, 355). The problem, of course, is that his writing seldom settled into a credible mode of address, suffering from what Njabulo Ndebele would later call, in another context, 'the obscenity of high seriousness' (1983, 217).[15] The poignancy of his legacy is not only that his manner was a 'Romantic-

Victorian effusion' (Gérard 1971, 236) and 'relentlessly elevated' (Chapman 1996, 213); it also lies in the consequences of this mode of address: his important (yes, at times revolutionary) ideas are seldom received with the degree of seriousness they ought to be. Having taken the high road to liberty, Dhlomo's language became asocial, strained, bloodless – frequently, it should be acknowledged, even absurd.

Ironically, Vilakazi's reputation before and after his death is that he was arrogant and aloof, as if, in his own mind at least, his university position and degrees qualified him to speak *ex cathedra.* C.L.S. Nyembezi notes that while he was perceived this way, he 'was pouring out his love of his people and his faith in their future into his poems' (1973, xix). Indeed, as we have seen, his entire position was an affirmation of his belonging within a particular speech community. Unlike Dhlomo, his language was credible. What Vilakazi lacked and Dhlomo possessed, was an ideological vision that extended from the page into a grander, historical self-consciousness, a consciousness in which later generations of militants might see their concerns reflected – provided the address was appropriate. Unfortunately, history would determine that amongst writers of this generation, with a Zulu background, there was to be no Dhlomo with Vilakazi's diction, and no Vilakazi with Dhlomo's ideological acumen.

IT REMAINS FOR us to assess the ways in which their positions become evident in Dhlomo's and Vilakazi's literary writing. Although these issues might be found in Dhlomo's English-language drama and Vilakazi's Zulu-language fiction, the place to locate them more acutely is in their poetry, which in both cases evinces a high degree of self-consciousness. To begin with Dhlomo: that his nationalism is articulated from a position of lofty isolation becomes apparent in a close reading of the poem for which he is most well known, *Valley of a Thousand Hills.* There are good internal and contextual reasons for this text to have acquired the reputation of being 'one of the early major poetic epics in South African literature' (Couzens 1985,

220). It is certainly a work of epic aspiration, from the opening section, which arranges the Zulu pantheon of gods and royal ancestors in an elaborate 'machinery'[16] and constructs the land as the fertile seed-bed of an heroic history, to the final three sections (V, VI and VII), which contrast an idyllic past of independent communalism, a degraded present of disarray under oppression, and a resurgent future in which the glories inherent in a revered landscape will once again find political expression. These features, coupled with the fact that the poem coincides with the stirring of militancy associated with the rise of the ANC Youth League, have given it its honorific reputation, all of which is borne out in its most frequently cited lines:

> The Seed of Shaka, Hintsa, Khama and
> Moshoeshoe, Go, Cetshwayo, and the band
> Of bards of old, cannot forever live
> Oppressed. To slavery they will not yield.
> Blood boils as they behold both spear and shield:
> We'll strike and take! if others will not give! (Dhlomo
> 1985, 318)

The more neglected aspect of the poem, however, is its struggle to find the voice with which to articulate this vision. From Couzens we know that Dhlomo's self-doubts were connected with the breakdown of his marriage and, partly linked to this, arguments with liberal patrons who questioned his ethical conduct and withdrew their support, events whose racial implications Dhlomo treated as implicitly political. These incidents find their way into the poem, as does Dhlomo's lingering grief over the death of his mother, Sardinia Caluza. Social displacement and personal anguish fuel a sense of despair that at times reaches a suicidal pitch, though the intensity is frequently vitiated by the derivativeness of the language. For example, a 'devil strange in me' will rail at injustice in Lear-like recklessness:

> There is no God! If any, hear!
> For I defy them to their faces – bold!
> Descend ye gods, take flesh, and let us fight!
> Why clothe yourselves and shelter, trembling, 'neath
> Invisibility or cowardice? (Dhlomo 1985, 305)

Similarly, the power of the Metaphysical conceit – not to mention rhyme, after the scorn inflicted on Vilakazi – proves irresistible in the midst of the apparent self-loathing:

> Fogs of despondence wrap me round
> In python-like death coils!
> And fling me to the ground
> Despised! A dog all full of boils!
> They blind me to all else but me –
> This putrid flea;
> This me I hate but cannot flee. (Dhlomo 1985, 306–07)

More significant, however, for our understanding of Dhlomo's uncertainties – that is to say, more significant than either his personal insecurities or his lack of sure-footed diction – is the fact that Dhlomo returns to and draws strength from the landscape of the Valley in terms of what can only be described as a displaced modern subject. We see this, for example, in the address to 'the arum lily of my native streams'. The lily is ambiguous in referring both to the regenerative terrain of the Valley itself, and to the imagined Zulu girl whose freshness and innocence represents everything he now misses in his wife (Dhlomo 1985, 303). He impresses her with his city background and stature as anguished artist and outsider:

> To storied countries strange and far I've been;
> The beauty of the sun and stars I've seen.
> Felt pain sweep on the soul like mellow tunes,
> Raising poetic dust from the Muses' dunes! (1985, 303)

More tellingly, the turning-point that brings Dhlomo out of despair – and ushers in the poem's militant final sections – is a moment of uncanny dislocation, in which the natural attributes of the Valley steal upon him, disarming his despair in their simplicity and hyper-reality. Dramatising the moment with Shakespearean tension ('. . . Who calls?'), Dhlomo presents the undisturbed continuity of the natural world and rural life as a source of wonder and amazement to a mind too long wrapped up in self-contemplation, and too long exposed to the maelstrom of modern turmoil:

> In mingled shame and doubt I blinked . . . 'Who calls?'
> There is no sound but purity and peace!
> Activity as silent, smooth, as song! . . .
> Silent, a bird floats past, and far away
> A drunken whisk of smoke staggers about
> this way and that, and wastes itself to naught!
> The distant mountain peaks peep silent, veiled!
> A dumb but busy ant has lost its way,
> And up my leg it climbs, silent . . .
> A snail jogs quiet by, all peaceful, mute.
> Curious, a root from some old tree, bobs up,
> Peeps naughtily, all shy, and down the earth
> It delves again leaving a part exposed –
> So hurried was its stolen silent glance! (Dhlomo 1985, 308)

And so on, for another two dozen lines. Couzens describes the line containing the jogging snail as 'the oddest . . . in all Dhlomo', and dignifies the passage as a version of Keatsian negative capability (Couzens 1985, 228). It may, in fact, be just the opposite: not a suspension of proactive perception that allows the mind to be rejuvenated by subconscious processes, but an attempt to concretise observation in an accession of self. In other words, it is not Keats after a draught of vintage wine, but Crusoe waking up beached on the island, joyfully running his fingers through the sand. It is the modern, bourgeois touch, so to speak, with its expansion of self. Eventually, it is a Wordsworthian cadence ('Tintern Abbey', specifically), which brings the desired resolution:

> Sequestered in this spot, 'twas joy to breathe . . .
> Living or dead, moving or still, all things
> Stood charmed with Beauty of deep Solitude!
> The Solitude not of these hills and vales,
> But Solitude of introspection deep. (Dhlomo 1985, 309)

Steadily, having weathered its crisis, the solitary subject is reconstituted:

> the Within dictates to the Without.
> Without the live within dead the Without. . . .
> Our world, our thought, our all is in the Self. (Dhlomo 1985, 309)

In subsequent lines, this self is transformed into that of the poet, and it is the poetic self that provides the historical sweep of past, present and resurgent future that is the poem's *raison d'être*. The preparation and authorisation of the poetic voice in Dhlomo's poem can be described in terms of the creation of a modern Prometheus, whose discovery of agency and independence is a precondition for the expression of the poem's nationalism. It almost goes without saying that like several of his Romantic forebears, Dhlomo's account of this process is strongly gendered:

> Ancestral Spirits great vouchsafe me power
> This beauty fierce to seize and rape and make
> My own . . . to express! The poet do not jilt (Dhlomo 1985, 295)

This tendency is confirmed in the prominence of the goddess of chastity and fertility, Nomkhubulwana, in the opening stanzas, the frolicking childhood of the mother-figure, the mysterious lover/arum lily, and so on.

In Vilakazi, the poetic self also seeks affirmation from the feminine. In 'Ugqozi' ('Inspiration') the poet waits, calling outside the gates of the Royal Place at Dukuza, and is eventually admitted by Shaka's great-aunt Mnkabayi, perhaps the most powerful woman of her time in Zululand. It is from her that he finally receives his commission (Vilakazi 1973, 76; 1980 [1945], 2; Ngwenya 1998, 135). But there is a marked difference from Dhlomo in the way Vilakazi seeks blessing from his sources of inspiration. In Vilakazi, this is always represented as a plea, an injunction, a promise, and seldom as an achieved state. He is usually deeply conscious of the possibility of failure, and success is held out as something that might flower only in the future.[17] He does not claim that he will, much less has already, fulfilled Mnkabayi's command; she says merely that it is his destiny to evoke the stories of battle ('Vuk'ubong' indaba yemikhonto') (Vilakazi 1980 [1945], 2). In 'Imbongi' ('Poet'), there is in fact a confession of deep uncertainty about his ability to fulfil the ancestral muse's injunctions:

> Konje ngabe yim' engikhulumayo,
> Noma ngabe nguwe Thongo likaMbongi?
> Ngabe ngizwe kahle noma ngiyahlongozelwa?
> (Vilakazi 1980 [1945], 3)

> Are these my words or yours, O deathless Muse?
> And do I voice the truth or fatuous nonsense?
> (Vilakazi 1973, 78)[18]

In his own poem on the inspiration provided by the Valley of a Thousand Hills ('KwaDedangendlale'), the assumption of the role of tribal bard is deferred to the future:

Ngiph' indaw' enjenga lena
Wena Thongo likababa,
Lapho ngiyoba namandla,
Ngiqoq' umqondo kaZulu,
Ngiwuvalel' embizeni.
Ngihay' amahub' enkondlo
UShak' ayihay' enqoba,
Eqa kwaDedangendlale,
Ayagqule ngoKhahlamba,
Adl'uLangalibalele. (Vilakazi 1980 [1945], 29)

Give me, I pray, a place like this –
O you spirits of my fathers! –
When I, one day, shall have the power
To glean the wisdom of the Zulus
And write about it in my books.
Then I shall chant our tribal songs,
Sung in victory by Shaka
Who crossed this valley of rolling hills
Until he reached the Drakensberg
And subjugated Langalibalele.[19] (Vilakazi 1973, 101)

The poem in which Vilakazi attempts to resolve the uncertainties around his sense of vocation is 'uMamina'. The title refers partly to the feminine side of the poet himself, and the nature of poetic inspiration is being addressed – 'museness', as it were. Friedman's translation simply calls the poem an 'ode to the muse' (Vilakazi 1973, 110), suggesting that the question of whether Zulu muses actually exist is unproblematic. D.B.Z. Ntuli, author of the only monograph on Vilakazi, states baldly that the notion of a muse is 'foreign to the Zulus' (Ntuli 1984, 99). Thengani Ngwenya is more nuanced than either of the foregoing, in arguing that Vilakazi 'is offering a culturally contextualised interpretation of the "foreign" conception of the muse' (Ngwenya 1998, 140).

The most persuasive account of Vilakazi's 'muse' in 'uMamina' is the one Ngwenya draws from, by Adrian Koopman. Using his own literal translations – as opposed to Friedman's rather free extrapolations – Koopman demonstrates that the obsessive and unresolved passions of the poet for Mamina convey the state of possession usually associated with the calling one receives from the *amadlozi* or ancestors – Mamina herself is a spirit-maiden – to become an *isangoma* or diviner. The poet's condition includes sobbing in grief, hallucinations, strange dreams, drunkenness, walking about at night, fidgeting, eating unusual herbs, washing in beach sand, becoming excessively delicate, and so on (Koopman 1980, 8–17). Koopman's suggestion is that Vilakazi, who felt his isolation intensely, encodes his poetic inspiration in terms of the *isangoma* in order to anchor his identity and achieve social acceptance (1980, 17).[20] A related suggestion, equally enlightening, is that just as the diviner, who as the 'interpreter of dreams, and therefore the link between the *abaphilayo* and the *abaphanzi*, i.e. the living and those below', manipulates ordinary objects and activities that have been reconstituted as signs, so Vilakazi imagines himself using writing to mediate between the living and the dead:

> Vuk'umhlwenga phimbo lami,
> Ungehlulwe yigekle lomhlanga.
> UNkulunkul' ukunik' amalaka,
> Nolimi nezindebe zokuphumesa
> Iminjunju nemizindlo, nemicabango
> Eqhuma emithonjeni yomphefumulo. . . .
> Dweba phans' okwaziyo nokuzwayo,
> Ithonga lizokuhumushela ngosiba. (Vilakazi 1980
> [1945], 48)
>
> Arouse yourself, O my throat,
> That you be not surpassed by a reed flute.
> God has given you vocal cords,
> And a tongue and lips of speaking out
> The pains and ponderings, and the thoughts,
> Which burst from the fountains of the soul. . . .

Write down what you know and feel and hear,
The spirit will interpret for you with a pen. (Koopman 1980, 18)

While Dhlomo seeks a poetic self of consolidated subjectivity from which to articulate a national vision, Vilakazi seeks a more vatic state, possession of a kind, a dissolution of the self, which would empower him to play the role of interpreter from within the culture. If Dhlomo's position is Promethean, Vilakazi's is Orphic, since he risks a 'death' of the self in a quest that emphasises the continuity and survival of cultural signs, and a lyrical voice and its songs (*inkondlo*) that carry the aspirations of his speech community. (That a number of Vilakazi's poems brood on the presence and pervasiveness of death is perhaps gratuitous confirmation of an Orphic tendency.)

The potential for successfully exploiting this orientation within the historical conditions associated with South African modernity – racial capitalism – is thoroughly borne out in Vilakazi's most militant poem, 'Ezinkomponi' ('The Gold Mines'). One of the poem's achievements is the integration of the speaking subject within the 'imagined community' he is writing about. The speaker is both miner and poet, sharing the miners' pain and interpreting it:

Umfoweth' uyolithwal' ipiki,
Nehalavu alibek' ehlombe
Efak'amagqukel' ezinyaweni.
Nay' angen' angilandele,
umhlab' usigwinye siyovukuza (Vilakazi 1980 [1945], 63)

My brother also carries a pick,
Heaves a spade upon his shoulder,
Drags on his feet a miner's boots
and enters the shaft to follow me.
The earth soon swallows us who burrow . . . (Vilakazi 1973, 126)

At times these personae become completely merged; in such moments, although Vilakazi uses the first person singular, he implies a collective subject. Accordingly, in her free translation, Friedman uses the first person plural:

> Yenzani kahle noma ngivathazela.
> Kuzona lezizingalwane ngeny'imini
> Kwake kwazululeka izijul' ezimbi,
> Engazizwiba kwafiphal' umhlaba,
> Kwanyakaz'umbuso weNdlovukazi,
> Kwancipha abakaPewula, kodwa ngadliwa.
> Ngiya ngiphupha njalo, mntanensimbi,
> Ngiphuph'umhlaba wawokok' ubuyela
> Ezandleni zamanxus' amnyama. (Vilakazi 1980 [1945], 64)

> Beware! Though now my hands are empty,
> These puny arms, in days gone by,
> Wielded the fatal assegais,
> Which as we hurled them, darkened the earth.
> Great Queen Victoria's realm was shaken,
> Paul Kruger's soldiers terrified –
> And yet we were defeated!
> But still I dream – O steel contraptions! –
> That lands our fathers once possessed
> Shall, by their sons be ruled again. (Vilakazi 1973, 127)

WHILE VILAKAZI WAS equivocal to the end about Dhlomo's poetry, especially *Valley* (Vilakazi 1946, 279), Dhlomo was more forgiving. Poems such as 'Ezinkomponi' may have helped to restore the friendship, though we cannot be sure. Certainly, by 1946, Dhlomo had decided to bury the hatchet, for in his review of *Amal'ezulu* he observed that the new volume 'reveals a revolutionary change or development in the poet's soul'. Previously, Vilakazi proved himself to be 'obsessed with the idea of classicism, an artist worshiping devoutly in the shrine of art for art's sake, a poet so enamored of the beauty and music and meaning of Nature that he was oblivious of the grim tragedy, the struggle, the pathetic conditions and the call of his people'. The 'new Vilakazi' was a 'cultural Bambatha' who identified with 'the struggles of his people', and by so doing, he has 'gained in breadth, strength and stature'(in Couzens 1985, 220–21).[21]

To argue this way, of course, is to ignore the poems in *Amal'ezulu* that are not especially militant, such as those about the moon and nightfall, or poems of personal sentiment such as the final piece on his father's death. There is also 'NgoMbuyazi eNdondakusuka', which opens up the ticklish question of Cetshwayo's assassinated brother, implying a lingering anxiety about the effects of succession disputes. In the light of the range of Vilakazi's concerns in his second collection, Dhlomo's review is very much an overstatement, in keeping with his own compulsions. Quite possibly, by 1946, having suffered several disappointments himself, Dhlomo had begun to feel that unity amongst the black intelligentsia was more important than the continuation of a feud.

On Vilakazi's early death by meningitis in 1947, Dhlomo wrote an elegy ('Ichabod') recognising what previously he had denounced: 'How beautiful our native speech resounded/In the mellowed tones you weaved in Race-pride grounded' (1985, 352). Dhlomo survived Vilakazi by ten years, dying during heart surgery in 1957. In this decade, his literary efforts were limited largely to journalism, working on *Ilanga Lase Natal* with his brother, Rolfes.

Both Vilakazi and Dhlomo died relatively young, and their dispute has about it a certain arrogance and assurance on both sides. That the argument was also deeply symptomatic of their period and its particular challenges, however, and that their conduct of it still speaks poignantly to our own times, testifies to their extraordinary talent.

4

Fugitive pieces

Es'kia Mphahlele in the diaspora

Two seemingly unrelated remarks by one of Es'kia Mphahlele's most perceptive commentators, Peter Thuynsma, provide our point of departure in this chapter. Firstly, he comments that Mphahlele is 'the first black South African to be so truly international', and secondly, that 'it should have come as little surprise that he eventually returned "to lay his shadow on ancestral soil"'[1] (Thuynsma 1989a, 1; 1989b, 101). That it should have come as little surprise that Mphahlele would return from exile so controversially – breaking the cultural boycott of those years – is a judgement that Thuynsma elicits from a sympathetic reading of Mphahlele's longer fiction of the exiled period, particularly *The Wanderers* (1984). However, Thuynsma's observations can be allowed to represent a larger pattern, for they define an essential paradox in Mphahlele's career.

In Es'kia Mphahlele we have arguably the most sustained record in South African literature of the encounter between a South African writer and the cultures of the wider African diaspora. Over a twenty-year period, between 1957 and 1977, he engaged with each of the major centres of intellectual ferment in the black world, in West and East Africa, with exiled francophone Africa, the Caribbean, and the United States. With the exception of the Caribbean where he was an intellectual, rather than an actual, traveller (with a particular affinity, it seems, for Martinique) he lived and worked as a cultural activist in these centres of literary volatility when they were either nascent or still flourishing. In Nigeria, he was a co-founder of the Mbari Writers and Artists Club and co-editor of the seminal *Black Orpheus*. In Kenya, through the Chemchemi Creative Centre, he sought to reproduce the successes of Mbari in East

Africa. In Paris, his problematic earlier encounter with the apologists of négritude would mellow through contact with Léopold Sédar Senghor, Aimé Césaire and others. At the University of Pennsylvania he would work alongside such prominent African-American writers as Sonia Sanchez and Houston Baker and he would deepen his immersion in the black American tradition notably, though not exclusively, the Harlem Renaissance. However, as emerges from Mphahlele's fiction, autobiography, and particularly – where there has been less critical attention – his scholarship or critical writing, this was a complex, shifting, even ambivalent encounter. In addition, it is one (I shall argue) in which Mphahlele's restlessness and irresolution, and ultimately his decision to return, have more than purely personal significance.

IF IT IS NOT altogether surprising (given what emerges from the exiled writing) that Mphahlele should have returned in 1977, it is equally unsurprising that he should have left in the first place, considering what he had been through. In *Down Second Avenue* he describes the sense of release on arriving in Nigeria in September 1957, in terms of 'having just climbed down from a vehicle that has been rocking violently for countless miles' (1971 [1959], 218). The rocking included, *inter alia*, years of professional harassment having been banned from teaching because of his opposition to Bantu Education, followed by the precipitous opportunism of life as a journalist and fiction editor on *Drum* magazine. Shortly before his departure, he had to undergo the properly Kafkaesque process (as we shall see) of petitioning for a passport in regular visits to the Union Buildings in Pretoria. The menacing imbecility of officialdom would have been pure gall to Mphahlele, crystallising years of accumulating resentment.

Picture the scene described in *Down Second Avenue*, of Mphahlele being called before the CID Chief in whose gift the granting of a passport lay, a passport to a more secure professional life, and beckoning intellectual horizons. Mphahlele's account of what transpired includes the following:

> The chief of the department whipped out his file on me. It told the whole story. Since 1950 when I became secretary of the provincial association of teachers; about my writings in the press, my speeches against Bantu education and one Government measure and another. During the years when I was walking the streets of Johannesburg I made a number of speeches at mass political rallies. Speeches which came hot from the anvil, speeches spitting vitriol. All these had been recorded. I knew they had been, and secretly I knew why the application for a passport had been rejected. (1971 [1959] 207)

The file containing the transcriptions of the speeches is now available in the State Archives in Pretoria. The security officers who informed on Mphahlele did so as follows:

> Op 9.1.1955 het hy hom as volg op 'n vergadering van die 'Orlando Rents Protection Association' uitgelaat [at this meeting he expressed himself as follows]: 'Slaves of Africa, I am one of those teachers who were expelled from the Orlando High School because the Government said I was a Communist. I appeal to you Orlando people to bring your children to me and do not send your children to the Government Schools. Bring your children to me they will be taught within three months, then they will be men and women of the future. I will also take them to Pretoria and will tell them that when they pass the [Voortrekker] monument they must spit at it instead of kneeling down and pray to the European God. They must rather pray to Chaka, Dingaan, Motshoetshoe and Sikukuni.'
>
> Op 26.6.1955 laat hy hom op 'n vergadering van die sogenaamds 'Congress of the People' as volg uit [at another meeting he expressed himself as follows]: 'Bantu Education is the most dirtiest thing you can think of. Your children are being taught that Chaka was a murderer. A cultural organisation must be opened for the black man, coloured and other Non-European friends. This culture

> must not leave room for Nationalists and we shall have a Nationalism in a Democratic form. I refuse to live in Group Areas. We want equal rights but I want to be better than the white man. We reject Bantu Education. We want to make the European unfit and we do not recognise his leadership anymore. There are a number of Europeans in this country who are joining us in our Democratic fight. Music and dancing and many other things can be the cause of Justice. . . .' (State Archives, Ezekiel Mphahlele, Ref. 1144/301)

How much of this is Mphahlele's own language, 'hot from the anvil', as he puts it, and how much of it has been filtered by the agent's racism, is difficult to discern. Certainly, Mphahlele's efforts at an event such as the Kliptown Congress of the People – that produced the Freedom Charter – to promote democratic non-racialism were not appreciated. Mphahlele's association with *Drum*, where he was fiction editor at the time, did not help his cause, since '"The Drum" [*sic*] is 'n uiters giftige tydskrif wat hoofsaaklik vir die nie-blanke leser gedoel is en hou niks goeds vir die Staat in nie' (*Drum* is an extremely poisonous magazine intended mainly for the non-white reader and contains nothing of any benefit to the state). Indeed, the file also shows that the application for a passport sowed considerable confusion in Pretoria. It was first approved by the Native Commissioner, then turned down by the Department of Internal Affairs on the recommendation of the Department of Native Affairs and the police. The disagreement led to correspondence being addressed to the relevant Minister, whose officials debated whether Mphahlele would do more harm inside or outside the country, though they did refuse the passport. Then, mysteriously, the police seem to have had a change of mind, because they recommended to Internal Affairs that the decision be reversed. This prompted inquiries from Native Affairs as to why, given the obvious 'linksgesindheid en kommunistiese neigings' (left-wing and communist tendencies) of the applicant, he should be allowed to leave the country. The reply from the police, as annotated by the inquirer in Native Affairs, takes the form of a particularly crude exercise of power: they believed they could use Mphahlele as an agent. There is nothing in the files that might serve as the basis for this proposition, nor is there any evidence of Mphahlele acceding to it. If we read between the lines of Mphahlele's own account of these negotiations, it is possible to conclude that what earned him the passport (not without a cliffhanger, since it was issued a day before his departure), in addition to the intercession of a black Dutch Reformed Church minister, was the dissonance evident to the 'cultured' CID Chief (by Mphahlele's account) between the man sitting before him and the intellectual poverty of some of his colleagues, not to mention the reporting of his underlings. It is also possible that the notion of Mphahlele's being used by the state was circulated by the same official to justify his decision to support the application. In which case, this policeman cuts an interesting figure: he does the right thing but has to account for his actions in a climate of corruption. Certainly, the correspondence is a bitter reminder, if one were needed, of the internecine complexity and hubristic arrogance of the official web in Pretoria that determined the fortunes of black intellectuals at the time.

AFTER MAKING MPHAHLELE endure a lengthy, hand-wringing monologue about the good intentions of the state, the CID Chief sent him on his way to take up a teaching appointment, first at the CMS Grammar School, then in the extension programme of the University of Ibadan (Mphahlele 1971 [1959], 208–09).

As its Epilogue explains, the second half of *Down Second Avenue* was written in the afterglow of this release: 'I'm breathing the new air of freedom . . . I shall soon know what to do with [it]' (1971 [1959], 220). Having left a kind of renaissance at home, that associated with the *Drum* generation, Mphahlele entered another one, represented by Mbari and *Black Orpheus*. The following three years, which saw the publication in quick succession of *Down Second Avenue* and the first edition of *The African Image*, and brief visits to Ghana, France and the United States, established Mphahlele as a public intellectual on the diasporic circuit, the first major consequence of which was that in 1961 he would move to Paris to become Director of the Africa Programme of the Congress for Cultural Freedom.

It was, however, West Africa that he would later say (in 1984), 'gave Africa back to me' (Mphahlele 1984a, 26). But what adjustments did this actually entail? The record of the intellectual encounters of these years suggests that Mphahlele was in fact struggling to adjust himself to, and at times even resisting, particular constructions of Africanity with which he had little intuitive affinity. In *Afrika My Music* (once again) he would later say that a 'solid sediment of Africanness' was taken for granted in South Africa, even repressed, 'in order that we might deal with the cruelties of the present', adding that the Congress tradition abetted such repression in its desire to counter the campaign of forced ethnicisation in apartheid (1984a, 29). We might add that the ethos of *Drum*, and the 1950s awakening in general, would have reinforced a distrust of ethnicity, encouraging as it did a fierce embrace of cosmopolitan modernity, against the intentions of the state, which were to imprison people in time-capsules of traditional identity. But in Nigeria, Mphahlele says, 'we came full circle. We knew that we had begun the Panafrican odyssey: shades of Orpheus' (1984a, 29). The epic and somewhat foreboding allusions here point to how difficult the adjustment would prove to be.

The most dramatic of the conflictual moments was undoubtedly the famous *cris de coeur* on the subject of négritude at a conference in Dakar on the place of African literature in the university curriculum. Mphahlele's scepticism about négritude had been accumulating for some years prior to this explosion, indeed since at least 1959 when, on returning to Ibadan after a period of leave in London, he had digressed to Paris where, with the artist Gerard Sekoto, he had met with the men of *Présence Africaine*, including Alioune Diop, Rabemananjara, and others. The mission, as reported in the first edition of *The African Image*, was to ask the négritudinists of the Society of African Culture, 'Where do *we* come in – we, who are detribalised and are producing a proletarian art?' The visit apparently included a two-hour lecture from the South Africans on their country's history, the purpose of which was to explain that the black South African intellectual's experience was one of urban restlessness and cross-cultural synthesis (Mphahlele 1962a, 27–28). Subsequently, the editors of *Présence Africaine* were gracious enough to publish a version of Mphahlele's vindication, in 'Negro culture in a multi-racial society in Africa'. But by 1963, Mphahlele's impatience had fomented into a formidable stew:

> Who is so stupid as to deny the historical fact of *négritude* as both a protest and a positive assertion of African values? All this is valid. What I do not accept is the way in which too much of the poetry inspired by it romanticises Africa – as a symbol of innocence, purity, and artless primitiveness. I feel insulted when some people imply that Africa is not also a violent Continent. I am a violent person, and proud of it because it is often a healthy human state of mind; someday I'm going to plunder, rape, set things of fire; I'm going to cut someone's throat; I'm going to subvert a government; I'm going to organise a *coup d'état*; yes, I'm going to oppress my own people; I'm going to hunt down the rich fat black men who bully the small, weak black men and destroy them; I'm going to become a capitalist, and woe to all who cross my path or who want to be my servants or chauffeurs and so on; I'm going to lead a breakaway church – there is money in it; I'm going to attack the black bourgeoisie while I cultivate a garden, rear dogs and parrots; listen to jazz and classics, read 'culture' and so on. Yes, I'm also going to organise a strike. Don't you know that sometimes I kill to the rhythm of drums and cut the sinews of a baby to cure it of paralysis? . . . The image of Africa consists of all these and others. . . . The omission of these elements of a continent in turmoil reflects a defective poetic vision. The greatest poetry of Léopold Sédar Senghor is that which portrays in himself the meeting point of Europe and Africa. This is the most realistic and honest and most meaningful symbol of Africa – an ambivalent continent searching

> for equilibrium. This synthesis of Europe and Africa does not necessarily reject the negro-ness of the African . . . . An image of Africa that only glorifies our ancestors and celebrates our 'purity' and 'innocence' is an image of a continent lying in state. (Mphahlele 1962b, 23–24)

Primitivism, it seems, can be valued positively or negatively. In reacting against négritude's overt lyricism, Mphahlele came dangerously close to defending something resembling the opposite, which would be irrational violence. The more sober version of the argument Mphahlele was working towards, appeared later in *The African Image* (1962). Indeed, the critical narrative implied in the sequence of essays in *The African Image* amounts to a vindication of the South African case, an elaborated record, in a sense, of the lecture given by the men from Johannesburg in the offices of *Présence Africaine*.

These essays begin with a brisk assessment of Kwame Nkrumah's version of the 'African Personality', which is seen as a useful, even inspiring political instrument but a false slogan for an artist, especially one from a ghetto in a multiracial society (1962a, 23). The francophone cousin of Nkrumah's thesis is addressed in 'What price "négritude"?', which distinguishes between négritude and the 'proletarian' art of South Africa, the ambience of which includes jazz, Hollywood, ballroom dancing, football, etc. By gathering a mass of detail from those forms of cultural life that thrive in the midst of South Africa's history of urbanisation, industrialisation, bureaucratisation, and segregation, Mphahlele produces an account of what he would later call 'a fugitive culture' – the implications of which phrase I shall return to later.

In 'Roots', he examines the images of Africa in the work of African-Americans, where he senses the emergence of a sustained tradition, unlike in the Caribbean where, he argues (somewhat anecdotally), the image of Africa is more problematic. What interests Mphahlele in African-American writing is this: what happens when the writers emerge at the other end of a process that begins with lyrical myths about Africa being complicated by a certain amount of contact, when African-Americans, in other words, effect the return to the United States after an encounter with Africa, and embrace the painful necessities of carving a cultural identity and sense of vocation out of heartless America. The process is traced through Langston Hughes, Richard Wright, and James Baldwin. Mphahlele's purposes, however, really emerge when he declares, 'If [the "native son"] finds the American civilisation frustrating, he should realise that it is not a parochial malady. Everywhere, especially in Africa, we are up against this invasion by the white world against our sense of values' (1962a, 52). In other words, for Mphahlele there is something paradigmatic in the African-American experience, a reality that is traduced in more romantic constructions of Africa, but one that he is able intuitively, because of his particular experience, to recognise. Our 'French-speaking brothers . . . just don't seem to know the social forces at work in African countries south of the Equator. They are too often apt to bring a philosophical mind to political and cultural questions in a changing continent' (1962a, 53). Indeed, it may be argued that the 'image studies' that comprise the more literary portions of *The African Image* – based on his Masters thesis for the University of South Africa on 'The non-European character in South African English literature' – implicitly affirm the principles of cultural contact and synthesis, or at least, the idea of history keeping identities in flux, which is Mphahlele's theme for most of the book. After all, stereotypes are investigated on the assumption that they may be sublimated. The first edition of *The African Image* is therefore, *inter alia*, Mphahlele's apology for the South African intellectual's estrangement in the face of négritude which was, at the time, the most talked-about of intellectualisations of identity in the black world.

THE SECOND, 1974 edition of *The African Image* would prove to be quite different. Before turning to it, however, we need to assess Mphahlele's most significant work of the intervening years, *The*

Wanderers, the novel that he submitted as the thesis component of his Ph.D. in Creative Writing at the University of Denver. The unpublished thesis carries a curious subtitle: 'a novel of Africa'. The preposition is ambiguous, pointing both to the subject matter of the novel and to its source, both the fictional setting and the condition from which it springs. Africa is, indeed, both subject and object, implying that the subject-position from which it is written straddles a boundary between inside and outside. And the complexities multiply: certainly, Mphahlele is the insider who is outside, the African in the West, but more crucially – as he had been in *The African Image* – he is the South African in the American reaches of the diaspora. As in the essays, therefore, Mphahlele is offering a self-vindication. However, since *The Wanderers* deals with the years of exile on the African continent itself, the emphasis falls not on négritude but on an assumption, held no doubt partly by Mphahlele himself, but also by those united to some degree by a loosely conceived pan-Africanism, namely, that Africa *ought* to be able to embrace the refugee brother from the South. That he presented this performance to an American readership (and Ph.D. committee) in Denver would, no doubt, have made the argument appear oddly framed and directed.

The Wanderers is essentially about the bitterness and sense of futility that accumulate in the life of the intellectual as refugee in Africa. Implicitly, it provides a retrospective explanation for Mphahlele's departure from Africa, having spent the years 1957–66 working as a cultural activist and teacher in Nigeria and Kenya, and his venturing into what would ordinarily be considered a state of more severe exile in the United States. That the continent should fail to provide a sense of belonging to a South African on the run from apartheid was something that needed explaining, both before the court of the diaspora and, as I hinted earlier, before the court of Mphahlele himself. But as Timi Tabane, the novel's chief protagonist, realises during his West African exile, his 'was a present that had gathered into its womb all the gall of the past. A past that came down to Timi's times with little or no romance . . .' (Mphahlele 1984b, 249).

The event with which the novel begins and ends is the death of Tabane's son, Felang, in a raid by troops of the Congress of Liberation through the border of Zimbabwe. Felang joins the Congress not, in the first instance, we are told, out of political commitment, but to compensate for failed relationships at home and a chequered school career, both of which give his parents much anguish. The son's failure is attributed to the family's, especially the father's, nomadism, and his death provides tragic release for the guilt and bitterness which accumulate in the father in his exile. There is sufficient evidence to note, as Thuynsma suggests, that the material for this relationship is directly autobiographical, reflecting Mphahlele's relationship with his own son, Anthony (Thuynsma 1989b, 94). The connection prompts Lewis Nkosi to ask the rather caustic question relating to Felang's death, 'is this perhaps a case of symbolic infanticide?' (Nkosi 1981, 97). Nkosi's demolition of *The Wanderers* in *Tasks and Masks* is founded on his knowledge of the biographical material, which, by Nkosi's own admission, makes it difficult for him to assess the work as fiction: 'The difficulty is compounded by the feeling we get quite early on in the novel that the author is out to settle scores with rivals and to vindicate himself at the expense of contemporaries whose personalities he did not like, whose careers he held in contempt, whose work he found trivial compared to his own' (Nkosi 1981, 98). So much of the novel owes its existence, Nkosi says, to the self-congratulatory presentation of the hero, who is close to Mphahlele himself, that it fails to rise to 'the level of art'. His criterion is the following: 'there is nothing wrong with autobiographical novels as long as the lives of the people involved are recast in a new and vivid light in such a way as to reveal some imaginative purpose or central design' (Nkosi 1981, 94).

Nkosi's laconic reading is too severe, because the narrative does, in fact, have a discernible symbolic design, one that goes further than Thuynsma's apt but limited conclusion that it 'registers his encounters in exile, not merely as self-indulgence, but as critical assessment' (Thuynsma 1989b, 101). What is that assessment, and by what core metaphor (to deploy Nkosi's criterion) is it defined? The inescapable assessment Thuynsma is working towards is this: the existential failure of pan-Africanism to support the intellectual refugee. The metaphor that carries this conclusion is the death and dismemberment of the son, which speaks of the protagonist's guilt and leaves Tabane stranded without continuity or a sense of the future. For Tabane's severance from his past and from home is also a severance from his future, and the distress associated with the son's death is all the more bitter for being metonymically linked to the void represented by the failed promises of the continent.

Throughout the novel, in fact, Tabane is plagued by memories and a recurring dream in which he is a fugitive. He is haunted by the memory of a mounted policeman towering over him, an icon of apartheid, 'the badge on his helmet [glittering] mercilessly' (Mphahlele 1984b, 109), while as a young herdboy he drank from a stream. The dream, which persists over the entire nine years covered by the novel, involves his being pursued by a 'gang of thugs' who cannot at first be identified, though by the time of the son's death it emerges that they are young, black South Africans (Mphahlele 1984b, 215, 319, 336). The course of the dream through Tabane's psyche suggests a process in which the threat of a brutal, external power is gradually internalised and turned into guilt, since the attackers are men like Felang whom he, as father, has failed. These events represent the fulfilment of the earlier foreboding that the present would produce a monstrous birth from 'the gall of the past' (Mphahlele 1984b, 249). The novel's opening sequence does seem gratuitously violent, in representing the bodies of the young freedom fighters being torn apart by crocodiles after being dumped in a river by mercenaries. But by the end of *The Wanderers* we come to appreciate that the dismemberment is chiefly psychic, a stripping of illusion in the consciousness of the narrator himself: 'I sensed that, in fact, his age – twenty – was less significant than the way he died', says Tabane, 'at the time when the wound in us gaped and defied any protection from the storm or the heat of emotion' (Mphahlele 1984b, 12).

Apart from this central metaphor, the narrative is organised around the development of Tabane's consciousness as he comes to terms with exile in three phases. The first exile is internal, taking place within the country of birth. Tabane is a reporter for *Bongo* magazine who agrees to investigate the disappearance of a prisoner on a potato farm, Glendale, outside the town of Goshen in what is recognisable today as Mpumalanga or the Lowveld (Mphahlele is, of course, fictionalising Henry Nxumalo's famous exposés of prisons and prison farms in *Drum*). The landscape brings a sense of crisis to Tabane: 'huge patches of squalor, of abject poverty, large numbers of people who were being moved about in whole communities; there was a large number of blind alleys; there were areas of heroism, of cowardice, both despicable and divine. The issue kept coming to the single conscience, like the endless ticking of a clock' (Mphahlele 1984b, 59). The phenomenology of a landscape 'corroded with power' focuses a sense of crisis and decision: if Tabane stays in the country, he must pit himself against the machine or shrivel up in bitterness; he must 'face up to [his] cowardice, reason with it and leave' (Mphahlele 1984b, 59). Interestingly, the temptation to sublimate this crisis by posing as the modernist *émigré*, a refugee of the soul, is rejected: 'things mattered only in relation to the time and place that contained them' (Mphahlele 1984b, 59). He decides to leave.

Tabane's arrival in Sogali repeats *Down Second Avenue*'s testimony of relief when Mphahlele reached Lagos. Very quickly, however, a sense of ambivalence accumulates, producing a dissonance that reminds Tabane that he is always a 'black foreigner' (Mphahlele 1984b, 229). The adjustments – comprising the burden of the narrative for the period spent in West Africa – include coping with the country's first *coup d'état*, being led into a bribe over a traffic offence, keeping servants and complaining about them in the way white South Africans do, negotiating hellish roads in the course of travelling to teaching appointments, and coming close to witnessing a thief being torn limb from limb in a public street. Such experiences, coupled with a failure to establish easy professional relationships, produce little amelioration of the violent impulses that were a feature of living in the burdensome south (Mphahlele 1984b, 230). Extraordinarily, the sense of alienation even includes a sequence in which Tabane and his group of cosmopolitan male peers visit the juju high-life clubs of Sogali, where class and cultural differences seem so severe that he imagines himself as the white frontiersman (Mphahlele 1984b, 247). 'Take your chances, tread softly', he subsequently muses in self-admonishment,

> human cultures have stone walls. Find the crevice and dig your way through that and don't try to go further than it allows you. Africa has several enclaves with walls around them and several crevices in the walls. Take your chances . . . maybe humanity must flow like water that cannot leave a crevice unflooded. (Mphahlele 1984b, 248)

Indeed, there are no 'ancestral springs' to unite him with the city of Sogali, despite the theatrical recreations of myth and cosmology he watches with his peers – shades of the activities of the Mbari club – since his ancestors 'had thrived in other climes'. With a quasi-Joycean ring we are told that the 'present had to be met not with the lyricism of the tongue, of the spoken word, but with the gun, with political cunning and a lashing tongue' (Mphahlele 1984b, 248).

Much of the third stage of exile, where Tabane is a university teacher of literature in Kambani, Lao-Kiku (clearly Nairobi, Kenya), is devoted to Felang's disintegration. Where we are presented with Tabane's own further development, it is to show us his disillusionment with the Eurocentrism of the East African élite – particularly when his teaching contract is not renewed. 'Africa is still a white man's paradise', he thinks, 'not a black exile's' (Mphahlele 1984b, 339–40). At an official function to open a new hospital on the escarpment of the Rift Valley, he hears a note of defeat in the drumming and the feet of the dancers, and imagines a troop of weary warriors from the south moving up the Valley, the implication being that the history of Southern Africa is continuous with that of post-independent East Africa: 'Why does that music sound so plaintive? Where's the roar of triumph, the triumph of black rule?' (Mphahlele 1984b, 340–41, 347). Under neo-colonial conditions, he realises, Lao-Kiku will not be able to embrace him and there will be no release from his anger. Perhaps at some point in the future he will return to Iboyoru, but not immediately: 'Meantime, I must wait somewhere outside Africa, contemplate the painful south and what I can do about it' (Mphahlele 1984b, 347). When his wife breaks this reverie, telling him that his face 'looks like [he'd] been out with witches . . . or seen a monster in the Valley' (Mphahlele 1984b, 348), she is quite correct: he is confronting the inescapable reality of his exile from the continent.

At this point in the narration, Mphahlele's novel exhausts itself. Felang's death – we are peremptorily told – occurs seven months later. Since there is no narration covering the intervening period, it is at this point that the loss of the son and the demise of the pan-African solution become irrevocably linked. Mphahlele's biographer, N. Chabani Manganyi, seeks a more consoling view of Felang's death than the one I offer here, which is written largely in response to Nkosi. Confirming the novel's autobiographical tendency, Manganyi suggests that the passage of the father-son relationship into fiction enabled Mphahlele to 'move closer to contemplating revolutionary violence as a solution to the problem of white racism' (Manganyi 1983, 224). While this reading is understandable in terms of the biographer's need to find wholeness in the disparate elements of his subject's life, and is made plausible by the context of Black Consciousness in which it was written, the novel does actually offer a bleaker view. Indeed, Felang's disintegration brings a repetition of the title's motif, 'we are wanderers' (Mphahlele 1984b, 346), a refrain that begins during Tabane's realisation of his foreignness in Sogali: 'Darkness, the darkness of exile, the long long road, a road full of wanderers, wanderers of no fixed abode' (Mphahlele 1984b, 229–30). This rootlessness and Felang's dismemberment remain painfully connected to the end. And Felang's death does not bring the consolation of tragic sacrifice: by the time it occurs, the family bonds have become irremediably torn, and without adequate motivation for Felang's joining the Congress of Liberation in the first place, it is a case of the best lacking all conviction (the phrase from Yeats's 'The Second Coming' that Mphahlele uses as his epigraph to *Down Second Avenue*). In his Preface to the dissertation submitted to the University of Denver, Mphahlele actually defends the *irresolution* of his text, claiming that it is apt for the condition that it explores (1968). That condition, which is an enigma only if we assume the inherent capacity of the continent to provide a literal or ideological home, is one of rootlessness, shading into aimlessness; without a consolatory myth to assuage the pangs of exile, it carries a sense of waste. What the death of the son achieves, in fictional terms, is not consolation but a rather brutal realism.

REVIEWING THE FIRST edition of *The African Image*, Nkosi says, 'to be a black South African is to be both unspeakably rich and incredibly poor'. Rich, perhaps – though he does not spell this out – because blessed with a dynamic, if anguished sense of community and history; poor, because despite a certain degree of cultural cross-fertilisation, 'one still suspects that the African has had to shed more of his heritage in order to accommodate himself to the ridiculous, and sometimes barbarous, demands of a society controlled by whites for the benefit of whites' (Nkosi 1983, 129). By the time Mphahlele came to revise *The African Image* for re-publication in 1974, he seems to have reached the same conclusion, with the result that his critical narrative had to be entirely turned around – re-aligned, in fact, by 180 degrees.

Perhaps the most startling evidence of the volte-face the second edition represents is provided by the chapters on nationalism. In the first edition, Mphahlele declared that he was not a nationalist, that he was opposed to 'medieval clannishness', going so far as to say that he had never been moved by Anton Lembede's slogan 'Africa for the Africans', which had inspired the Youth League and contributed to the development of Africanism within the ANC, and eventually the formation of the Pan-Africanist Congress. Africanism in this form, he declared, was 'unwittingly joining the Afrikaans [*sic*] in their ambition to create parallel streams of legislative, political, economic and cultural growth: separate trade unions, places of entertainment – the lot' (Mphahlele 1962a, 71–73). Describing the necessity of non-racialism as 'cold realism', meaning a shared destiny was inescapable, he envisioned a future in terms that were anything but coldly real: 'We are aiming at a common society and to prove that multi-racial societies can thrive and become a glorious reality in Africa' (Mphahlele 1962a, 74).

By contrast, in the 1974 edition he would argue: 'The white man has done everything to drag into the mud any ideas of non-racialism and it would be futile to try to evoke this ideology at this and at any future time.' While the multiracial leadership of the Congress alliance pounded the theme of non-racialism, 'The rank and file . . . were nationalist-minded. They never did think that in an open society the African majority would yield to minority groups.' Even to the Africans in positions of leadership in the alliance, non-racialism was merely a 'ploy': 'Still less did the Blacks in the Congress Alliance believe in what they were telling the whites.' 'And so we are back to the freedom wars our ancestors of two centuries ago waged against the whites' (Mphahlele 1974a, 52–53). Far from attacking the Pan-Africanist Congress (PAC), as he had done earlier, he now deduced from statements by Nelson Mandela and Robert Sobukwe that

> their attitudes towards the other racial groups in South Africa were fundamentally the same; that indeed the nationalism of one was at the root of things the same as that of the other; that in terms of strategy they could both visualise a united front somewhere along the line, of the ANC, the PAC, the Indians and Africans of mixed descent. (Mphahlele 1974a, 56)

The position Mphahlele was beginning to articulate, of course, was becoming increasingly familiar at home as Black Consciousness (BC).

Indeed, in his Preface and elsewhere, he uses the term several times, as well as other BC code-words, notably Boer in reference to whites in general, including the English. Not all of BC's lexicon was taken over in the same way, though: 'these college-boy theorists who broke away from the Pan-Africanist Congress and who indulge in naming antics must retract the name "Azania" which they arbitrarily gave South Africa, a name some misguided Afro-American militants have also adopted' (Mphahlele 1974a, 58). Ripples of BC's explosive vocabulary were reaching him, therefore, and he was adjusting to them, selectively. The challenge Mphahlele seems to have had to confront in the second edition of *The African Image* is that having repudiated racial thought so volubly early in his career, various factors, historical and personal, were driving him towards a *rapprochement.* These factors are not too difficult to enumerate: the hardening of apartheid as it moved towards totalitarianism; in this context, the failure of multiracial alliance politics; the rise of a properly revolutionary discourse as a feature of the movement in exile; and the emergence of BC at home. Added to this, the pressures of exile itself seem to have fed the racial bitterness:

> There is something about the act and fact of communal survival *inside* a situation of racism that either tones down, or lends another complexion to, the hate that is mixed with anger. *Outside* the situation, you are on your own, you have little communal support: at best, it is intellectual. So you hate the whites you left behind with a scalding intensity. Could it be that distance creates a void and that the burning lava of hate *must* fill it? (Mphahlele 1974a, 42)

Surely, we must also assume that the influence of those very streams of identitarian thinking that he had earlier found so exclusive of his own, peculiar history, began to have an effect, especially since his circumstances in the United States were those of a member of a racial minority that has to look deep within itself to find the resources to survive. Indeed, there is ample evidence, both in the second edition of *The African Image* and in *Voices in the Whirlwind*, of a sustained intellectual search on Mphahlele's part for points of contact between his own particular sense of racial identity and those of diasporic origin. The path he had to walk in finding these points was littered with evidence of his own previous volatility, particularly with regard to négritude. Mphahlele's later position on this question, therefore, entails opening négritude to diverse historical circumstances and interpretations – repeating Césaire's *chacun à sa négritude propre* – and then plotting this diversity in terms of a continuum between two poles, with the lyricism of Senghor at one end and, at the other, forms of black consciousness that are in tune with the realities of power. Mphahlele aligns himself with the latter end of this continuum, and does so by invoking a Fanonist position that ties the problematics of racial identity to a vision of an ongoing social revolution sustained by the struggle for independent nationhood.

Apart from Frantz Fanon, the other Martiniquan whose work enabled Mphahlele to resituate himself in relation to négritude was, of course, Aimé Césaire. Césaire's account of négritude was always 'historical rather than dogmatic', says Mphahlele; he 'kept returning to [it] as a weapon against power' (1974a, 93). That Mphahlele should declare a truce with négritude by invoking these two figures is not altogether surprising, if we take as our point of reference Abiola Irele's assessment of them. Irele describes a shift in Césaire's poetry from collective identity to social consciousness. It is a movement still more acutely and sharply defined, of course, in Fanon, suggesting that a Martiniquan take on négritude carried the philosophy from the fields of aesthetics and black subjectivity, to ideology and secular, social critique (Irele 1981, 142–43). Mphahlele's revisiting of racial identity may, therefore, not have been a complete break with the restless historicity that he had earlier associated with his South African background, since a synthesis was being sought between a black and an urban or secular self-consciousness. Citing Réne Dépestre, Mphahlele concludes his discussion of négritude by saying that the unifying elements in constructions of the philosophy in the Caribbean, Africa and the

Americas were historical first, rather than racial, and that négritude is essentially 'the modern (cultural) equivalent of the old condition of the fugitive slave' (1974a, 95). In the figure of the fugitive, therefore, Mphahlele's South African and diasporic selves could become one.

Whereas the critical narrative, then, of the first edition of *The African Image* explained to the black world the South African position of Congress affiliation, that of the second edition was more inwardly directed, being principally a series of reflections on the growth of racial self-consciousness. As such, it was in tune with BC's quest for black self-reconstruction. The way Mphahlele's prose bends back on itself around the word 'Except' in the following passage, is typical of this shift:

> We had to grab the tools by which the white man pillaged and plundered his way to power. The arms, we couldn't have. Education we could have, albeit literally at a price. With education went the mastery of English . . . We had jazz, we had European music. European music was in an uncanny way a symbol of conquest for the individual. It took one to far-away lands where we imagined ourselves elevated above the tyranny around us. Jazz also spoke to us of an imaginary land where Blacks were achieving things we couldn't dream of. Except that jazz also grounded us deeper in our Black experience because we did sense its other dimension: a state of mind rooted in a life that knew slave ships, whips, back-breaking labour, break-up of family life, alienation, and so on. (1974a, 27)

The project of the second edition involved establishing a position of black self-definition, but this had to be accomplished without traducing the historical reality of a transcultural existence. The resolution of this tension that emerges in key passages entails a 'dialogue', a culture that is both 'synthetic' (transcultural) and 'self-sufficient' (African):

> It comprises among other things the continuous dialogue between the present and the living traditions that first inspired the négritude movement; the imperatives of our modern existence and those we have inherited from our ancestors; the colonial oppression and white racism that still harass our people in Southern Africa; the several cycles South Africans have lived through in their encounter with whites; out of which has evolved a synthetic but self-sufficient native culture, a living culture that is quite adequate to our political imperatives. . . . This dialogue will certainly determine in time the direction of our literature. (1974a, 84)

This synthesis introduces us to Mphahlele's notion of 'African humanism', a feature of his writing after his return to South Africa, but it is worth observing that the resolution that emerges in the second edition of *The African Image* came only after a considerable struggle, part of which is reflected in *Voices in the Whirlwind and Other Essays* (1972). These essays, in fact, come between the two editions of *The African Image*, having been written in the mid-1960s while he was still a doctoral candidate at the University of Denver, teaching black literature. The title essay, on poetry written out of situations of racialised political conflict, is a sober assessment of the prospects of Black Aesthetics, so sober, indeed, that it attracted unfavourable attention from one of the spokespersons of that poetics, Addison Gayle. Nevertheless, what is self-evident in this and the other essays of the collection is that Mphahlele is immersing himself in the cultures of the diaspora in order to find a position that does justice to the several parts of himself. In other essays, he reveals an awareness that the historical subject he represents, and for which he is trying to find an appropriate language, is one of some philosophic importance, involving an attempt to imagine a subject position within African modernity – a case, really, of ideas catching up with reality.

In an essay on rivalling traditions in African literature, for example, he says, 'While I am prepared to stake a lot on the survival of African humanism and the social relationships it informs, Emerson's voice keeps sounding back of my mind: "There are no fixtures in nature. The universe is fluid and volatile. Permanence is but a word of degrees"' (Mphahlele 1972, 150). Similarly, he revisits Sartre's endorsement of the poets of négritude, saying, 'The image of Black Orpheus conceived by Sartre in which he dramatises the black man searching for his Eurydice . . . is only part of the story. Because not only is the African present seeking out the past, but the past is seeking out the present' (Mphahlele 1972, 151). And in an essay on African writers and commitment, he contrasts the modern African subject with the *angst*-ridden modernist subject represented by Kafka – the perspective described by Lukács in terms of 'a trapped and struggling fly' – by saying, 'At the moment our [African] literature in the European languages is of a frontier kind. We are pioneers at the frontier, seeking a definition of ourselves and the past from which we have come.' Switching the metaphor, he speaks of 'the stream of modern life in Africa and the stream of its *living* traditions' (original emphasis) coming together in a dialogue that 'may yet determine the idioms of the literature to come' (Mphahlele 1972, 198).

If the second edition of *The African Image* marks Mphahlele's gradual adjustment to racial thought, however, this resolution does not bring an equivalent adjustment to the pain of living in exile, despite the fact that his career had reached a high water mark with an appointment at the University of Pennsylvania. Already in *The African Image* he is contemplating a return, though it comes with fears of having to compromise, fears even of assassination (Mphahlele 1974a, 42–43). At a symposium on contemporary South African literature in Austin, Texas, in 1975, which brought together most of the literary exiles in North America, Mphahlele risked reading a poem ('Death III: Variations on a theme by John Keats'), which pointedly confesses to a desire at mid-life to return home before mortality sets in. Clearly, a philosophical accommodation to a broadly diasporic identity was not a sufficient answer to Mphahlele's existential longing for rootedness, for *place*. In retrospect, Mphahlele speaks of having come to the realisation that, 'Journalistically, you can establish the connections between the black peoples of the world. You can capture the general mood, the yearnings of militants to assert a Pan-African identity'; nevertheless, a prophet who could speak to all the diverse constituencies of the black world would be a 'freak' (Mphahlele 1984a, 167). 'One must sacrifice authenticity somewhere – place – in order to let one's poetry speak for peoples across cultural boundaries' (Mphahlele 1984a, 168).

AND SO WE come to Mphahlele's return. Both as teacher and as writer, particularly of fiction, Mphahlele had arrived at the conclusion that he needed a community and a milieu to which he was viscerally attached. The phrase that has served as an explanation of this decision is 'the tyranny of place'. The following statement is typical:

> I must know whom I'm speaking to. Not a place in the theatre of the mind. But a place whose real life I can feel in my blood and bones. There's the rub. I must stay with the South African reality. A reality so deeply rooted in my life that I could never lose it, dare not lose it. That is its tyranny and its value as the root of commitment to culture. (Mphahlele 1979, 41)

In *Afrika My Music*, Mphahlele says that what he sought in coming back to South Africa, he found: 'community', 'an identifiable culture', 'an ancestral ground'. What he lost was 'liberty – freedom of association, expression, mobility' (1984a, 250). The retrospective long view offered here does iron out the difficulties of the return, which we can summarise as calumny, compromise, and contradiction. He had to endure the calumny of the exiles, some of whom denounced him. As a school inspector in Lebowa, before taking up a fellowship at the University of the Witwatersrand, he had to accept the compromise of working in the very system of Bantu Education that had been the principal reason for his departure twenty years earlier. And there is certainly contradiction. The account of a lecture at the University of Lesotho at Roma in 1978 is revealing. Mphahlele finds himself resenting the assertion of a white woman in the audience who suggested he was negating his political responsibility: 'I knew my constituency, to which I was answerable, because I was communicating with it. It was African, and she was not in it as she, a white person, did not share my culture, my constituency's culture.' In the same audience, a group of young refugees, BC activists who had left South Africa in the wake of the Soweto Revolt, were just as vociferous, unsurprisingly, since they were taking on the very role of militant exile that Mphahlele seemed to be abandoning. The constituency in which Mphahlele sought refuge from white arrogance was itself conflicted.

But Mphahlele's attachment to place, and the meaning of place as the vessel in which a community pours its historical experience, ran deeper than such contradictions. It is here that we discover the larger import of the African humanism that he declares as his manifesto after his return. Mphahlele needed a conceptual frame of reference that was grounded in an intuitive loyalty to his home, but that could, nevertheless, answer to the complexity of his experience in the twenty years of his exile. Having been a committed anti-racist, indeed a non-racist in the Congress tradition, he found himself adrift in West and East Africa, unsupported when it counted, by Pan-Africanism. He then experienced the same sense of alienation from Europe and America, which led the intellectuals of an earlier generation – from francophone Africa and the Caribbean – to cling to the mast of négritude, and thus he began a journey into the racial self-consciousness he had earlier declined. Even that journey was inconclusive. Its ambience, we might say, like the source of much of the mythic power of diasporic thought, was the sea, whereas what Mphahlele most needed, he came to realise, was land, place, community, and home, all of which comprised an historical reality. Yet, the experience of landfall would have been bittersweet, since he was not returning in triumph as his fellow exiles would seem to be doing on their return at the demise of apartheid. As an umbrella term, African humanism answers, broadly, to Mphahlele's sense of being a creature buffeted by history, a child of modernity, but being, at the same time, in possession of a cultural code that owes nothing to modernity's bland universality. This blend of an acute sense of history with the knowledge that one is part of a distinctive culture is hard-won in Mphahlele, though it informs his sense more generally of what it means to be a black South African. Towards the end of *Afrika My Music* Mphahlele describes a Soweto funeral procession, complete with footballers loping theatrically between the cars and buses, and a loudspeaker blaring metallic hymns from the roof of the hearse:

> In the midst of this I am at pains to extract a meaning. I begin to wonder if the whole show is not an expression of, and at the same time an antidote to despair. So much violence is with us, so much death. To ritualise it, however grotesquely, may be a way of conquering the fear of death, of coaxing it, containing it. I begin to wonder if Soweto, as the paradigm of black South African life, is not striving in its own burlesque fashion to define something of communal experience that the collective memory still cherishes; the disinherited personality trying to salvage something from the collective memory and to give it definition so that people may survive the cruelty of the times. A survival culture, a fugitive culture. (Mphahlele 1984a, 256)

The influence of diasporic thinking is strong here, in the notion of the disinherited personality, the recourse to collective memory to endure history's nightmare, and the culture of survival, yet these reflections also rely on the continuities provided by notions of community and place. To return to the paradox with which we began: whilst Mphahlele's restlessness and his attachment to home are in tension for much of his career, by the time of his return to South Africa they have reached a mature equilibrium. This equilibrium is as well served by the term African humanism, as any other. The journey towards this position can be measured by the fact that when he left South Africa, Mphahlele sought to interpret the diaspora via home; by the time he writes the passage on a Soweto funeral, he is interpreting South Africa via the diaspora.

5

Lyric and epic

The ideology of form in Soweto poetry

Between, let's say, May 1984 and May 1986 . . .
There was a shift out there
From lyric to epic.
Jeremy Cronin (1997)

This chapter shares Jeremy Cronin's observation, but moves his dates back by a decade. Cronin is right in his own way: he is referring to the launch of the United Democratic Front (UDF) in 1984 and the period of insurrectionary alliance politics it spawned, events that led to the government declaring a State of Emergency in June 1985. By 1990, the year of transition, the genre of South Africa's politics would change again. However, to speak of a shift from lyric to epic is to speak of the ways in which intellectuals respond to a wholly new rhetorical situation. The particular changes identified by Cronin occurred, I would argue, a decade earlier than he suggests. It was a key feature of the careers of writers who came to be associated with the Black Consciousness movement from the late 1960s to the end of the 1970s.

In this chapter I explore the roles of lyric and of epic in the poetry of Black Consciousness, principally in Mongane Serote but also to a lesser extent in the other poets making up the quartet most commonly associated with the term 'Soweto poetry', namely, Oswald Mbuyiseni Mtshali, Sipho Sepamla, and Mafika Gwala. My purpose is to reach an understanding of the relationship between these poetic modes and modernity in the context of South Africa in the late 1960s and 70s.

Let's start by describing one event that actually happened, and another that could not have occurred under the circumstances, although it nearly did. The event that did happen was an unusually lively poetry festival, amongst largely white poets and critics. In January 1974 a festival of readings, lectures and workshops on South African poetry arranged by the University of Cape Town's adult education unit turned out to be particularly auspicious. Since it was off the education syllabus, the subject – the current state of South African poetry – had a kind of non-official glamour and a direct bearing on the participants' sense of their moment. It is difficult now to imagine how a festival on the current state of poetry could gather such intensity. No doubt, the wider historical situation had something to do with it: in the preceding months, a series of strikes in Durban had signalled that the country's economy was becoming subject to rapid and radical politicisation. The Black Consciousness movement, which had become the most volatile and visible of new political developments in opposition to the government, had organised a number of rallies in support of Frelimo in Mozambique. (Three months after the event, a coup in Lisbon signalled the beginning of the end of Portuguese colonialism in South Africa's neighbouring states, bringing decolonisation much closer. By June 1976, of course, an internal revolution was under way.)

At 'Poetry '74', the most memorable contest of ideas, and the one to attract much commentary in the succeeding years, involved Mike Kirkwood – soon afterwards, editor of Ravan Press and *Staffrider* magazine – and Guy Butler, professor of English at Rhodes University and the figurehead of an English-speaking South African identity and literary self-consciousness. Kirkwood challenged Butler through a critique of the psychology and ideology of colonialism drawn from Frantz Fanon and Albert Memmi. Kirkwood also shared the Marxist revisionism that had by then made its mark in South African social history (Kirkwood 1976, 102–33). This clash has been seen as marking a serious rift in English-speaking intellectual culture between liberalism and radicalism as the country moved towards what Nadine Gordimer later called its 'interregnum' years (1989, 261; Attwell 1993, 30–32) Participants at the festival, however, would have been conscious of the potential, at least, for a far more serious clash, one in which the Kirkwood-Butler debate would have been merely a sideshow: a clash between liberalism and Black Consciousness. Indeed, this was the real conflict, though it did not come to a head.

There was, in fact, a black presence at the festival. Mongane Serote is quoted in the proceedings as saying: 'I am looking at what has happened to me as a man in South Africa. I am trying to understand it and this is what I write about' (Polley 1976, 8). Serote's assertion of black personhood (as well as his emphasis on masculinity) are typical markers of Black Consciousness. The movement he represented, however, which was, in a sense, the black template onto which was etched much the same anti-colonial subject-position and analysis of which Kirkwood was speaking, was not foregrounded in the discussions. For the most part, white academics spoke about or for a black position that was off-stage. Tim Couzens located local black poetry within major developments in African writing elsewhere on the continent (1976, 47–59), and Geoffrey Haresnape – bravely quoting writing banned at the time, by Lewis Nkosi and Es'kia Mphahlele – referred to what was being called 'the new black poetry', but he was anxious to ward off a growing sense of polarisation by defining a position common to all South African poets (Haresnape 1976, 35–46).

It was already too late for consensus politics, however. Only the day before 'Poetry '74', a well-known figure in the Black Consciousness movement, a student leader who had been expelled from the University of the North for his activism, Onkgopotse Tiro, was killed by a parcel bomb in Botswana where he had gone into exile. Mafika Gwala, who had suspended his editorial work on *The Black Review 1973* in Johannesburg to travel to Cape Town for the festival, withdrew as a consequence of Tiro's death. On the very day of the assassination, Gwala had, in fact, telephoned Tiro in Botswana to seek his advice about whether he should take part in the festival at all (Gwala 1984, 42–43). A position of principled withdrawal from non-racial or multiracial meetings or programmes organised by whites was already well established in the Black Consciousness movement. The most obvious example of this was the formation of Saso (the South African Students Organisation), which four years earlier had broken away from Nusas (the National Union of South African Students). A black presence in Cape Town was therefore, to some degree, already anomalous. Serote and Mtshali, who were in Cape Town, saw the report of Tiro's death in the press on the way to the university. Later, Serote made it clear that they went to the festival in a sense of crisis and remained guarded during the discussions (Serote 1977, 24).

Serote and Mtshali observed the Kirkwood-Butler clash from the wings, therefore, and Gwala missed it altogether. What might have been the Serote/Mtshali/Gwala-Butler clash, or even for that matter, the Serote/Mtshali/Gwala-Kirkwood clash, and all that *they* might have represented, remains a tantalising historical possibility.[1] It is not strictly a non-event, but an event that could not take place: contiguous historical moments that have a bearing on one another do not always coalesce and we construct their significance afterwards. Why is it, however, that the main issue never materialised? Much of the debate at 'Poetry '74' had the direction and texture of the maturation of a settler-colonial culture into a relatively autonomous though still contentious cultural formation, a process that in Canada and Australia was to produce what, from the outside, looks like a national, though largely white, literary-intellectual idiom. The debate in the wings in Cape Town, potentially upstaging the main action and to some degree undermining its self-assurance (a crisis of doubt that, apart from Kirkwood, only J.M. Coetzee's novel of the same year, *Dusklands*, seems to have properly captured) was the product of the belated arrival in South Africa of other, more aggressive forms of postcolonial self-definition: the cultural products of wars of liberation in Africa, notably Algeria, and the civil rights movement in the United States. At least, these were the currents that had the most obvious implications for black mobilisation in South Africa.

We should also mention the general sense of political – and epistemological – awakening of the 1960s, and the emergence of the idea of 'consciousness' itself as a resource or a programme around which plans of action could be drawn up. The distinctive edge in this concept has behind it a mélange of existentialism, politicised psychoanalysis, négritude, structuralism, Maoism, and cultural revolution. Admittedly, in their own spheres, these are all rather different movements, but their cohesion is more than the sum of their parts, especially as they were received by South Africans at some remove from their sources. Their combined effect provided a touchstone, or principle of comprehensive conceptual refashioning that, as we shall see later in this chapter, drove the artists influenced by it into dramatically revisionist forms of discourse. In his account of the 1960s, Fredric Jameson captures this *zeitgeist* by referring to Jean-Paul Sartre's Preface to *The Wretched of the Earth*: 'Not so very long ago, the earth numbered two thousand million inhabitants: five hundred million *men* and one thousand five hundred million *natives*. The former had the Word; the others merely had use of it.'

'The 60s,' Jameson continues, 'was the period when all these "natives" became human beings, and this internally as well as externally: those inner colonised of the First World – "minorities", marginals, and women – fully as much as its external subjects and official "natives"' (1988, 181).[2] The emergence in such numbers of new 'subjects of history' following decolonisation (the process that, Jameson argues, was the engine behind many of the new social movements, as much in Europe and the United States as in recently decolonised countries) suggests the extent to which apartheid was actually a hopelessly quixotic attempt to hold back these forces and ideas, to withhold or, at best, to manage by force the autonomy, agency and world citizenship of black South Africans. In much of the country's internal memory, the 1960s were the darkest days of apartheid and a low point in the history of resistance, but world-wide a very different modernity with its roots in anti-colonial struggle – to follow Jameson's lead – was gathering. Its local reception was largely and most powerfully felt in Black Consciousness, so that by the early 1970s South Africa was ripe, first for discursive violence, and then for more serious street-battles.

Prior to June 1976, one of the places where we can witness a clash of consciousness between apartheid and the new postcolonial currents is in what came to be called the Schlebusch Commission. The cabinet minister Alwyn Schlebusch was appointed by the government to establish a Commission of Inquiry into a range of liberal and radical organisations and report to parliament, which he did in December 1973. In a sense, the unspoken conflict at 'Poetry '74' had already happened in the preceding months, but in the political sphere where it properly belonged – that is to say, in the context of the interrogations, forced testimony, and threats associated with Minister Schlebusch's Commission. The coercive context did not prevent the Commission's hearings and later its report from reflecting a real contest of *ideas*, and its view of Black Consciousness emerges in its investigation of Nusas, which is presented under the heading, 'Polarisation' (Schlebusch 1974, 391–521).

Polarisation is the Commission's term for the cultural and political climate of the 1960s, encoded in its anxieties around the possibility of a race war. (The role of apartheid itself in promoting such a war is, by definition, not addressed.) Essentially, Schlebusch and his commissioners tried to prove that the polarisation came from elsewhere, not from South African conditions. Thus, Black Consciousness was imported from the United States by individuals in the University Christian Movement, who latched onto Stokely Carmichael's book *Black Power* (1967) and who later became instrumental in launching Saso. In fact, the Commission tries to argue that key figures in Nusas and Saso simply plagiarised Carmichael's book. The anxieties extended beyond Carmichael, however, to the Black Panthers, whose admiration for Maoism is discussed, and also to Fanon: 'a very alarming aspect of this philosophy is to be found in the writings of Frantz Fanon, which appear to glorify the use of brutal physical violence against Whites' (Schlebusch 1974, 463). The commissioners were somewhat confused as to whether Black Consciousness espoused Marxist dialectics or the Maoist proposition of a peasant-led revolution, *swart gevaar* (black danger) or *rooi gevaar* (red danger). (Perhaps this confusion was understandable since, if the truth be told, the activists of the period themselves were unsure which paradigm was more important.) Either way, the Commission was certain that the outcome would be damaging to white rule and it recommended the prohibition of funds from abroad and further censorship (Schlebusch 1974, 515–16). These findings prepared the ground for later, more vicious state action, including the trial in May 1976 of the Saso leadership and the eventual banning and banishment to King William's Town of Steve Biko.

The Commission's insistence that Black Consciousness was a foreign import misses the point in a precise and revealing way. Black Consciousness was, indeed, a diasporic mode of thought, as the Commission suspected, but since this is the case, let me risk the following observations. Black Consciousness may enjoy the distinction of being the only mid- to late-twentieth-century movement of a specifically *racial* self-consciousness to be wholly born from *local* African conditions. To be sure, it has affinities with earlier movements, especially with the négritude of Aimé Césaire and Leopold Senghor; perhaps also with négritude's older, Liberian cousin, the idea of an African Personality that had been developed by Edward Blyden. Common to all these positions, including Carmichael's brand of black power, are assertions of a distinctive selfhood, of counter-myths to racist categories, of a tactical withdrawal that enables a recovery of agency, and of a future in which black and white might co-exist on some yet-to-be-discovered, universal basis. These propositions are made under varying conditions and with different degrees of militancy in their various contexts. What is unique about Black Consciousness, however, is that it developed not in the encounter with First World racism outside of Africa, nor out of exile, which is the case in the other movements mentioned. It is a measure of the invasiveness of apartheid, then, of its erosion of fundamental ideas around subjectivity and personhood, that Black Consciousness and its diasporic precursors shared such a great deal in common *except* their geographies of origin. To some degree, apartheid seems to have turned its own citizens into cultural exiles, who developed a language of racial solidarity that was similar to the ideas of the heirs of slavery in the diaspora, and it established conditions in which a local intelligentsia would give to South Africa a Black Atlantic cultural formation, but of the townships – to adapt Paul Gilroy.

To come back to the more limited focus of this inquiry: what were some of the cultural forms that the intellectuals associated with this movement developed in pursuit of their goals? How did those forms evolve? What pressures led them, finally, to adapt, as the country moved into its crisis years from the mid-1970s onwards? I will pursue these questions by focusing closely on poetry, leaving aside, apart from incidental references, much else – theatre, the novel, performance poetry, the political and cultural manifesto. I will look in particular at the career of Mongane Serote, the poet described by Mbulelo Mzamane in his Introduction to Serote's *Selected Poems* (1982) as the leading poet of the 1970s.

WHEN WE REVISIT Mongane Serote's early poems, which were published in *The Classic* and then in *Yakhal'inkomo* in 1972 and *Tsetlo* in 1974, it is somewhat surprising to discover that they do not disturb the Anglo-American tradition of the lyric poem as much as we have come to assume – if by the lyric poem we mean something like the poetry of personal statement, or the poetry of what Northrop Frye once called 'overheard utterance' (Frye 1965, 249; Culler 1985, 38). It's surprising, because what we have come to call 'Soweto poetry', including and especially Serote's, is supposed to have jettisoned the European forms learned in the classroom (Chapman 1982, 12; McClintock 1987). This now generally accepted critical assumption needs revision or clarification: in particular, what needs explaining is how and why the lyric tradition was actually useful under South African conditions, and then why the poets of the period moved on to write something else, something that we could call epic.[3] The context we've already established, relating to Black Consciousness, will help us to understand why that trajectory was both necessary and inevitable.[4]

Serote's first published poem, 'Cat and Bird', which appeared in *The Classic* in 1969, is a straightforward performance of the lyric that seems indebted to Ted Hughes's animal poems. Mzamane would like us to read it as a political fable (Serote 1982, 7), a reading that is also possible with Hughes. Here is Serote:

> Soft steps
> Expressed fully by the teeth
> Meeting each other through the road of flesh
> And blood, the last sweat of the bird
> Dripped,
> The cat slid across the green grass,
> Glowing hunger in its dark eyes,
> Into the dry, dust leaves,
> It hid. (1974, 35)

What confirms that this poem is consistent with the lyric tradition is not simply the similarity with Hughes, but more fundamentally, the individuality and intensity of the speaking voice, or its drama of personal observation. The lyric poem has at its origins in early modernity the sonnet, which is quintessentially the performance of the individualist, the exhibitionist, the courtier, the lover. After the Romantics, and still more so after the Modernists, the lyric poem comes to instantiate the isolated, intelligent, contemplative observer-self, a place of writing that is also a space of recovery or self-reconstitution, even or perhaps especially, in one of its most favoured of tones, that of irony. The dominance of the speaking voice in lyric poetry is so well established that recent Anglo-American criticism has come to question its assumptions, revealing the extent to which this voice is indeed a fiction that is dependent on certain conventions, and one that is permeated by various kinds of written inscription (Parker 1985, 16–21).

Something close to this personalised, even exhibitionist voice, is a trademark of Serote's early poetry as well. When we read the prefatory note, however, to the title of his first collection, *Yakhal'inkomo*, it seems inappropriate even to begin to question, as criticism of the Anglo-American lyric has done, the authority – the moral authority – of this feature of his work. For Serote's title refers to the cry of cattle at the slaughter house, and his explanation of its significance makes it representative of what it means to observe and give witness to a crisis of pain and terror, a situation that has obvious human and societal implications in South Africa. Serote's cry, 'yakhal'inkomo', is a kind of multi-disciplinary modernism of a fierce and fiercely local, kind:

> Dumile, the sculptor, told me that once in the country he saw a cow being killed. In the kraal cattle were looking on. They were crying for their like, dying at the hands of human beings. Yakhal'inkomo. Dumile held the left side of his chest and said that is where the cry of the cattle hit him . . . Yakhal'inkomo. The cattle raged and fought, they became a terror to themselves; the twisted poles of the kraal rattled and shook. The cattle saw blood flow into the ground.
>
> I once saw Mankunku Ngozi blowing his saxophone. Yakhal'inkomo. His face was inflated like a balloon, it was wet with sweat, his eyes huge and red. He grew tall, shrank, coiled into himself, uncoiled and the cry came out of his horn.
>
> This is the meaning of Yakhal'inkomo. (Serote 1972, iii)

The cry is not that of cattle being slaughtered but of cattle *watching*: it vocalises empathy and suffering. In the transference of the cry of cattle to the human drama, there is a further metamorphosis that has to do with the role of art in giving witness, as we see in the saxophone of Mankunku Ngozi, and indeed (need it be said) ultimately in the poetry of Serote himself.[5]

To summarise, it would be reasonable to assert that Serote's gut-wrenching sound-image, 'yakhal'inkomo', puts a local pain into the lyric tradition. Or, to put it the other way round, Serote's cry is a striking, local appropriation of the lyrical voice. Is this move a reflection of Serote's proximity to an *oral* culture? That interpretation is certainly possible, but it is also the case that there is no reference here to the genres, codes and conventions of oral poetry, that is to say, to the institutionality of oral tradition. It is not the oral poet who interprets the cry of the cattle, it is the *sculptor*, and his empathy would be recognisable in any culture broadly sharing the post-Romantic and modernist sensibility.

There are many other appropriations of the lyric tradition by the Soweto poets, from Renaissance to modern examples, but they do not have quite the same intensity and stamp of bodily authenticity as Serote's. A few examples will suffice. Mafika Gwala's 'We Lie Under Tall Gum-Trees', in his first collection, *Jol'iinkomo* (1977), revisits Donne's 'The Flea', substituting mosquitoes for fleas as the bearers of sexual intimacy. In his first collection, *Hurry Up To It!* (1975), Sipho Sepamla's poem, 'To Whom It May Concern' (which later became the title poem of a representative anthology of the period), takes off from Auden's 'The Unknown Citizen'. Oswald Mtshali's is an interesting case, which makes extensive use of Blake's *Songs of Innocence and Experience*. The subjects of several of Mtshali's poems, like the shepherd watching the farmer's children going to school, or the boy on a swing, ask questions that, following the example of Blake, scandalise innocence by confronting it with the nasty reality of apartheid. Unfortunately, Mtshali is rather self-consciously literary: the poets of the classroom (not only Blake but also Wordsworth and Hopkins) are often looking over his shoulder, as when in 'Reapers in a Mieliefield', his subjects

> stop for a while
> to wipe a brine-bathed brow
> and drink from battered cans
> bubbling with malty 'maheu' (Mtshali 1971, 10).

Serote, too, knows his Wordsworth. Here, in 'I Will Wait', it is the Wordsworth of 'Tintern Abbey':

> But O! often, now and then, everywhere where I have
> been
> Joy, as real as paths,
> Has spread within me like pleasant scenery,
> Has run beneath my flesh like rivers glitteringly
> silver . . . (Serote 1972, 36)

For the most part, however, Serote eschews this kind of derivativeness. His themes in the early poems have to do with the futility and violence of township life, and they are presented in tones of anguish, bitterness, disgust, and ironic condemnation, rhetoric that is seldom less than passionate and authoritative. 'What's In This Black "Shit"' is such a poem, which begins by evoking racial self-consciousness under apartheid as a kind of bile on which the speaker gags:

> It is not the steaming little rot
> In the toilet bucket,
> It is the upheaval of the bowels
> Bleeding and coming out through the mouth
> And swallowed back,
> Rolling in the mouth,
> Feeling its taste and wondering what's next like it.
> (Serote 1972, 8)

The climax of this disgust is an act of recovery, where the speaker pronounces 'shit' in the face of the official at the pass office, something, it pleases him to recall, his father would never have done: 'That's what's in this black "Shit",' he says, flinging the disgust back to its point of origin.

In pointing out this predominance of the lyric tradition in the early work of the Soweto poets, is it the case, as Duncan Brown asserts (1997, 7), that we are 'recuperating' that tradition in some conservative sense? Not necessarily; rather, we are raising the honest question, which is, as I suggested earlier, why the tradition should have proved so useful to poets whose formation was in the South

Africa of the 1960s. Michael Chapman has said that 'in the late 1960s – in literary journals such as *The Classic* – the voices of Mtshali, Serote, later Sepamla, Gwala and others challenged many assumptions about the well-wrought urn of Western-romantic lyric tradition' (Chapman 1997, 1). The evidence of what was actually published in *The Classic* suggests otherwise. Certainly, to take up Chapman's terms, the glassy polish of the 'well-wrought urn' is not especially important in these poems, in the sense that they are memorable more for the force of their statement than their construction as art-objects. Nevertheless, their reliance on the lyric's contemplative voice is strong. The answer to the question of why the tradition was useful is surely that the performance of the 'overheard utterance' was a defence against the programme of radical dehumanisation that had been under way in apartheid for a generation or more. The lyric poem, in other words, conveyed a distillation of agency to the distinctive human subject, and the installation of a contemplative (and sometimes angry) voice – these were powerful, appealing weapons in the prevailing climate.

Mafika Gwala opens his first collection, *Jol'iinkomo* with exactly this affirmation:

> Thoughts jet north and south
> Like migratory birds trailing season
> stopover here,
> stopover there;
> The trips go on
> in shuttle system
> B
>   U
>   T
> one thought never leaves:
> that one is human
> with feelings of love and hate
> with pangs of desertion and embrace
> with inner urge to destroy and create (1974, 9).

Gwala's typographic arrangement here shows that it was not only the voice and individual agency of the lyric that were taken over, but many of the formal tricks of modern poetry. Frye rather laconically speaks of the lyric poem being about babble (sound-play, onomatopoeia), doodle (verbal design on the page), and riddle (complex, semantically encoded interpretations) (Frye 1957, 275–80; Culler 1985, 40–41). All three of these elements were of service to South African poets of the 1970s, as even a cursory glance through their early production confirms. Duncan Brown has argued that paradoxically, in one of the later Soweto poets, Ingoapele Madingoane, typographical experiments are a sign of a commitment to *orality* rather than to print-culture, since they facilitate the poems' performance (1997, 14–16). That may be the case but, in fact, the lyric tradition as a whole, particularly in its more modern forms, used typographical and other experiments *precisely* in imitation of the voice. Indeed, the whole tradition is *based* on imitations of the voice in print, and therefore Madingoane (or Gwala, in the above example) was not really departing from it. The important point cannot be that the lyric tradition and its bag of tricks were eschewed by the Soweto poets, an argument that is unsustainable, but that the tradition was made tougher and became politicised through the process of its localisation.

Ingrid de Kok is one of the few South African poets who has spoken of the political potential of the lyric tradition. At a conference that launched the vanguard publication of the mid-1980s, *From South Africa: New Writing, Photographs and Art* (a special issue of the journal *TriQuarterly*), she said, 'the traditional features associated with the lyric, things like reflection and irony and analysis, must be put to the service of the historical moment in all its urgency'. Her defence of the lyric was part of an argument to the effect that South African poets (women, in particular) 'are particularly well placed to disassemble, to reassemble and interpret, to reimagine, the self. This work could help in a small way to reconstitute a fuller story of our internal life and of our history, not the partial one we still privilege as "true", as "real"' (in Gibbons 1989, 56–61). De Kok was speaking speculatively, in the manner of a manifesto, but her argument had already been given a practical demonstration in the early work of the Soweto poets.

To continue with Serote: while it is clear that as with other poets, the lyric was useful, there are also signs of discomfort. For example, he shows anxiety about whether the tradition (and print in general) could convey or contain the extent of the voice's anguish. A poem such as 'Prelude' – another Wordsworthian touch – illustrates this:

> When i take my pen,
> my soul bursts to deface the paper
> pus spills –
> spreads
> deforming a line into a figure that violates my love,
> when I take a pen,
> my crimson heart oozes into the ink,
> dilutes it
> spreads the gem of my life
> makes the word I utter a gasp to the world, –
> my mother, when I dance your eyes won't keep pace
> look into my eyes,
> there, the story of my day is told. (Serote 1974, 9)

The vessel of the poem is too static to hold the subject's volatility. This suggests Serote's discomfort with using a borrowed language and tradition, which fall outside of the family's, or the community's intuitions, as is suggested in the anticipated reactions of the mother. The problem addressed in 'Prelude' is also, in part, the problem of temporality, of the 'nowness' of the experience encoded in the poem, since the speaker is concerned that the mother's gaze might not 'keep pace' with his performance. In more abstract terms, the question Serote faces is how the lyric as a form relates to the particular experience of modernity that the subject is facing.

At the risk of being slightly digressive, let me pursue this further as a theoretical issue. How, in general terms, has the relationship between the lyric and modernity been understood? One of the oldest functions of the lyric, as I have suggested, entails anchoring the isolated, speaking subject in the convention of the 'overheard utterance'. This was a useful defence-mechanism under South African conditions as apartheid waged its campaign of dehumanisation. The lyric, in other words, gave to local poets a vehicle for expressing selfhood and autonomy, key features of modern, post-enlightenment thought.[6] Apart from the lyric's *ideological* usefulness, however, what about its language and formal properties, and the possible ways in which their modernity could be construed? I am alluding here to the fact that since Baudelaire and Symbolism, there has been a modernist infatuation with the process in which the lyric actually *gives up* its claims to mimesis and representation, and gives itself over to obscurity, or to put this more positively, to music. In this view, modernity is associated with the lyric as something like 'pure sound', and the ideological freight of the post-enlightenment or perhaps Romantic instantiation of the subject, has been judged to be passé.

Paul de Man's analysis of the lyric's relationship to modernity renders this debate still more interesting. His argument is that the lyric is necessarily an unstable structure, which is the result of its being partly representational and partly not, in the sense that it is historical and situational but that it also reaches beyond representation to something like pure performance. Via a discussion of Mallarmé, De Man shows that even where there is an apparent tendency towards irrationalism in the lyric as pure sound, there is frequently also a thread of representational or mimetic logic that anchors the reader in a cognitive and affective space. Only in such a space, in fact, can the pull towards pure form be recognised for what it is, as a movement supposedly *away* from the real. However, a purely representational poetry is also a contradiction in terms, since straightforward representation is not effected best in the devious language of poetry. (As Albie Sachs once memorably put it, 'a gun is a gun is a gun' [1998, 240].) It is this aspect that De Man defines as the lyric's modernity: its ambivalence – its dual nature, or its capacity both to say something and to reach beyond that which is actually said. There is something in the tradition, says De Man, which 'makes lyric poetry into an enigma which never stops asking for the unreachable' (1983, 186).

Serote's restlessness, which is partly a feature of his absorption in the conditions of South African city life, and partly a feature of his anguished, always unsatisfied, voice, would seem to illustrate De Man's argument precisely. Serote's poetry 'never stops asking for the unreachable'; to that extent, he is in touch with the inherent possibilities and enigmas of his form, indeed as a poet of modernity. However, in addition to the lyric's inherent qualities, in Serote there are other pressures that propel him beyond the conventional statement. In the first place, as is sharply revealed in the poem 'Black Bells' (the last of the poems in *Yakhal'inkomo*) there is the problem of being trapped in the language and forms of white culture and looking for a black alternative:

> I know I'm trapped.
> Helpless
> Hopeless
> You've trapped me whitey! Meem wanna ge aot Fuc
> Pschwee e ep booboodubooboodu blllll
> Black books,
> Flesh blood words shitrr Haai,
> Amen. (Serote 1972, 52)

It is not 'pure sound', exactly, but the sound of anger and frustration. Secondly, there is the question of capturing the obscure logic of the *apartheid* city, which mauls its subjects as it shuttles them between work and ghetto, an experience Serote captures in such well-known poems as 'City Johannesburg' and 'Alexandra' in *Yakhal'inkomo*. In 'The Face of a Happening', the subject's struggle to find a language in which to frame this headlong chaos is given precise definition:

> And I sit and look through the gap between the
> curtains
> And I feel like saying this is not the way to look at
> the world.
> Where's the world? How do you look at it?
> It's like trying to put the wind into bed. (Serote 1972,
> 37)

Thirdly, the crisis around finding an appropriate language is also a function of the way in which the rhetorical context around Serote is developing – the situation with which I began this chapter. The culture is demanding radical adjustments of the voice, indeed of the basic rhetorical relationships between writer/speaker and reader/listener. All of these challenges are registered in a voice that struggles to thread the fragments of chaos together, as in 'Made of Broken Pieces':

> I picked pieces of my bro-
> ken heart early one morning
> from the ceiling
> and pillow
> while I lay
> think-
> ing
> feel-
> ing
> so
> low like a man his head below
> trying hard to creep beneath a sagged low barb wire
> which wove his soul
> hanging
> in Cape town. Durban. Swaziland. Al
> ex-
> andra's head has been chopped off
> the tail remains

> wags
> awkwardly in my gut
> while those other places clutch me
> so
> pulling this way and that way
> so
> my
> heart
> bro-
> ke
> because it's so soft
> like a baby's bones
> twisted
> in the camp yellow walls of District 6
> Langa . . . (Serote 1974, 27)

In this extract, a pattern that will grow from this point on in Serote's poetry (and indeed, later in his fiction) can be readily identified: it lies in the conjunction between a subject who registers the violence of history on the body, and a developing, communal and more encompassing historical perspective.

This is the basic structure of Serote's next two volumes: *No Baby Must Weep* (1975) and *Behold Mama, Flowers* (1978). The turn in these poems is towards an integration of the personal and existential – the legacy of the lyric, as it were – with the historical and the national. A seamless connection is sought between the self and the nation, a connection that demands – not to put too fine a point on it – both longer and stronger forms, forms that seem best described as epic in their aspirations. It is here that we can identify Serote's attempt to find adequate formal vehicles for conveying Jameson's notion of 'subjects of history' coming into being to claim their own. This turn will also take Serote into the novel, but let us pause over the longer poems first. The quest for epic, we might say, begins for Serote in *No Baby Must Weep*. The subject of the poem is the 'blackmanchild' who is on a journey of self-discovery and self-emergence. No longer the heterogeneous speakers of the many and various lyrics of *Yakhal'inkomo* and *Tsetlo*, the focaliser has become unified and more widely representative. This formal adaptation would also seem to be a very precise response to a crucial aspect of Black Consciousness, in which, as Biko put it, 'the interrelationship between the consciousness of the self and the emancipatory programme is of paramount importance' (1978, 49). The journey of the blackmanchild begins in childhood and family relationships; appropriately, the addressee of the poem at this stage is the mother. Steadily, there is the growth of adult consciousness that comes with a sense of loss, indeed of parturition, and the separation from the mother is recurrently presented in terms of a bleeding wound. At the same time, there is the growth of an identity that takes on the wider social character of township life. Here Serote gives free rein to ideas of the body in various states of crisis – wounded, in child-birth, aged, scarred – imagery that registers graphically the pressures of history on the emergent subject. The final stages of the poem involve a search for larger, organic metaphors in which the agonies of the self's relationship to history are assuaged – images of landscape, sky, sea, trees and, most powerfully, following Langston Hughes's example, rivers. The isolated subject of the lyric has, in this metamorphosis, begun to give way to the heroic and representative subject of epic and, along with it, a more revolutionary vision:

> i am the man you will never defeat
> when the trees rattle you shall hear my last footsteps
> this won't be your world
> i am the man you will never defeat
> i will be your shadow, to be with you always
> and one day
> when the sun rises
> the shadows will move, heaving like a tired chest
> there shall be millions of shadows

heaving
and the earth shall be cold
and the river will freeze
and the plants will refuse to grow
and the earth shall be dark
and the river shall be dark
and we will be alone (Serote 1982, 86).

The difference between *No Baby Must Weep* and *Behold Mama, Flowers*, the next collection, is that the latter is more systematically in tune with international black and anti-colonial intellectual life. From the artist Skunder Boghossian, Serote learned the story of a man who chopped a body into pieces and threw them into a river; a child observing them said, 'Mama, look at the flowers'. The poem puts this symbolism into narrative: the speaking subject witnesses suffering, recalls it in memory over the generations, and looks for resources to overcome it through a collective will that is located in the anti-colonial struggle. The river, in this poem, runs through both the diaspora and the former colonial world: it is the Limpopo, the Zambezi, the Nile, and the Mississippi, but also the Amazon and the Ganges. The blackmanchild of *No Baby Must Weep* is now a larger and more precisely referenced historical persona that includes Angela Davis, Malcolm X, George Jackson, Eduardo Mondlane and Amilcar Cabral. This new expansiveness is no doubt connected with the fact that *Behold Mama, Flowers* was written mainly during Serote's period of studies towards a fine arts degree at Columbia in 1975. For the first time, we are told the places of the poems' composition: New Orleans, Washington, DC, Berkeley, New York. The internationalisation of Serote's vision also seems to have left him in no doubt about the need to cast in his lot with the political movement in exile. The most politically uncompromising of the poems in the collection (interestingly, still entitled 'Song of Experience') is written in Francistown, Botswana, where he has finally chosen ANC company:

> the word is here: change
> there can be no bottom or top
> only people who put brick on brick
>
> we choose the weapons now
> either we live or we die (Serote 1978, 78).

Serote's novel, *To Every Birth its Blood* (1981) gives further definition to this moment of choice. With reference to June 1976 and its aftermath, it incorporates what it calls 'the days of Power'. This phrase gathers together several threads: Stokley Carmichael's 'black power' recontextualised, and the gathering of exiled liberation forces for a final thrust. The novel's structure confirms the directions already taken by the poetry: Part One tells of the formation of Tsi Molope as a rather dissolute, unfulfilled activist and intellectual; Part Two tells of his absorption into a collective struggle, with the consequences of 1976 beginning to take effect. The communal awakening Serote charts in Part Two is to some degree an attempt to bring together different ideological positions and generations into a single political unit, one that of necessity has to remain fairly loosely defined as the Movement, but which is suggestive of a shift from Black Consciousness towards ANC politics, a function of exile and the absorption of Black Consciousness refugees as cadres of the liberation forces (indeed, in this period the term 'Movement' was used colloquially with reference to the ANC). The mature political intelligence of Michael Ramono, representing an older, ANC-aligned generation, in dialogue with his daughter, Dikeledi, of the generation of Black Consciousness, suggests the basic elements out of which the Movement is to be constructed.

Whether the Movement is indeed so easily identifiable with the ANC, or whether it represents Serote's somewhat utopian efforts to bring into being an image of collective, purposeful struggle through the use of unifying organic metaphors – a literary patriotic front, in a sense – is perhaps a moot point. Criticism of the novel has sought to explain the shifts of emphasis between Parts One and Two, with Kelwyn Sole arguing convincingly that there is never a sharp division between Serote's secular, political vision, and his more expansive, poetic-symbolic aspirations (Sole 1991, 51–80). The point is, the novel's structure is pivotal, illustrating in a precise way the shift from lyric to epic with which this chapter is concerned. Moreover, the structure of *To Every Birth its Blood* suggests very tidily the overarching developmental logic of all of Serote's writing as he moves progressively towards attempts to speak in a representative voice, with selfhood recontextualised through political struggle and national formation.[7]

In the 1980s, Serote continued producing poetry that defers to the Movement for its authority. *The Night Keeps Winking* (1982) is committed unambiguously to 'national revolution'. Written in Botswana, it builds memorably to a celebration of a sabotage attack on an oil refinery, and uses imagery of natural justice throughout. In *A Tough Tale* (1987) there is a shift of tone: as the title suggests, there is some reference to the human costs of the struggle, but Serote also proposes that the full historical demands of the times are beyond the capacity of language to grasp. These are, indeed, the years of the States of Emergency and of Nadine Gordimer's 'interregnum'. It is a time of news blackouts, tens of thousands of detentions, thousands of deaths: a time, in other words, when narrative seems superfluous, given the scale of what people are being called on to endure. Curiously, however, *A Tough Tale* lacks energy, and its closing gestures defer to the authority of the ANC and its allies, Cosatu (the Congress of Trade Unions) and the Communist Party, calling on them to tell their own story directly through their actions. In a sense, Serote seems to call into question the power of all poetic statement, with these organisations assuming responsibility for telling their own 'tough tale'. From its opening paragraphs, *A Tough Tale* never achieves the intensity that has been Serote's *sine qua non,* and the overriding spirit is one of enervation:

> We page through each other's faces
> we read each looking eye.

> it has taken lives to be able to do so.
> we move like a tortoise
> as we journey home.
> home –
> where are we that we are not home?
> ah
> it is a long story this
> that is why we page every face
> and read each look
> and move like a tortoise.
> please
> spare our tongue, do not make us relate the long story
> because when your mother goes mad
> you would rather help her to sanity than just talk about
> her madness.
> we want to help ours –
> in this long bewilderment
> she's done and shown us the most strange things
> so: we stalk her
> that is why we are not home. (Serote 1987, 7–8)

The enervation is not relieved in *Third World Express* (1992), another poem of epic aspirations. Despite its attempts to begin to address the post-apartheid situation, its many repetitions suggest uncertainty on Serote's part as to where his next formal innovation will lie. The problem persists in *Freedom Lament and Song* (1997). Looking back over Serote's career, it seems to inscribe a parabola: beginning with a powerful lyrical voice it builds with lively representational chaos and formal instability. Steadily, this restlessness stabilises as Serote discovers the appeal of longer and stronger, indeed epic forms. Increasingly, however, there seems to be a price for this: as the poetry is nationalised, there is a sense of exhaustion, as if epic has begun to cancel lyric rather than to absorb it into something new, a platform from which a new phase of vision-making could be launched. As Yeats put it, the falcon cannot hear the falconer.

WHAT DOES SEROTE'S trajectory tell us about the period and the challenges that he and his fellow poets faced? Firstly, it seems clear that as the Black Consciousness movement gathered strength, it changed the social and rhetorical conditions under which the Soweto poets operated. It is not that the lyric tradition was not reconcilable with Black Consciousness – indeed, as we have seen, it facilitated the affirmation of selfhood that was at the heart of the movement's social programme. But Black Consciousness discourse, especially after 1976, tilted away from the reflective, contemplative voice of the lyric towards more collective, public and declamatory modes, such that poets like Mtshali, Serote, Gwala, and Sepamla, who had begun publishing some years earlier in vehicles that were by no means populist, found themselves adjusting to the new demands and possibilities.

As Kelwyn Sole and Duncan Brown have documented, after 1976 there was, in particular, a shift from publication to performance, with a slightly younger generation of poets challenging the predominance, and the literariness, of their elders (Sole 1987, 259; Brown 1997, 10–11). The currency of Ingoapele Madingoane's *Black Trial* and *Africa My Beginning* is a measure of the new circumstances: Madingoane's poems were performed on many occasions in the late 1970s; they also circulated in manuscript before being collected and published by Ravan Press in 1979 (Brown 1997, 2). Apart from the emergence of *Staffrider* magazine and Ravan's accompanying book series, in which Madingoane was published, the growth of performance poetry in this period is perhaps the most dramatic of the shifts of culture that took place in the 1970s. How did our quartet of poets, and Serote especially, relate to it?

Adapting Walter Ong's theories of orality, Duncan Brown writes about what he calls a 'secondary' orality in the poets of Black Consciousness. For Ong, 'primary' orality reflects the speech and oral culture of illiterate communities, whilst 'secondary' orality occurs in the electronic media – especially radio, television and (in the period Ong was writing) the cassette recorder. Brown, however, gives a different meaning to 'secondary' orality, which seems more appropriate to the local context: '[it] usually involves the mobilisation of indigenous oral forms by literate or semi-literate individuals as an act of political and cultural resistance' (1997, 2). In other words, oral poets such as Madingoane, in Brown's account, who are more than literate themselves, address speech communities who are both literate and non-literate (and somewhere between), adapting themselves strategically to gain maximum rhetorical advantage. (Mzwakhe Mbuli, as a poet who came into prominence in the 1980s, was in a similar position, although Mbuli was also able to exploit more favourable conditions of censorship to make use of Ong's version of secondary orality as well, that is, by using the recording industry.)

Did Serote and his peers follow this shift, then, from publication to performance, which is reflected in the role that was afforded an increasingly public poetry in the context of the events of 1976? Not strictly: rather, it would seem that the implications of speaking *on behalf of* (rather than literally *to*) a wider audience became encoded into what remained a largely print-bound *oeuvre* for the early Soweto poets, who by this stage became recognisable as elder statesmen. By definition, it is not possible to perform epic poems on the scale that Serote wrote them, at large gatherings (though, of course, he did perform extracts at festivals and conferences). In any event, Serote's 'post-lyrical' work was written largely under conditions of exile. Mtshali's career is also instructive in this regard: *Sounds of a Cowhide Drum* (1971) was followed by the more militant *Fireflames* (1980), a shift that is particularly responsive to the Soweto Revolt (*Fireflames* is dedicated to 'the brave schoolchildren of Soweto, who have died, been imprisoned and persecuted in the grim struggle for our freedom'). However, like Serote's, much of Mtshali's later poetry was written in the United States. Whilst there are many poems that represent a *mimesis* of oral discourse (several of them with repetitions, slogans and the naming devices of the *izibongo*), and also, whilst there are poems translated from originals in isiZulu (which are, nevertheless, not printed), *Fireflames* was published essentially as an art-work, complete with linocut illustrations. Related observations could be made about Gwala's *No More Lullabies* (1982) and Sepamla's *Children of the Earth* (1983): there is a good deal of playful and at times declamatory language in these collections, but it is a case again of the printed poem imitating orality, rather than bearing obvious signs of having been written expressly for performance. (Interestingly, after *No More Lullabies*, Gwala's work was deeply involved with oral culture but on more scholarly terms, leading to *Musho!* [1991], a collection of *izibongo* co-edited with Liz Gunner.) In Serote, particularly, the long, written epic poem becomes a way of responding to a general historical situation rather than an attempt to develop a performance style and mode of speech that would have an immediate, affective charge to an audience of listeners.

The mixed success of Serote's later epics – *A Tough Tale*, *Third World Express*, *Freedom Lament and Song* – raises the question of whether the epic mode of discourse can be sustained over time. To put it simply: can one remain for long in a state of cultural revolution? Gwala and Sepamla were noticeably sensitive, in their later poems, to the dangers of speaking in consistently heroic terms. In 'A Wish' from *The Soweto I Love* (1977), Sepamla hits a rather valedictory note, with the speaker imagining himself as Atlas – bending the sky, holding back rivers, changing their course, rivalling the birds, pulling himself out of the earth's womb – a true subject of epic – but then the poem concludes, 'but a wish of mine remains/peace at all times with all men' (Sepamla 1984, 111). Similarly, in 'Fruits Not Seeds' from *Children of the Earth* (1983), there is a sense of doubt about his vocation:

> I should write no more poems but tributes
> read at night vigils and funerals
> I sing dirges for those whose dances
> have ended in bloody pools
> for our life is a commentary of wasted moments
> a purge of the unfaithful who ride chariots
> of the condemned soon to be labelled numbers

carted by impotent porters
yet why should I go on bleating
when others feed me bullets (Sepamla 1983, 132).

Much of poetry of the 1970s dealing with the future and the anticipated moment of liberation was apocalyptic. Such is Mtshali's poem, 'The Dawn of a New Era', for example, which speaks of history 'spring cleaning the cobwebbed corners of the earth', and sending the moon 'baying like a dog skulking for shelter' (Mtshali 1980, 17). By contrast, Gwala's poem 'Time of the Hero' is a rare example of a poet using irony to speak of the final moments of liberation. It suggests that when the 'time of the hero' actually arrives, people may still be as ordinary, and as unheroic, as they frequently are in the present:

Time of the hero
is when blacks start
pissing on Mankunku's lament
refusing to bemoan their blackness
– is when music fans drop out of the pancake blues
and appletart classics
– is when Mannenberg's untoothed mamas
chew 'druiwe by die tros'
– is when Ngoye students
blow Graffitti Blues on the System
– is when the ghetto goes
for imbuya herbs & butterbean chitterlings.
Time of the hero
is when leftovers give blacks constipation
– is when ghetto trains
spill out racecards thru the windows
with blacks refusing to bet on their poverty anymore.
Time of the hero
is when Durban's Golden Mile
stops being golden
– is when Jo'burg The Big Apple turns fluffy

with Soweto massing the City streets.
Time of the hero
is when the struggle weeds out
alcoholic glances & syphilitic frowns.
The moment of the times shall have come (Gwala
1982, 71).

By the end of the poem, the 'time of hero' (singular) has become the heterogeneous 'moment of the times' (plural), a move that shifts the moment of liberation from the realm of myth to a more ordinary reality. It is also a move that anticipates Njabulo Ndebele's intervention of the mid-1980s, which shifted the emphasis from the 'spectacular' to the 'ordinary' and developed the latter perspective as a new, and nuanced, mode of critique.

The issue that remains to be addressed, one that Gwala's poem implicitly raises, and one I discussed previously in relation to the lyric, is the question of temporality, of how epic discourse positions its speakers or writers in relation to the present and to the modernity that is unfolding around them. Let us begin with the seemingly simple question, what is epic? The traditional definition provided by M.H. Abrams is a useful point of departure: 'it is a long narrative poem on a great and serious subject, related in an elevated style, and centred on a heroic or quasi-divine figure on whose actions depend the fate of a tribe, a nation, or the human race' (1981, 50). Serote's male child of *No Baby Must Weep*, as well as the subjects of the later epic poems, would fit this description. There is, however, a feature of Abrams's definition that is not spelt out but that is nevertheless implicit: epic heroes normally belong to the past, whereas Serote's heroes belong in the present. Serote's subjects are, after all, metaphoric distillations of the community as it exists, a community struggling to bring itself into being as a modern nation, or perhaps as a modern *nation-state*, since what drives the quest is the yearning for citizenship, sovereignty, and power. To understand Serote's project, then, we need to take a position on the question of what it means to rewrite the present in epic terms.

Mikhail Bakhtin's discussion of epic in *The Dialogic Imagination* would suggest that to attempt to write the present as epic would be inadvisable, perhaps even impossible, since by definition epic belongs to the time of the 'absolute past'. Unlike the novel, which for Bakhtin is the quintessential genre of modernity because of its dynamic qualities of incompletion, open-endedness, and receptiveness to the present, epic as a genre has ceased to develop. Moreover, the resources of epic, its heroic narratives, lie in tradition, the problem for Bakhtin being that tradition in this particular sense is 'inaccessible to personal experience'. One cannot 'glimpse it, grope for it, touch it; one cannot look at it from just any point of view; it is impossible to experience it, analyze it, take it apart, penetrate into its core. It is given solely as tradition, sacred and sacrosanct, evaluated in the same way by all and demanding a pious attitude toward itself.' As all of this implies, the mode of relation to its material that is prescribed in epic is one of *distance.* Epic narration implies detachment from the living contact zone and familiarity in the present on which the novel thrives (Bakhtin 1985, 14–17). Where a writer such as Gogol, Bakhtin says, attempts to write about Russia from an epic perspective (using as a model, the *Divine Comedy*), the result is a failure because Gogol 'got muddled somewhere between memory and familiar contact – to put it bluntly, he could not find the proper focus on his binoculars' (Bakhtin 1985, 28).

How appropriate is Bakhtin's account of epic to the work of South African poets? It must be recognised that Bakhtin's view of epic is mildly tendentious insofar as its main purpose is to serve his account of the development of the novel, but apart from that, the major source of epic discourse in South African literature is the praise poem, which is certainly a dynamic genre that has continued to adapt all the way into the present. Furthermore, the social weight of the past on which epic discourse relies in South Africa continues to be felt in particularly painful ways, so that the pastness of the past, so to speak, can hardly be taken for granted, as Bakhtin seems to do. Consequently, the epic's temporality, or what Bakhtin would call its chronotope, changes considerably in South Africa. Indeed, instead of being wholly associated with the past, the dignity of epic discourse is tied to the present. In fact, on the basis of an ethical imperative, the absoluteness of epic, as Bakhtin would have it, is in South Africa transferred to the *future*. It is possible, then, under these conditions, to associate epic discourse with openness to the ongoing production of modernity, and Soweto poetry in particular seems to hold the possibility of an *epic of futurity*.[8] This would seem to be the essential distinction between the epic discourse of Serote, in which we have the iteration of the present and future as epic, as compared with Mazisi Kunene's *Emperor Shaka the Great* and *Anthem of the Decades*, where, despite the fact that these epics resonate in the present (not least when they are read by troops in the barracks of a liberation army), they nevertheless do not have quite the same purchase on the present and future as Serote's do.[9] The basis and historical modality of Serote's epics would seem to be the progress of the black subject in contemporary history, in an expanded horizon made possible by its articulation within the wider diaspora.[10] There is continuity here with the post-Romantic lyrical subject, but also a radical departure, with its collectivisation and instantiation within a more encompassing vision. Perhaps this is why it seems possible for Serote to move quite easily between epic poetry and the novel, something that would be difficult to account for in Bakhtin's scheme. In Serote the process of novelisation (the emergence of the individual subject, the foregrounding of contemporary reality, the presence of polyphony as the text takes on the social discourses of its time, etc.) occurs comfortably alongside the reinvention of the epic as one of the modes of narrating the present, a mixing of genres and their historical possibilities that Bakhtin could not have envisaged. This also helps to explain why several critics have suggested that the most appropriate sense in which we might speak of epic discourse in Soweto poetry is that of the epic theatre of Brecht, which is concerned not with past mythic heroes but with the present of economic hardship and political education (Brown 1997, 19; Msimang 1982, 204–05; and Chapman 1984, 200–01). This is a suggestive idea, although there is little evidence of a direct Brechtian influence and therefore we must also account for the local epic's modernity in other ways.

In one respect, Bakhtin's analysis does seem applicable to Serote and to South African conditions: whether what Bakhtin calls *absoluteness* is tied to the past or to the future, it does detract from a sense of the ordinariness of the present and the kind of dynamic historicity that Bakhtin associates with the novel. This is the concern of Gwala's poem, which renders the future ordinary and surprises the reader with comic, anti-climactic effects while still sustaining a sense of community familiarity and solidarity, since the whole poem is rendered in a local idiom. To write always in the name of a radical epistemological shift and of momentous change is, as I have suggested, to carry a heavy burden, and the noticeable enervation in Serote's later epics would seem to confirm this. However, that remark cannot be the last word on this subject. While the literary price to be paid might be that of exhaustion, the historical and visionary claims that are inherent in the epic discourse of Soweto poetry and in Serote in particular remain a powerful legacy, one that was continued into the 1980s by other writers, notably Njabulo Ndebele who reinscribed the epistemological energy of Black Consciousness in a sustained articulation of a theory of the cultural imagination of the oppressed.[11] The underlying relationship of the poetry of Black Consciousness with modernity, therefore, is one that insisted uncompromisingly that the present be reinvented in every conceivable way. The vision, courage, and even the exhaustion associated with this insistence, lives on as a powerful legacy in the post-apartheid era.

6

The experimental turn

Experimentalism in contemporary fiction

Our survival depends on a tactical cosmopolitanism

Njabulo Ndebele (in Lindfors 2002 [1986], 245)

Since the late 1960s, a truism in discussions of black South African writing – fiction, in particular – has been that conditions have militated against the development of a fully-fledged experimentalism. The predominant mode, it is said, is the literature of witness, documentary, and protest – varieties of realism, although with the exception of Alex La Guma, local practices of realism are not easily described in terms of their European counterparts such as naturalism, or social and critical realism. Indeed, so axiomatic has this position been, that it seems naïve to propose a critical archaeology in pursuit of anything resembling a local black modernism or postmodernism.

The reasons for this tendency are not hard to find. Lewis Nkosi, who represents something of a lone voice in his consistently trenchant interventions in this field, once suggested that what is generally expected from South Africans is 'not so much art as confidential reports about the condition of society, its health or lack of it, its ability to survive' (1981, 76). What is exceptional about this remark is its tone: it is seldom that anyone treats the subject ironically. On the contrary, more often than not with regard to black writing the claim is that realism of a direct and polemical kind is the most logical and principled of modes of representation and of responses to apartheid and apartheid conditions. Writing about the 'rhetoric of urgency' in South African literary culture, Louise

Bethlehem (2001) rightly speaks of a tendency to conflate a 'trope-of-truth' and the 'trope-as-truth'. In other words, Bethlehem discerns a narrowly instrumental view of language in South African literary culture, where mediations inherent in language as a semiotic system are wished away simply because it seems ethically desirable to do so.

Nadine Gordimer's reflections on this subject are instructive in revealing how consequential this position has been for South African authorship. She distinguishes between her own self-chosen immersion in the novelistic tradition, and the kinds of demands that are appropriately made of black writers. The latter, she says, who have responded not so much to an orthodoxy but to a genuine impulse, reached a point where they decided 'to discard the lantern of artistic truth that reveals human worth through human ambiguity, and to see by the flames of burning vehicles only the strong, thick lines that draw heroes' (1989, 293). She qualifies this by referring to work of the early 1980s by Njabulo Ndebele, Es'kia Mphahlele and Ahmed Essop, which reserves the right to interpret, 'for the post-revolutionary future', 'that nobility in ordinary men and women to be found only among their doubts, culpabilities, shortcomings: their courage-in-spite-of' (Gordimer 1989, 293). Even here, Gordimer's acknowledgement does not speak of formal or literary or experimental self-consciousness in black writing, merely a more complex realism. For the most part, her sense of a neighbouring black tradition whose aesthetics she generally finds inimical to her own, despite being drawn to it in a spirit of comradeship, has helped to define her own, rather different course. It is one that has been, in some respects, the much lonelier one of struggling, as she represents it, to reconcile social responsibility with art. The ideal of the writer, she poignantly remarked, lay in Walter Benjamin's storyteller, who 'could let the wick of his life be consumed completely by the gentle flame of his story' (Gordimer 1989, 300). The tendency to polarise white and black in terms of their relationship with experimental traditions therefore runs deep, entering the self-construction of as prominent an *oeuvre* as Gordimer's.

Like Gordimer, Nkosi accepts that the polarisation is a historical reality, but in his essay 'Postmodernism and black writing in South Africa', he says candidly that the tendency to avoid experimentalism is the result not of a principled abjuration (the way Gordimer and others credit it) but simply of the deprivation and isolation of the black writer. Indeed, Nkosi goes so far as to argue with a kind of spade-calling relish that the 'breadline asceticism', 'prim disapproval of irony', and 'petty realism' of much black writing gives it an essentially 'colonial status' (1998, 77–80). Despite this forthrightness, Nkosi's purpose is actually benign: it is to open a more complex debate about how we might recognise and theorise literary experimentalism in black prose fiction when we see it.

Nkosi makes the obvious but necessary point that if a black experimentalism is to emerge, it will do so under its own animating conditions and along its own paths of development, not those that have obtained for Western and white South African writers (Nkosi 1998, 84). The distinction marks a departure from an earlier version of the argument, which first appeared in 1967, involving the often-cited statement that black fiction was filled with 'the journalistic fact parading outrageously as imaginative literature' (Nkosi 1979 [1967], 222). That intervention led, at the time, to a productive exchange with J.M. Coetzee (well before the appearance of Coetzee's first novel, *Dusklands*) who responded by asking, 'What value does the experimental line hold for Africa? . . . does not the experimental line assume *and perpetuate* a rift between the writer and society at large which is a fact of life in the West but need not become a fact of life in Africa?' (Coetzee 1973, 6). Coetzee's question later led him to examine Alex La Guma's critical realism, which he treats as a form of experimentalism that does *not* fall into the conservatism that haunts Nkosi's argument (compare Attwell 1993, 12). We now know, of course, that when his own novelistic career got underway, Coetzee did not pursue the idea of weaving critical or any other realism into his own experimental practice, except by way of parody. In Nkosi's more recent essay, the questions he raises are essentially about the origins and development of South African epistemologies and forms of subjectivity, rather than the fate of European modernism in the country. Indeed, in his insistence that if a local experimentalism is to develop it should not be understood in linear terms with Western practice at the high point, Nkosi's position is close to the question Coetzee put to him.

One possible response to Nkosi must be, however, that black writing is indeed replete with instances of aesthetic self-consciousness, not excluding the very kinds of experimentalism that we associate with modernism. This assertion may seem remarkable in the face of so much commentary to the contrary, not only of an academic kind but also statements of cultural activism (dating especially from the 1980s) in which affirmations of the transparent political message are to be found in prominent manifestos, such as those of the Congress of South African Writers (Cosaw), the cultural desks of the ANC, UDF and Cosatu, as well as in arguments reiterated in festivals such as 'Towards a People's Culture' and 'Culture in Another South Africa', which celebrated the culture of resistance (compare Parry 1994, 12). It is worth observing that a great deal of this kind of statement, however, is circular and self-perpetuating. In other words, assertions about the overwhelming prevalence of documentary realism all too frequently involve generalisations based on other critical statements with little or no discussion of the literature's actual qualities: its range, its idiosyncrasies, its very unfinishedness, and sadly, also its high points. In an unguarded moment, Coetzee once remarked on what he saw as a 'programmatic refusal' in the fiction of Serote and Sipho Sepamla 'to create a structure in which there is some centre of intelligence', a refusal, that is, to recognise that 'making sense of life inside a book is different from making sense of real life – not more or less difficult, just different' (Coetzee no date, 4). The appropriate way to read this statement is to see in it Coetzee's determination to carve out a space for himself and for the possibility of a late-modernist or postmodern or broadly self-reflexive metafictional enterprise in South Africa, in the unwelcoming climate described by Bethlehem. Indeed, if we are to speak of a lonely poetics in

South Africa, Coetzee's of the 1970s and 80s was perhaps the loneliest of all. But Coetzee himself would probably agree that we should not mistake this reaction for a general description of black writing, from which we can quickly cull enough anecdotal evidence to suggest a widespread and even at times a surprisingly orthodox interest in modernist experimentalism.

What does it mean, for instance, that Njabulo Ndebele confesses that while reading for the English Tripos at Cambridge in the early 1970s (with an undergraduate degree in English already behind him) he experimented with Joycean internal monologue in isiZulu (Lindfors 2002 [1986], 226)? And perhaps we should take seriously the fact that despite the aggression of his language, Muthobi Mutloatse is going down the well-trodden road of the modernist manifesto when he declares, in his notorious Introduction to the collection of short fiction of the Black Consciousness period, *Forced Landing*:

> We are involved in and consumed by an exciting experimental art form that I can only call, to coin a phrase, 'proemdra': Prose, Poem and Drama in one!
>
> We will have to *donder* conventional literature: old-fashioned critic and reader alike. We are going to pee, spit and shit on literary convention before we are through; we are going to kick and pull and push and drag literature into the form we prefer. (Mutloatse 1980, 5)

As Nkosi points out, readers familiar with the twentieth century's long history of aesthetic revolutionising will look on this as 'defiant insouciance' (1998, 77). Nevertheless, it declares an experimental horizon, one which, furthermore, is more than apparent in several of the contributions to Mutloatse's collection itself, which does not contain much 'proemdra' but does include samples of allegory, political fable and even science fiction. For an earlier example, we might turn to the 'Interludes' in Esk'ia Mphahlele's autobiography, *Down Second Avenue* (1971 [1959]). The following passage – which deals with a child's insomnia in a crowded township home and his identification with fugitives from the curfew outside – is typical:

> Saturday night and it's ten to ten, I can hear the big curfew bell at the police station peal 'ten to ten, ten to ten, ten to ten' for the black man to be out of the streets to be home to be out of the policeman's reach. Year after year every night the sound of the bell floats in the air at ten minutes to ten and the Black man must run home and the Black man must sleep or have a night special permit. The whistle is very near now and the hunted man must be in Second Avenue but the bell goes on peeling lustily and so Black man you must run wherever you are, run. (Mphahlele 1971 [1959], 45)

The passage is experimental in a number of ways: its visceral pacing, and its fusion of the boy's consciousness with that of the imagined fugitive, a fusion that seems to stand for a collective self, the speech of which is captured in an imagined black (diasporic) argot. In Nkosi's own *Mating Birds* (1987) we find a different kind of inventiveness: the novel crafts a dispassionate, self-ironising introspection on the causes and consequences of interracial sexual violence, in a voice that keeps company with Albert Camus's outsider and Richard Wright's Bigger Thomas. Another example might be Dugmore Boetie's *Familiarity is the Kingdom of the Lost* (1969) – the very title suggests an experimental impulse – which blurs the distinction between artist and con-man. Yet another would be Part One of Mongane Serote's *To Every Birth its Blood*, where Tsi Molope's subjectivity is filtered through narration modelled on jazz. We could go on, but for the moment it is enough to name what these examples represent: black South African writing *has* been touched by what Coetzee calls 'the experimental line'. If garden variety forms of realism do abound, it is not true to say that they have crowded out altogether the more adventurous flowerings of experimentalism. We should add that the phenomenon we are observing (inchoate, perhaps, but objectively present) goes well beyond the improvisational bricolage of the earlier generation, that of the 'New Africans' such as Sol Plaatje and Herbert Dhlomo.

Definitional dangers could beset us at this point. The simple procedure of defining what modernism or postmodernism are, and applying these crude categories to local black writing – thus ignoring Nkosi's cautionary note – is not available to us. Coetzee's phrase, 'the experimental line', is useful precisely because it recognises that attempts to be categorical can be artificial and misleading. Nevertheless, since I prefer the term experimentalism to the more overdetermined categories of modernism or postmodernism, it seems necessary to offer a working definition of what I mean by experimentalism. In *Sources of the Self*, Charles Taylor refers to twentieth-century modernisms collectively as 'epiphanic art', meaning self-consciously aesthetic practices of the late nineteenth and twentieth centuries that try to initiate an epistemological renewal in response to conditions we associate with modernity. This is close enough (because it is general enough) to what I mean by experimentalism, although at certain points in the argument I shall have to refine or qualify it. Something I do wish to emphasise as a general assumption in my argument, since it is so relevant to black writing, is that as Taylor also points out, all the modernist revolutions (like their Romantic precursors) may detach themselves from various kinds of worldliness or from prior cultural monoliths or institutions, but what they share is a desire to affirm the *agency* in terms of which the new subject or practice they are heralding would like to be understood (Taylor 1989, 456–93). This emphasis on the agency that is carried in projects of epistemological renewal is fundamental to the writing under discussion.

In order to understand this phenomenon properly we need to add other terms: shortly, I shall speak of 'reflexivity' and of 'cultural struggle'. Before doing so, however, I shall pick up once again Nkosi's insistence that the black South African context imposes its own caveats. Nkosi argues that certain features of modernism and postmodernism, which we may think of as definitive – for example, the break-up of the Cartesian, rational self, and the veneration of the decentred subject – are inherent in *traditional* culture. The example he gives is the celebrated one of Nongqawuse in the Cattle

Killing of the mid-nineteenth century, who provided that movement with a millenarian symbolic language. Her language (and that of her mentors and followers) was not entirely autochthonous since it was already informed by missionary teaching. Consequently, the kind of splitting Nkosi is referring to may equally be a function of the syncretic epistemologies emerging from the colonial encounter. A different example might be that of the initiate who feels the call to become an *isangoma* or diviner as a disruption of the rational self, as the ancestors badger and irritate him or her into service. Indeed, in his poem 'uMamina' in *Amal'ezulu* (1945) Vilakazi uses this as a metaphor for poetic inspiration, in order to ground the concept of the muse in a local field of reference. Whilst Vilakazi's experiments with English rhyme might not have been wholly successful, as I mentioned earlier, this aspect of his experimentalism is decidedly an African modernism, one that draws on the pre-modern in a manner not procedurally different from European primitivism.

Nkosi's argument therefore points to ways in which the temporal axes of modernism and postmodernism may need to be revised in the local context. The same could be said for their spatial dimensions. To take an obvious example: when European modernism registers spatial dislocations, it frequently does so in terms of the expatriate or exile (Conrad in Africa, Hemingway in Paris, Lawrence in New Mexico, and so on). This pattern is not absent from black South African writing – think of Mphahlele's reflections on a man in a glass house, in this case the places of exile being Denver and Philadelphia (Manganyi 1983, 288–89). Equally and more powerfully, though, black South African writing can reflect a sense of dislocation *at home*. The force of this can be gauged from the fact that before the term 'township' became the standard descriptor of the black dormitory suburb, the common term was 'location'.[1] Ironically, the location names a place of permanent unease or unsettlement, a place where one experiences one's *dislocation* from rural life, economic independence, political representation, and citizenship. The boy's consciousness in the passage from *Down Second Avenue* cited earlier on page 174 develops precisely around this disorientation, as does Tsi Molope's in *To Every Birth its Blood.* This is where modernist decentring speaks to the spectral nightmare that was apartheid, the disempowering effects of which Ndebele will try to resist in his theory of the 'ordinary' (I shall come back to this issue).

Thus far I have collected examples of black experimentalism that must complicate the critical orthodoxy with which I began, and begun to suggest (following Nkosi's leads) that what is required is a more contextual theorising about what we are looking for and what the phenomenon might mean when we find it. Let me now come to the nub of my argument, in which I would like to focus on a particular, recent moment in the history of black fiction in South Africa. I wish to argue that in the work of Ndebele and Zakes Mda we have an experimentalism in which a process of epistemological recovery and revision is fully under way. Far from being partial or inchoate, the experimentalism of their practice is self-conscious and programmatic (to refer to Coetzee's 'programmatic refusal', mentioned earlier). Their practice is also, I suggest, reflexive (to pick up that term now), in the sense in which John Noyes speaks of a reflexive theorising. By this he means a practice that is concerned both with identity, and with the ways in which its 'conceptualisation relates to the moment of its performance', that is to say, 'how in the act of theorisation, a specific constellation of ideas comes together to define and delimit the individual's position in a particular social and historical order' (Noyes 2000, 49). For Graham Pechey, this is the deeper meaning of the term 'cultural struggle', one that is not fully registered in the instrumental senses given to it in debates about resistance. 'To emphasise "culture" as struggle', says Pechey, is 'to speak of that struggle's subjects, the birth and growth of its forms of subjectivity, the complex socially symbolic acts whereby it makes it makers' (1994, 25). What we are concerned with here, then, is how this reflexivity and sense of cultural struggle have come to be encoded in black fiction. What we find in Ndebele and Mda is indeed an attempt to develop a transformative fictional practice answering to the specific situation of black South African subjectivity under the conditions of modernity defined by the apartheid city.

This description begs the question of other modes of experimentalism in black writing: Bessie Head, for instance, or, more recently, Zoë Wicomb. Undoubtedly, their work is both modernist and postmodern in specific ways, some of which have to do with gendered modes of representation and their implied subject-positions. However, I would argue that the case I am making can be formulated all too easily with respect to Head and Wicomb, whose gender-positions and whose exilic relation to their material weighs more heavily than it does with writers such as Ndebele and Mda. What I am pursuing, in other words, in terms of the larger dimensions of the argument, is the meaning of a fictional practice informed by a desire to articulate a black, urban South African epistemology. Ndebele and Mda offer the most sustained examples of this project in recent fiction.[2] It is quite possible, as Anthony O'Brien has suggested, that Head, in her efforts to reconstitute a 'private sphere' in the context of a Botswana village, is an influence on Ndebele (O'Brien 2001, 59). This may be so, but it is a different question.

A final, brief word of theory before turning to the writing. Debates around Theodor Adorno and Georg Lukács's positions on the political legacy of modernism might be useful as further points of reference. In the mid-1980s, Neil Lazarus published a path-breaking essay in which he explored the relevance of Adorno's thinking on modernism to South Africa. Adorno's defence of modernism affirms the value of the insider's 'immanent critique', a critique associated with the power of difficult language to resist reification. Lazarus argues that this position, which sees modernism as an attempt to refashion a world sunk in the torpor of the administered society and demoralised by fascism, applies *mutatis mutandis* to the work of Breyten Breytenbach, André Brink and J.M. Coetzee in the context of apartheid in the 1970s (Lazarus 1986, 134). By definition, however, surely this account of modernism cannot apply in any straightforward way to black writers, whose relationship to social conditions is such as to position them not *inside* the headgear of apartheid – to use a mining metaphor – but *outside* it? In other words, we would expect black writing to establish a certain distance from the apartheid insider's consciousness, locating itself in a different subject-position altogether. Adorno's argument, of course, comes to us as an alternative to Lukács's rather stringent critique of the 'ideology' of modernism, a critique of the kind of self-consciousness that paralyses living connections between the subject and society. It was this principle that Gordimer invoked in her critical review of Coetzee's *Life and Times of Michael K* when it first appeared, a position that would in all likelihood have been informed by Gordimer's sense of what black readers might make of the novel's quietist hero (Gordimer 1984, 6).[3] The Lukácsian position would be common cause for black South African writers, who have sought to protect their connectedness with their readerships. As Mutloatse puts it, 'no black writer can afford the luxury of isolation from his immediate audience' (1980, 1). As we have seen, however, from Mutloatse's own concerns and those of others, it would be inaccurate to say that black writing is untouched by modernism. What we are trying to understand, then, is an experimentalism that is both socially connected and aesthetically reflexive, a practice that, in Nkosi's terms, is both 'task' and 'mask', one that enables the critique that we might associate with realism but that also announces the epistemological invigoration and subject-construction that we might associate with the modernist movement.

IN HIS CRITIQUE of Ndebele's *Fools and Other Stories* (1983), which he reads in the light of Ndebele's essays in *Rediscovery of the Ordinary*, Michael Vaughan (followed later by Benita Parry) points out that despite the claims Ndebele makes for fiction that is close to the orality of black communities, a mode that in some ways echoes the storytelling traditions of rural life, in his own fiction Ndebele does little to disturb Western realism (Vaughan 1990, 191; Parry 1994, 17). We could endorse this to a degree by pointing out that certain features of Ndebele's theory of fiction – for example, that part of it which contrasts irony and depth with the repetition of stereotypes – are part of realism's stock-in-trade, adding little to what E.M. Forster said about character in *Aspects of the Novel.* What deserves more careful consideration, though, is the fact that Ndebele dramatises a process of epistemological recovery.

The stories seem straightforwardly representational in the way they lay out certain dynamics of South African society, such as tensions between the generations, class divisions and aspirations, political alliances, clashing accounts of tradition, and so on. However, this is not where the emphasis lies. Instead, it falls on the growth of consciousness and its connection to the data of daily life in a black community. The stories are profoundly about language, knowledge and cultural agency, and how *these* instruments of power are to be understood, acquired, and developed. Their formal properties serve this inquiry, and in a sense I shall shortly explain, their overarching project is to make 'form' their 'content'.

Ndebele's fiction and essays would not have been possible without the Black Consciousness movement, which was founded, essentially, on a theory of the self. That is to say, against apartheid's denigration of blackness, its relegation of black agency to minor (rural, and underclass) regimes of labour, political representation and citizenship, Steve Biko and his associates claimed a modern identity on behalf of black South Africans. It is an identity defined eclectically with reference to Third World and African-American intellectual currents, but one that participates nevertheless in post-enlightenment, modern assumptions about selfhood: namely, its autonomy and agency. Ndebele's fictional project brings aspects of realism into this social movement, its particular contribution being to stage an epistemological recovery. In doing so, it implicitly critiques the legacies of Bantu and missionary education, both of which disrupted the continuities there might have been between the black subject and the practices of literate culture. Such continuities have had to be re-created ever since by writers' re-appropriating the instruments of culture, using and developing them on their own terms. Indeed, it is possible, as A.C. Jordan and his successors in black literary history have done, to read the history of black writing in South Africa on precisely these lines. This process of self-recovery is staged in *Fools* in terms of an implicit *bildungsroman* that underlies and links all of the stories in the narrative of a boy who comes to develop the kind of social imagination out of which an appropriately subject-centred activism is possible. It would be wrong to suggest that *Fools* is typical of the literature of Black Consciousness, which was decidedly a literature of militant advocacy. Rather, Ndebele explores the conditions of possibility – epistemological primarily, but also ethical – under which programmes of advocacy might either thrive or die.

One way to approach Ndebele's recovery of a self-directed epistemology would be, once again, via the work of Charles Taylor. Taylor is relevant not only in the general terms of his inquiry into what he calls the 'sources of the self' in modernity, but more specifically in terms of his suggestion that the modern concern with selfhood starts with an affirmation, in early modern society, of ordinary life. This affirmation, says Taylor, is theological in origin, indeed it is inaugurated by the Reformation, and what we have come to think of as later, fundamental shifts of culture, including the Enlightenment and Romanticism, really secularise and deepen this original moment (Taylor 1989, 211–33). Arguments involving aesthetic revolutions are really arguments over the appropriate 'symbolic goods' that will serve this affirmation at given moments of history. 'Affirming ordinary life', says Taylor, 'has meant valuing the efficacious control of things by which it is preserved and enhanced' (1989, 232).

Seen from this longer perspective, in his call for 'the rediscovery of the ordinary' (the coincidence of terms with Taylor is felicitous but non-essential) Ndebele is laying claim to what Taylor is naming, that is, the symbolic goods of modern selfhood, on behalf of black South Africans. When Vaughan says that Ndebele, despite himself, is writing within the Western tradition of realism, he misses the reason for Ndebele's doing so, which is that Ndebele wishes to access one of the historical forms by which a self-conscious expansion and affirmation of selfhood has been achieved. The progress of the self in the context of what Ian Watt famously called 'a full and authentic report of human experience' (1957, 35) is in these stories being placed at the feet of a social and intellectual community that is still working out the terms of its historical actualisation. The underlying purpose of all life-writing, including autobiography and the *bildungsroman*, says Taylor, is to distinguish 'the life-shape from the events', and these forms provide the intellectual spine of *Fools*.

Following Vaughan, Benita Parry suggests that Ndebele's interest in formal experiment is limited. Her view is that Ndebele treats form as 'the handmaiden of the new content, enabling the assumed reader to recognise an authentic version of a familiar world, and not as the means of representation, which can . . . reveal that what is being offered is a fabrication, thereby interrupting expectations, defamiliarising "the real", and resituating the reader as interrogator rather than recipient' (Parry 1994, 17). This critique seems to me to undervalue the degree to which the issues Parry is raising are implicit in the stories' own concerns, for the formal inventiveness Parry wishes from Ndebele would principally serve the recovery of epistemological agency, which is at the heart of Ndebele's project. Moreover, it is not strictly true to say that Ndebele wants his reader simply 'to recognise an authentic version of a familiar world' because what he is doing, in fact, is *instantiating* a world and more especially a subject-position that, in a crucial sense, has not been fully present to literary representation at all.

When I speak of experimentalism in Ndebele while acknowledging his realism, this might be seen as tempting contradiction. Indeed, I *am* arguing that Ndebele brings these things together, and that his realism ought to be understood as participating in the afterlife of modernism. In his own time and place, after all, Ndebele is drawing on the symbolic goods of realism long after the effects of modernism have been widely felt. Moreover, the history of realism's emergence in Europe is being reprised under critical conditions, such that the social intensity and historical telescoping inherent in the project give it the force of an intervention, a revisionism that is more characteristic of twentieth- than nineteenth-century aesthetic history. We could argue, in fact, that Ndebele's project recovers some of the epistemological freshness that once adhered to realism itself.

At the centre of *Fools* lies an experiment in projecting a contextually nuanced subjectivity. The trick the reader is required to catch in the opening paragraphs of the first of the stories, 'The Test', is to recognise the historical weight that supports this apparently ingenuous project: 'As he felt the first drops of rain on his bare arms, Thoba wondered if he should run home quickly before there was a downpour. He shivered briefly, and his teeth chattered for a moment as a cold breeze blew and then stopped' (Ndebele 1983, 1). Self-consciousness and timidity are matched by a certain aesthetic sensuousness: 'He looked down at his arms. There they were: tiny drops of rain, some sitting on goose pimples, others between them. Fly's spit, he thought' (Ndebele 1983, 22). As it does in *The Portrait of the Artist as a Young Man*, of which this image-making is surely an echo, the child's sensitivity isolates him to a degree from his peers and from the soccer game in which he is, and is not, a participant.

Ndebele takes palpable risks in opening his collection this way, not least risking the accusation of fiddling while the townships burn; of distracting readers from the mature resistance that had become a reality in the Black Consciousness movement and the Soweto Revolt that it had inspired five years before the stories were written. That 'The Test' unfolds around a group of boys – carefully delineated in class terms, revealing the proximity of the middle-class black child to his impoverished peers – reflects the irruption of June 1976, is implicit in the situation. 'The Test' is an archetypal tale of self-actualisation, encoded in the events of the story as a challenge by the boys to withstand the elements of a highveld storm on one's bare torso, like a 'horse in the rain'. This simple drama tracks a moment in Thoba's emergence as he runs home in the falling rain and cold, through familiar but now unhomely streets, mindful of a folkloric beast who might swallow him, past the AME and Dutch

Reformed Churches, and especially, past the humiliating women who are known to his mother. When he reaches home, he curls up in bed and contemplates his soreness and humiliation as badges of honour.

What is important here is simply the fact of focalisation, which collects together a sweeping historical legacy. The subject-position is an act of epistemological leverage on Ndebele's part. The very boundedness of the child's world, in which he cannot recognise the apartheid social engineering that has shaped Charterston township, is an affirmation of this experiential reality and perspective. It is from this consciousness, and *no other*, that maturity and autonomy must develop. The gesture here is not substantially different from that of J.M. Coetzee's in *Waiting for the Barbarians*: it is a difference of scale, not of kind. Where Coetzee uses a deliberately non-South African and to a degree ahistorical milieu in order to challenge the comprehensive capturing of space and consciousness that was under way in late apartheid, Ndebele, too, clears a space, in this context one in which a mode of consciousness and agency can begin to extend itself, independent of the political discourses that swirl around him.

I have intimated that the subjectivity at the centre of Ndebele's stories is provisional and unfinished. Its dynamic and, as we shall see, dialectical attributes are intimately connected with questions of language. This emerges most forcefully in 'The Prophetess', where the boy – perhaps the same boy – visits a prophetess from an independent church to have water blessed for use by his ailing mother. As she sings and prays, the boy is in awe, and while it is clear that her creed has no particular meaning for him – his middle-class background seems to preclude him from uncomplicated belief in what she represents – what he takes away is her potency, simply her power to speak and symbolise. On the way home, the bottle breaks in a street encounter, whereupon the boy fills it with unblessed tap water that he gives to his mother, who drinks it and feels revived. This turn of events confirms our impression that the boy is a child of calculation, indeed of modernity, but the absence of guilt on his part, and the rush of pride and affection with which the story ends, imply continuity between the generations. More importantly, they imply a compacting of the prophetess's powers into the boy's subject-position, his feelings and familial relationships (Ndebele 1983, 51–52). What heals the mother, obviously, is love – fuelled by the boy's experience of poetic elevation. Ndebele's subject, who is on his way to claiming the rights and powers of a secular democratic order, achieves expansion through contact with a tradition of indigenous spiritualism. It is not the content of this spiritualism that matters, but its epiphanic charge.

This pattern is developed further in 'Uncle', in which Ndebele places the same developing consciousness in contact with a cultural order we have come to associate with the 1950s. The itinerant uncle, Lovington, who takes the boy under his wing for the duration of his visit to the family, is a jazz musician and to some degree a proponent of cultural pan-Africanism. He teaches the boy how to turn a clichéd school exercise on 'places I have visited' into a lesson on reclaiming a personal and communal geography, providing instruction, *inter alia*, on the pride and antiquity of Egypt. Most memorably, he turns evening bathing into a ritual activity in which the boy, having cleansed himself – his awakening to sexual potency is very much in the background – is encouraged to imagine himself a volcano. Steadily, Lovington's catechism links the child's developing masculinity to the idea of revolution, as he imagines himself a member of a throng moving through history, undaunted by the oppressive armoury of the alien modernity that confronts them – the factories, towns and jets in the sky 'like hundreds of vultures' (Ndebele 1983, 107). It is an induction into the unashamedly masculine culture of the epic (qualifications to this troubling virilism arrive in the subsequent story, which foregrounds the moral authority of women over the men) with, once again, a telescoping effect in which the energies of Africa's mid-twentieth century moment of decolonisation become the personalised heritage of the child of apartheid.

In the most complex of the stories, however, the novella *Fools*, Ndebele resists suggesting that an achieved, much less a revolutionary, consciousness is easy to hand. Indeed, the subject-position is split at this point between two characters: the older, corrupted and cynical schoolteacher Zamani, and his young antagonist, the idealist Zani. It is here that agency becomes dialectical, something that is reinforced by careful historical contextualisation. The story is set in 1966, a moment falling precisely between the demoralisation following the Sharpeville massacre, and the utopianism of Black Consciousness, when resistance has to reinvent itself, with the exiled movement beginning to organise for armed propaganda and internal resistance caught between generations. These are the historical coordinates of what Zani calls Charterston's 'stagnant isolation' (Ndebele 1983, 170).

As their complementary names suggest, Zamani and Zani are elements of a composite dilemma. Indeed, the plotting suggests their connectedness: when the story opens with their encounter on the platform of Springs Station, they are both in the midst of compromising love affairs: Zamani with a mistress, Candu, and Zani with a girlfriend who may be pregnant, Ntozakhe. Later, Zamani turns out to be the rapist of Zani's younger sister, Busi, an event from which a child is born whom Zamani refuses to acknowledge; Zani becomes the supportive friend to Zamani's injured wife, Nosipho, and so on. The point is, Zani is really Zamani's younger self, and they represent complementary positions on the issues the story confronts. Ndebele adopts a similar view of historical agency in his well-cited poem, 'The Revolution of the Aged', which stages a debate about acts of resistance needing to be correctly timed. The poem suggests that such acts must await the arrival of actors who can understand, with due historical weight, the implications of their actions:

> now is the time
> pluck the apple
> and feed the future with its ripeness (Ndebele 1983, 388)

The tension between the protagonists comes to a head when Zamani, at the risk of losing his job since he is at the mercy of an intellectually colonised headmaster, agrees to Zani visiting his classroom to proselytise the children over a demeaning national holiday, the Day of the Covenant. Zani addresses the ten-year-olds as Ladies and Gentlemen, haranguing them with the historical events of Blood River and its consequences, when the Boers defeated the Zulu king Dingane's troops and vowed afterwards to keep the day in religious memory. Zamani's reflections on Zani's performance follow:

> That they heard, I was sure; but that they understood, was impossible. . . . and it struck me at that moment how evenly serious Zani's language was. He had become his books, and when he moved out of them, he came out without a social language. He spoke to me in the same way he spoke to those children. Is that how he had spoken in the bar, and then got stabbed? I wondered if he was not another instance of disembodiment: the obscenity of high seriousness. (Ndebele 1983, 217)

'Disembodied', 'obscene' high seriousness has just shown itself in another form in the classroom, in the uncomprehending recitation by a child of an epic poem on one of the Zulu kings. These examples of discourse drained of subject-centredness are linked with another kind of disembodiment: a piece of amateurish pornography showing locked genitalia, which Zamani discovers being passed around, drawn (significantly) on the back of a poster calling for resistance to the national holiday. These connections are harsh indeed: autochthonous tradition, black history, and pornography. The point of the connections is to insist that revolutionary language must be 'social', that is to say, it must speak to and elicit the consciousness of those who are to be its agents. The larger context for this, what amounts to a critique from within of resistance culture, is not difficult to map. It lies in the legacy of Bantu Education and in the structural constraints on black intellectual life that has had to rely on what

Ndebele elsewhere calls an 'information order' that has been fashioned by others, notably liberal and radical historians, universities, and publishers (Ndebele 1994, 29–30). Seen in this light, Ndebele's project is about *reconnection*: linking subjects as agents-of-meaning with the resistance culture that is their proper heritage.

Zani and Zamani's failures and achievements are again juxtaposed at the end of the story. Zani's attempts to mobilise the community end in disarray when he flees the whip of an outraged 'Boer' who attacks black picnickers on the disputed national holiday. His tortured reflections ring with the story's title:

> What have I found anywhere? Everything seems so small. Am I that small too? Tell me. Have there been many years in which this smallness has turned into a tradition; many years of this crushing sleep of smallness? What is there to be done? It is so easy to make plans, and then everything comes crashing down because the proper act seems so rare. So many acts get done, and so few of them are proper. . . . But I ran too. And the wind that blew against my face as I ran sounded like the very sound of shame. The sound of victims laughing at victims. Feeding on their victimness, until it becomes an obscene virtue. Is there ever an excuse for ignorance? And when victims spit upon victims, should they not be called fools? Fools of darkness? Should they not be trampled upon? (Ndebele 1983, 278)

Given that Zani's despair is one position amongst others that the story offers, and that it is the predictable result of his *hubris*, it is curious that Ndebele should emphasise this outburst in his title. I suggest that the importance Ndebele attaches to the notion of 'fools' here – victims feeding on their victimage – is related to the principle of subject-centredness and the ownership of agency. Auto-critique, the argument would run, is a necessary condition for a thoroughgoing autonomy. Where the prize to be won by collective action – nothing less than a democratic revolution – is of such magnitude, it is of signal importance that an over-reaching immaturity such as Zani's be expunged. Zani's chastening self-discovery, in other words, in which he confronts his weaknesses and gauges the extent to which they represent a common condition, is a crucial step on the road to individual and collective empowerment. His discovery is very like that of the artist Mandla's in the story, 'Uncle', who finds the recognition he achieves in Johannesburg's élite galleries demeaning. He later carves a figure, 'The Hunchback', which he explains in part by saying that in the township of Orlando East: 'I do not have to pretend. I am nothing, and that is where I begin, rather than from an imagined somethingness. My mind can never rot here because I've learnt to humble myself before the people, beginning from the somethingness that has always sustained them' (Ndebele 1983, 80).

Zani's humiliation is matched by a moment of triumphant rehabilitation in Zamani. Instead of fleeing the white man with the whip, he stands and takes the blows in a moment of what O'Brien calls 'a Ghandian parable of the truth-force of African presence' (2001, 49):

> The blows stopped; and I knew I had crushed him. I had crushed him with the sheer force of my presence. I was there, and would be there to the end of time: a perpetual symbol of his failure to have a world without me. And he walked away to his car, a man without a shadow, the sun couldn't see him. And the sound of his car when he drove away seemed so irrelevant. There he went: a member of a people whose sole gift to the world has been the perfection of hate. And because there was nothing much more in them, they will forever destroy, consuming us and themselves in a great fire. But the people of the north will come down and settle the land again, as they have done for thousands of years. (Ndebele 1983, 276)

This quietism is not offered as a general solution, because of what it represents in *Zamani's* development: his victory over self-hatred, his overcoming of the very kind of debilitating consciousness of one's failures that Zani has expressed and that has turned Zamani into a cynic. Nor does the passage have to be seen as a moment of Africanist essentialism, for Zamani's image of the Africans who will come down from the north to resettle a land destroyed by whites is his grasping at metaphor in the resolution of a personal drama. However, whilst it cannot be taken as a last word, it certainly resonates with the assurance of Black Consciousness. At the Hector Peterson Museum in Soweto you are able to view video footage of Biko explaining that blacks will never oppress whites when they are in power since their sheer numbers will preclude them from having to protect their ascendancy. Shortly before his death, Biko said the following in an interview:

> So if you can overcome the personal fear of death, which is a highly irrational thing, you know, then you're on the way. . . . And in interrogation the same sort of thing applies. I was talking to this policeman, and I told him, 'If you want us to make any progress, the best thing to do is for us to talk. Don't try any form of rough stuff, because it just won't work.' And this is absolutely true, also. For I just couldn't see what they could do to me which would make me all of a sudden soften to them. If they talk to me, well I'm bound to be affected by them as human beings. But the moment they adopt rough stuff, they are imprinting in my mind that they are police. And I only understand one form of dealing with police, and that's to be as unhelpful as possible. So I button up. And I told them this: 'It's up to you'. (Biko 1979, 296–97)

O'Brien points to another moment in which Ndebele articulates a principled autonomy, about the same time as the completion of *Fools*. This involved his intervention in the naming of an anthology of black poetry to be published by Ravan Press, the publishers of S*taffrider* magazine. Before it became *The Return of the Amasi Bird*, the title was to be 'Ask Any Black Man', to which Ndebele responded, 'who should ask any black man? Surely not another African'. He goes on to argue that the time for implicit appeals for dialogue with whites is over: 'I have gone *far beyond* begging to be "heard". I am not even demanding. It is the pure force of my people's inevitable presence that I want to consolidate'. As O'Brien points out, Zamani's moment of truth-force matches Ndebele's own (2001: 49).

In his discussion of Ndebele's essays, O'Brien shows the degree to which their core project is indeed a developmental analysis of black intellectual agency. They conduct 'an inquiry into rethinking and remaking power/knowledge – "breaking down closed epistemological structures", "freeing the entire social imagination of the oppressed" – on the basis of an actual historical emergence of . . . a new hegemony, borne by the historically new subjects of the mass movement' (O'Brien 2001, 40). I have to agree with this emphasis and add that the project is intrinsic to the fiction as well. What the fiction, especially the title story, enables us to gauge, however, is the extent to which this project in subject-formation represents a putative ideal; it is, in the best sense, an inquiry: the *bildungsroman* is never rounded off.

We might develop O'Brien's observation that there is some autobiographical pressure behind the project. In some of Ndebele's writing as a student, such as his contribution on 'Black development' to Biko's collection, *Black Viewpoint* (1972), two things stand out. Firstly, his precociousness, in judgements such as the following: 'The peasants on the white farms have almost no political consciousness' (Ndebele 1972, 16); 'The urban blacks are the most socio-politically aware among the black groups' (1972, 17–18); 'The black middle class is also characterised by a general lack of creative imagination' (1972, 22); and

> the black must set about destroying the old and static customs and traditions that have . . . made Africa the world's human zoo and museum of human evolution. When customs no longer cater for the proper development of adequate human expression, they should be removed. Almost all the so-called tribal customs must be destroyed, because they cannot even do so little as to help the black man get food for the day. (1972, 26)

This is the kind of Zani-speak that falls under the scrutiny of *Fools*. The second observation, however, is the consistency of his most deeply held views:

> The blacks must ignore the frustrated black journalist who says that South African blacks must win the political kingdom first before they begin to create artistic works of any meaning and merit. Indeed, it is the great art works that inspire a bondaged people towards seeking freedom. An imaginative exploration of the miserable human conditions in which people live, touches the fibre of revolt in them; the fibre that seeks to reassert human dignity. Indeed, an intellectual awakening is a vital pre-requisite to any significant social change. (Ndebele 1972, 27)

> It is now for the black man to begin to work. It is work that involves a whole human re-orientation. The blacks must awaken intellectually, spiritually, socially, morally, culturally and in many other ways that make life worth living. If the whites do not want to change their attitudes, let the blacks advance and leave them behind . . . The black must know what they want when they cry for freedom. They should not be put in the situation whereby when they get this freedom they do not know what to do with it. The struggle is more than a racial one; it is also a human one; a human struggle involves development in all human activities that are the marks of true civilisation. (Ndebele 1972, 28)

The overarching thesis of 1972 is much the same as it is in 1994, the date that marks the publication of the collected, re-authorised version of *Rediscovery of the Ordinary*. What is different in that interim, however, is the degree of reflexivity with which the project is conducted – Ndebele's study in fiction of the conditions under which the emergence of the 'social imagination' is possible.

IF NDEBELE REDEPLOYS realism's resources in an experimental intervention, Zakes Mda takes us further down the same road. Let us begin with Toloki in Mda's first novel, *Ways of Dying* (1995). Toloki is theatrical – his signature outfit of top hat and cloak is acquired in a costume-hire shop – and his diet and personal habits (Swiss roll and green onions, a refusal to wash) set him apart. He has an eclectic mysticism that has nothing to do with oral culture, nor has his role as Professional Mourner, which is self-invented. Part ringmaster, part shaman, his practice is, however, empty of explicit metaphysical comfort, since his mourning takes the form of incomprehensible grunts. Toloki has no message other than to teach people that they must grieve. Later, through his companion, Noria, he learns 'how to live', but this knowledge does not translate into a programme. When the children of the township view Toloki's drawings, or his and Noria's shack that they have turned into a place of intimacy by the appropriation and transformation of imagery torn from the pages of *Home and Garden*, 'they cannot say what the meaning is. It is not even necessary to say, or even to know, what the meaning is. It is enough only to know that there is a meaning, and it is a profound one' (Mda 1995b, 187).

My claim here is that Mda is toying with modernism's characteristic position of non- or anti-instrumentalism. The notion that it is possible to refashion the world by style, that complex language is in itself a mode of resistance (to refer again to Adorno), is given a new, anthropomorphic embodiment in the figure of Toloki. If I may be allowed to draw on the author's own account of Toloki's genesis, the decisive influence on Mda was the figure of Vercueil in Coetzee's *Age of Iron*.[4] Vercueil is a tramp with a history of seafaring, a wanderer who smells of fatality. For this, amongst other reasons, Elizabeth Curren, Coetzee's protagonist who is suffering from terminal cancer, constructs him as her Angel of Death. The connection with Toloki is obvious, in the asocial behaviour and the association with death. More importantly, Vercueil is the key figure of alterity in Coetzee's text and as such, the agent of that novel's estrangement from the real. The intertextuality between *Age of Iron* and *Ways of Dying* is an explicit instance of the movement of modernist practice across the racial divide of authorship in South Africa. Indeed, Mda has mentioned to me another instance of his indebtedness to Coetzee: the arms-length treatment of the historical period to which his novel refers was developed under the influence of *Waiting for the Barbarians.* It is interesting and telling that Mda has come in for some of the same criticism that Coetzee faced in the 1970s and 80s, for displacing the social landscape of apartheid onto a symbolic or allegorical plane (compare Farred 2000).

Toloki embodies, then, a certain experimental practice of the South African township. His empty showmanship derives, via Coetzee it seems, from that feature of late modernism that is apparent in Beckett's defence of Joyce's *Work in Progress*, where he argues that 'form *is* content, content *is* form. . . . [Joyce's] writing is not *about* something; *it is that something itself*' (Beckett 1998, 451). However, in Mda we will not find Beckett's scorn for what he calls the philistinism that insists on finding a core of rationality in the literary text: 'the rapid skimming and absorption of the scant cream of sense is made possible by what I may simply call a continuous process of copious intellectual salivation' (Beckett 1998, 450). (Let me note in passing, though, that this tone is similar to Coetzee's in 'The novel today', where he says that stories are not messages plus a covering of art: 'on the keyboard on which stories are written, the plus key does not work' [Coetzee 1988, 4].) Mda would not deride instrumental modes of thought to this extent. If I may put it so awkwardly, Mda re-instrumentalises modernism's anti-instrumentalism, bringing it into an effective relationship with a given context and history. This contextualisation precludes the delivering of messages, the flattening out of performance or its reduction to simple meaning, but what Mda dramatises is the power of non-instrumental art to awaken listeners to their precariousness, to stir up affective capacities, and to remind them that despite the brutalisation that is their daily lot, they are still agents of culture. This makes Mda's writing a development from Ndebele's. The historical context of Toloki's performance is the wasteland of city and township in that narrow interregnum of South Africa between

1990 and 1994, that is, between the unbanning of the liberation movements and the first democratic election, when death has become a way of life, with Third Force killings engineered by security agents, the massacre of squatters by vigilantes, and the necklacing of child activists accused of being collaborators. To the African subjects who inhabit this space, Toloki offers not words of consolation but a symbolic presence whose function it is to symbolise. What Mda places before his readers is a performance that stands for the symbolic function, the point being to restore the image of the man-of-ritual, and the maker-of-culture.

The pattern is not restricted to Toloki in Mda's fiction. We also find it in Dikosha in *She Plays with the Darkness* (1995), whose dancing is a peculiarly celebratory mourning, and to some degree also in Camagu in *The Heart of Redness* (2000), who is drawn to the mysterious NomaRussia at a wake on the roof of a Hillbrow building. In these examples, modernity seems endemically linked to death, something also apparent in the actions of the unbelievers in *The Heart of Redness*, the non-traditionalists who need bouts of public grieving to cope with the consequences of their abandonment of their cultural past. The point is, Mda renders history – colonialism, apartheid – as a process of creeping death that necessitates modes of aesthetic production – the professional mourner, the dancer, *ritual*, in general – which are offered as sources of hope. Mda pits stylised aesthetic humanism against historically-induced death. By so doing, he participates in Coetzee's 'experimental line', but on his own terms.

The Heart of Redness, Mda's most ambitious work to date, is filled with a rather different aesthetic self-consciousness. The title echoes *Heart of Darkness*, as does the character, Sir Harry Smith, Mda's version of the historical colonial governor, who leads his troops into battle against the Xhosa with 'Extermination!' emblazoned on their hats (Mda 2000, 20). The novel also locates itself in other traditions: Xhosa narratives such as S.E.K. Mqhayi's *Ityala lamawele* ('the trial of the twins') and A.C. Jordan's *Ingqumbo Yeminyanya* ('the wrath of the ancestors'), which in their own ways are texts that deal with the Xhosa encounter with modernity. It also refers to Chinua Achebe's early fiction. There are a number of strong allusions to *Things Fall Apart*, including a memorable linking of the governor of the Cape Colony, Sir George Grey, with the district commissioner of Achebe's novel who writes Okonkwo's story as an episode in the history of 'pacification'. Like Achebe's aesthetics, Mda's go beyond the literary to the anthropological: he uses the Xhosa principle of twinning and, as Johan Jacobs has shown, the tradition of split-tone or overtone singing, *umngqokolo*, as a structural device. This occurs both in a generalised use of diglossia (unitalicised terms from isiXhosa used extensively alongside English) and in the arrangement of the narrative itself. The text is organised around two historical moments as well as two opposed social tendencies, one involving *ubuqaba* (conservatism, traditionalism, the 'Believers', their 'redness', from the red ochre with which the women adorn themselves and colour their skirts), the other involving *ubugqobokha* (literally 'piercedness', or enlightenment, the 'Unbelievers', with their faith in schooling and modernity). In addition to the gnomic traditions of isiXhosa and traditional music, Mda uses the set-piece debates that are typical of theatre-for-development, another arm of his expressive practice. All told, the novel is multi-voiced and multidisciplinary, an elaborately colourful, allegorical, historiographic mural, infused with the freeing of representational energy that the post-apartheid moment seems to promise. If black fiction comprises a unified tradition, then the effect of *The Heart of Redness* will be to put an end to the generalisation that this chapter has sought to confront, that it has not risen above elementary forms of realism.

This is perhaps not even the most significant of the novel's innovations. Instead of focusing on racial conflict, or apartheid and its counter-histories, *The Heart of Redness* foregrounds the encounter with modernity, not as completed event, but as unfinished business, over which the amaXhosa – and through figures such as Dalton and Camagu, South Africans in general – must take charge. The decisive de-privileging of the apartheid years and their struggles comes in the form of their relegation to the relatively unexplored 'Middle Generations'. Mda's larger canvas serves his mapping of the Xhosa response to modernity at a number of levels, beginning with the shock of its intrusion in the form of the demise of Xikixa, who becomes the 'headless ancestor' when during the war of Mlanjeni, in a moment of iconographic reversal, he is decapitated and the flesh is boiled off his skull to preserve it for future studies in phrenology. The psychic disturbance of this moment, which is witnessed by the old man's sons and which robs them of the means to lay him to rest, produces the splitting referred to earlier, with Twin and Twin-Twin falling into the rivalling camps of Believers and Unbelievers, answering respectively the call of indigenous and exogenous allegiances. The contemporary heirs of Twin and Twin-Twin, Zim and Bhonco, and their homesteads, are similarly caught in this division. With the apartheid years in the background, two historical moments encapsulate the ongoing struggle over modernity. In the first, around 1857, it is the prophetic movement started by Nongqawuse and sustained by her uncle, Mhlakaza, which provides the point of reference. In the second, it is the emergence of democracy in 1994, and more especially the period immediately after the elections when political freedom needs to be translated into autonomous social development. In choosing these moments as narrative *foci*, Mda, like Ndebele, implicitly places in question the problem of agency.

In the mid-nineteenth century, 'belief' takes the form of the millenarian Cattle-Killing Movement; 'unbelief' a readiness to cast in one's lot with what calls itself civilisation. Both positions bring degrees of catastrophe: to the believers, it brings famine, loss of land and power; to the unbelievers, it brings loss of self. The believers resent their neighbours' charge of backwardness; the unbelievers engage in their bouts of mourning. The contemporary version of this crisis takes place in the same rural, seaside village of the nineteenth-century story, Qolorha, whose residents must now decide how to take possession of their freedom. To a degree, the novel resembles a *roman a thèse* as it stages the debates in the community over appropriate modes of development: do they welcome the developers who will turn the village into a casino and hotel resort, cashing in on globalisation with all its dangers, or do they try to manage eco- and cultural tourism on their own terms?

The subject-position in terms of which these choices become personal, affective, and ethical is principally that of Camagu, who holds a Ph.D. in communications. He returns from exile to vote, only to find himself marginalised by the new élite and its nepotism, which has already proved to be the forte of the 'Aristocrats of the Revolution'. Camagu is about to abandon his country and return abroad when he discovers the true meaning of his presence, indeed his quest, at a roof-top wake that he stumbles upon in Hillbrow. The mysterious NomaRussia's singing stirs in him an irrepressible longing, and he pursues her to Qolorha. Her name suggests the Cattle Killing, with its allusion to the Xhosa belief of 1856 that since the Russians had recently finished off Sir George Cathcart in the Crimean War, the very man who had given them so much trouble in Mlanjeni's war of 1852, they would assist the ancestors on their return to drive the settlers into the sea. NomaRussia dies before Camagu finds her, but his romantic life takes on other forms, centrally an allegorical love-triangle in which he must choose between Qukezwa, who is mystically in touch with indigenous natural life, and Xoliswa, the school teacher who wears smart suits and shoes and who imagines that the America that is represented by Eddie Murphy and Dolly Parton is the apogee of everything desirable and sophisticated.

Camagu's quest reverses that trope of South Africa's literature of modernisation, the 'Jim-goes-to-Jo'burg' theme that we find in Alan Paton and an earlier generation of black writers (notably R.R.R. Dhlomo in *An African Tragedy*). The reversal is telling: instead of narrating the emergence of the African as modern subject – the end of innocence – the novel attempts a *reintegration* of the already-modern subject into the dilemmas of southern Africa's post-coloniality. Like Soyinka's figure of the interpreter, Camagu is a returnee who needs to discover who he is, in the professional sense, but more importantly in cultural terms, and the choices before him are modelled by Qukezwa and Xoliswa. In the final analysis, it is the side of belief that receives Mda's endorsement, with Qukezwa becoming the chosen one and the believers winning the strategic battle over the village's development. The decision is affirmed in the conception and birth of Heitsi, Qukezwa's child by Camagu, who is conceived by a kind of immaculate conception as the lovers are out horseriding.

As the resolution of Camagu's quest suggests, Mda is not content to allow the central choice imposed by modernity – return to the source or, as it were, cash in – to remain unanswered. Camagu, and therefore the novel, offer a modernised Africanism as the inevitable path into the future. Of particular interest to the concerns of this chapter are the tropological moves Mda makes to nudge his text towards resolutions at the deeper symbolic levels. Undoubtedly, modernity introduces splitting, a splitting of political allegiances and subjectivities, but against this, Mda asserts the metaphorical and ontological power of twinning. In Mqhayi's *Ityala lamawele*, conflict over inheritance and patriarchal authority between twins is resolved by the court's insistence that they are to rule jointly and wisely. This is in keeping with a traditional position that interprets twinship as a *single* identity. In Mda's hands, splitting and twinning comprise a warp and woof, a weaving of pattern and tension that gives definition to South African postcolonial modernity.

Mda's closing paragraphs are enigmatic. One of the reasons for this is that he brings together different registers that we may loosely call the politico-economic and the prophetic. Here is the politico-economic:

> As [Camagu] drives back home he sees wattle trees along the road. Qukezwa taught him that these are enemy trees. All along the way he cannot see any of the indigenous trees that grow in abundance in Qolorha. Just the wattle and other imported trees. He feels fortunate that he lives in Qolorha. Those who want to preserve indigenous plants and birds have won the day there. At least for

> now. But for how long? The whole country is ruled by greed. Everyone wants to have his or her snout in the trough. Sooner or later the powers that be may decide, in the name of the people, that it is good for the people to have a gambling complex at Qolorha-by-Sea. And the gambling complex shall come into being. And of course the powers that be or their proxies – in the form of wives, sons, daughters, cousins – shall be given equity. And so the people shall be empowered. (Mda 2000, 319)

The powers that be – the state, no doubt, and those who drive the economy – are mistaken, even treasonous in siding with unbelief, which is what capitulating to globalisation and material acquisitiveness amounts to. The bitterness of that final phrase – 'and so the people shall be empowered' – is made more deeply ironic by its echo of the Freedom Charter, which has been debased in its association with 'equity' in the financial sense. This register offers critique, therefore, the passage's implication being that freedom will never mean freedom from having to make hard ethical decisions in relation to development – to that extent, tradition cannot supply ready answers either. But then there is the prophetic register, such as we find in the novel's final paragraph:

> Oh, this Heitsi! He is afraid of the sea. How will he survive without the sea? How will he carry out the business of saving his people? Qukezwa grabs him by his hand and drags him into the water. He is screaming and kicking wildly. Wild waves come and cover them for a while, then rush back again. Qukezwa laughs excitedly. Heitsi screams even louder, pulling away from her grip, 'No, mama! No! This boy does not belong in the sea! This boy belongs in the man village!' (Mda 2000, 319–20)

At this point, Mda has conflated the two narratives, bringing about a deliberate merging of identities such that the Heitsi of this passage, the child of Qukezwa and Camagu, carries within himself the identity of Heitsi, the child of Twin and his wife Qukezwa of the nineteenth century, and behind both stands the figure of Heitsi Eibib, 'the earliest prophet of the Khoikhoi' (Mda 2000, 24), a touchstone of indigenous symbolic power. Similarly, the early and later Qukezwas have become less distinct, and prior to this passage, somewhat disturbingly, John Dalton, the white man who sides with the believers and whose 'heart is an umXhosa heart' (Mda 2000, 7), has nearly been murdered by the unbelieving Bhonco for the part the historical Dalton, John Dalton's predecessor, played in the humiliation of the 'headless ancestor'. In this general merging of identities, is Mda trying to impose a cyclic, pre-modern conception of history – the eternal return – on his tale?

This is possible, but the conclusion is not quite that straightforward. In the coda, Qukezwa wants Heitsi to learn to be comfortable in the sea, water being the element from which the shades will return; it is the element of prophecy, of millenarianism, of salvation. But the story is too multi-faceted, the tensions of Xhosa symbolic life are too contradictory, for Qukezwa to have the final word. It is given to Heitsi, who chooses not the sea but the village – therefore people over prophecy, and the future over the past. There is nothing in this resolution to qualify Mda's overarching thesis that the future must entail the working-out of an African modernity, but the emphasis is tilted, finally, towards open-endedness. The position is Fanonist, in the sense of the famous lines from the essay on national culture:

> It is not enough to try to get back to the people in that past out of which they have already emerged; rather, we must join them in that fluctuating movement which they are just giving shape to, and which, as soon as it has started, will be the signal for everything to be called into question. Let there be no mistake about it; it is to this zone of occult instability where the people dwell that we must come . . . (Fanon 1963, 227)

National cultures are not to be discovered, pre-formed, Fanon is saying, by returning to icons of indigenous purity forgotten in the wake of colonialism. Rather, they are to be made from all the resources at a people's disposal, in acts of appeasement not to the past, but to the future, for at the end of the quest to make peace with the past, there is still the question of living in historical time.

THIS CHAPTER HAS turned on two conceptual axes: the first is realism and experimentalism, the second is the real and the subject. My contention is that the positions circulating in the critical literature about black South African fiction are the result of privileging the first set of terms over the second, that is, realism and the real predominate over experimentalism and the creativity of subjects. I began by saying that the reasons for this privileging are not hard to find: the climate of expectation around the literature has appeared to necessitate it. The trouble with this emphasis is that it comes at a heavy price: unwittingly, and despite the protest value of realism, it has always suggested that black fiction is epistemologically naïve, wide-eyed in its confrontation with history, a rabbit caught in the headlights.

Why does it seem so important to be able to claim an 'experimental line' for black South African writing? The simple answer is that *not* to do so is demeaning and, in any case, inaccurate. Behind the question of whether laying claim to a tradition of experimentalism is necessary or not, lies the trickier, political problem – one the reader would have anticipated – of whether black writing repeats the subject-construction of European modernism, or whether it offers something distinctive and original. At the heart of *that* question lies the vexed issue of humanism, and the problem of whether the subject-construction I have described in Ndebele and Mda repeats Europe's – or liberal South Africa's – desire to perpetuate a reactionary subjectivity that has proved itself to be politically evasive and socially exclusive.

This, essentially, is the argument offered by Kelwyn Sole in his critique of Ndebele. Ndebele may be a radical humanist, says Sole, but he is still a humanist (1993, 91). Presumably, in his more flaunted aesthetics and his construction of symbolic rituals to oppose apartheid's deathliness, Mda would come in for similar criticism. Sole argues that Ndebele's conceptual framework bears the hallmarks of intellectual humanism: moral abstractions, binary oppositions, and a tendency to wish 'for a certain type of human nature to prevail in South Africa' (1993, 96). Ndebele also overrates the role of literature in providing instruction, its capacity 'to form certain types of human experience and perception' and install 'reason and knowledge into citizens' (Sole 1993, 97). The price of this tendency is 'the absence of any concentrated attention given . . . to those social forces which divide human beings and position them in antagonistic groups within the nation' (Sole 1993, 97).

The skeletons that Sole sees lurking in Ndebele's theory cupboard are Matthew Arnold and his successors, with their efforts to position literary humanism at the centre of public education and civil society. Accordingly, the debate in which Sole positions Ndebele is the one that dominated South African literary-critical politics in the 1970s and 80s between liberal-humanism and Marxism. I argue that this is not appropriate. To entertain Sole's critique, we would have to accept that the Njabulo Ndebele of the 1980s shares in some equivalent way Arnold's defensiveness and concern for literature to acquire a middle-class social mission. Surely, even if we were to concede that Ndebele's protagonists are middle class, the historical project defining their endeavours is politically emergent rather than reactive. The critique would also imply that the tendency of liberal-humanism to seal its preferred modes of subjectivity off from history and the influence of ideology is repeated in Ndebele. This would certainly traduce Ndebele's writing, its particular social formation, and its sensitivity to the class positions of its protagonists. In fact, Ndebele's concerns are generally coded not in terms of humanist ethics at all, but the social conditions of agency against a particular historical background. Indeed, Sole's conclusion, to the effect that 'when all is said and done, aspiring writers have to trust their own judgement, and the direction in which their own particular priorities and vision are taking them' ('it is the writers themselves, as they struggle to develop identity, direction and technique, who will have to choose how best to express their chosen concerns' [Sole 1993, 98]), is an apt summary of Ndebele's project. It precisely defines Zani's development and, as we have seen, in certain respects, Ndebele's own.

My claim, then, is that the subject construction in this writing carries a post-humanist urgency. But perhaps a full and final answer to the question of whether this writing represents repetition or renewal is not really possible, since the question itself is open to the future as a utopian gesture. As Graham Pechey puts it, '[h]aving helped to worst its foes under the old order, [post-apartheid reason] now has the challenge of reminding its friends under the new that democracy is a hypothetical point in socio-political infinity rather than an accomplished fact in the gift of a sect' (1998, 14). It falls to this reason 'to ensure that the (modern) tragedy of the country's earlier efforts at hitching a lift into the future . . . does not repeat itself as (postmodern) farce' (Pechey 1998, 14). John Noyes also offers valuable counsel. To apply his more general theory to the context: Ndebele's dialectical account of agency, and Mda's imaging of the tensions arising from Xhosa responses to modernity, may reveal the 'collapse of a [prior] discourse of truth', but equally, they could lead us to 'what enables the enactment of human rights in practice' (Noyes 2000, 60). The optimism here is conditional: it is positioned between one mode of reason that has been corrupted by historical failure, and another that is called into being by a different historical task. That space between – of incomplete, fugitive, yet necessary reinvention – is a suitable place for me to leave the argument of *Rewriting modernity*.

Notes

Introduction

1. The poem was originally published in isiXhosa in *Isigidimi Sama-Xosa* on 1 June 1882. André Odendaal attributes it to Isaac Wauchope. Hoho is the site of the Rharhabe paramount chief Sandile's death in 1878. See De Kock (1996 199, footnote 1) for a succinct summary of scholarship on the poem.
2. H.I.E. Dhlomo writing as 'Peregrine', with the possible assistance of Jordan Ngubane. See Couzens (1985, 265).
3. Hereafter 'the Enlightenment' refers to the intellectual environment of rationality, autonomy and selfhood of eighteenth-century Europe; 'enlightenment' refers to transcultural versions of these ideas developed elsewhere.
4. See Mbembe and Posel (2004), and Gilroy (2004), in the inaugural issue of the *WISER Review*, which was launched as part of the University of the Witwatersrand's commemoration of the first ten years of democracy under the heading, 'The Promise of Freedom and its Practice: Global Perspectives on South Africa's Decade of Democracy'. These terms bear comparison with Homi Bhabha's notion of a 'vernacular cosmopolitanism' (see Bhabha and Comaroff 2002). See also Pechey (1998).
5. For a summary of this debate, see Attwell (2004). See also Gray (1989); Smit, Van Wyk, and Wade (1996); Green (1997); De Kock (2001); and Chapman (2003).
6. See Attwell (1984). The injection of 'theory' into these paradoxically conservative discourses via postcolonial studies has, arguably, been a productive development, despite conservative claims to the contrary.
7. When colonial discourse analysis is attacked, for example (surprisingly frequently by South Africans working in the Anglo-American academy) it is not clear to me why that particular construction of the field should receive such privileged attention, unless it is, paradoxically, because of a lingering sense of cultural displacement from the 'centre'.
8. This view has been shared by militant commentators and conservative detractors alike.
9. This point bears comparison with Mark Sanders's account of 'complicities' in South African intellectual life. See in particular his comments about the relationship between Black Consciousness and liberalism (2002, 168–69).

10. Some might observe that I am seeing continuities between settler-colonial writing and properly nationalist or 'Third World' resistance. Indeed, that would be a fair observation, although 'continuities' need not imply identical formations. I am in agreement with Stephen Slemon (and before him Alan Lawson) who have argued that the inherent instability and continual, structural negotiation of 'here' and 'there' that has always characterised settler-colonial writing could be taken as a paradigm of postcolonial resistance more generally, including 'Third World' nationalism that, if adequately theorised, is also deeply relational. For how does resistance get recognised as such, without participating in the same representational economy? (Gayatri Spivak's much-misunderstood position on subalternity is a reflection on aporetic notions of resistance that fall outside of a common representational economy altogether; it is only in this sense that the 'subaltern cannot speak', a point that has nothing to do with oppressed people not being able to articulate their oppression [1988, 294–308].) The local gloss I would put on this debate in postcolonial theory, however, is that whereas Slemon speaks of different national cultures and forms of resistance across the postcolonial world, I am arguing that the South African case locates these modes of relational tension within the same national context. They may not be equivalent, but their mutual visibility is partly constitutive of the South African situation. See Slemon (1995).
11. Young (2001) has done much to correct a malaise in postcolonial theory by demonstrating that postcolonial discourses frequently have their roots in anticolonial struggles (and that poststructuralism has its origins in the Maghrib). This implicit emphasis on the historical formation and genealogies of postcolonial theory is likely to signpost much work needing to be done in future.
12. Stephan Meyer and Thomas Olver (2002) have usefully disaggregated the various concepts of modernity at work in African literary and cultural studies.

Chapter 1: The transculturation of enlightenment

1. The use of European objects as protective icons occurs elsewhere in 'frontier' skirmishes: John Laband reports that some of Dingane's troops led an attack on a Voortrekker patrol wearing European clothing taken in previous engagements (1995, 95–96).
2. The historiographic implications of this view are spelled out by Martin Legassick in a review essay of Crais's *White Supremacy* and Mostert's *Frontiers* (see Legassick 1993, 329–68; see also De Kock 1996, 200 n.6; and Switzer 1993). Legassick speaks of a fresh synthesis in which the emphasis in the inquiry into the foundations of apartheid shifts from Afrikaners to British settlers and the Cape Colony

(1993, 332). Crais, whose exposition is most explicit, argues that while the British settlement of 1820 projected a culture of civilised, manorial benevolence based on white 'free labour', the scheme failed partly because of harsh agricultural conditions and partly because of conflict among settlers themselves. This produced a new crisis that directly threatened the Xhosa: whereas the scheme had proposed a relationship of civil detachment with the Xhosa, or at best their absorption into a modernising economy, the failure of settlement made subjugation a more attractive proposition as a means of securing black labour and thereby extending pastoral agriculture, increasingly through sheep farming. The shortage of labour and traditional patterns of resistance were finally dealt with in the aftermath of the Cattle Killing of 1856–57, but even before that a fairly tight weave of administrative measures was already in place: the Masters and Servants Ordinance, the vagrancy laws, and the 'D'Urban system' of control over settlement patterns, all of which were reinforced by a narrow ethnographic code pertaining to the character of 'the Kafir' (in Legassick 1993, 333).

3. I am grateful to Tony Voss both for this quotation, and for his insightful account of the eighteenth century in South Africa's cultural memory (see Voss 1994, 59–75). Voss's essay is an important precursor to this account of the post-apartheid recurrence of the Enlightenment. As far as Soga's own use of English is concerned, it was not enough for him to have mastered the language with the nuance of a mother-tongue speaker. Mrs Charles Brownlee, wife of the Ngqika Commissioner, observed of his preaching, 'the classic English, in well-tuned sentences, melodiously flowing from his lips, was indeed surprising; but as the discourse proceeded, and the heart and mind became enthralled, the thought would unconsciously arise: "Is this possible?"' (in Chalmers 1877, 387).
4. Taylor was a white member of the Unity Movement. See also Cochrane (1987).
5. In their Introduction to *Colonial Discourse and Post-Colonial Theory*, Patrick Williams and Laura Chrisman remind us that among its many attributes and functions, the discourse of enlightenment became, under certain conditions, a mode of resistance. The intellectuals who figure prominently in the early history of African nationalism, say Williams and Chrisman, 'were engaged both in instrumentalising and immanently critiquing [e]nlightenment cultural forms (novels, newspapers, historiography, ethnography), political forms (parliamentary petitions, delegations), ethical and political emancipatory values (universal human equality, enfranchisement, self-government) in ways which require much critical attention today' (1994, 15).
6. Compare this with Rian Malan, author of *My Traitor's Heart*, who remarked of the new constitution, 'In my heart, this I believe: this [new] constitution is not for us. It is not an African constitution. It is a mission boy constitution, a hodge-podge of sorry borrowings from old colonial powers.' (1994, 42). It is

the mission-boy constitution, of course, which entitles Malan to disaffiliate ideologically, while still enabling him to claim his place as a son of the soil.

7. I am adapting Said's phrase 'the voyage in' from his discussion of George Antonius and C.L.R. James, whose dependency on Western humanism enables them to lay claim to values that the West has repudiated in practice (Said 1993, 239–61).
8. Donovan Williams points out that there had been widespread disillusionment among missionaries since the 1840s and that Chalmers's views were by no means exceptional by the mid-1860s (see Williams 1978, 94).
9. 'Interior Africa solemnis gaudii proximi Ecclesiae triumphi particeps fiat' (in Mudimbe 1988, 46).

Chapter 2: Time and narrative

1. Following Hayden White's description of the genres of historical writing, Leon de Kock uses this phrase to describe the eschatology of the Stewart regime at Lovedale in the mid-Victorian period (De Kock 1996, 64–104).
2. I refer here to Marks's analysis of Dube and A.W.G. Champion (Marks 1986) and La Hausse's work on 'second tier' Natal politicians (La Hausse 1992).
3. Isabel Hofmeyr points out to me that some of the missionary influence itself would have been quite ardently counter-modern (Personal correspondence). The libertarian undercurrent of A.K. Soga's lyric suggests that this was possible even amongst the Lovedale Calvinists. Another test case for the Catholic influence would be B.W. Vilakazi, a product of Mariannhill mission. Vilakazi (together with H.I.E. Dhlomo) is the subject of Chapter 3.
4. Of course, we should temper enthusiasm for this experimentalism with the recognition that the passage of any manuscript through the mission press was fraught with danger. There are well-documented cases of manuscripts being bowdlerised or 'disappeared' (see Peires 1979, 170). However, it would be equally unwise to assume that the published writing is not a reasonable reflection of the diction of those who produced it.
5. Derek Attridge raises the question of whether the future-directedness of modernity can be so violently yoked together with the Christian idea of timelessness and the eternal now. The former suggests restless movement, the latter permanent stasis. The explanation for Gqoba and Dhlomo's connecting the two, however, might be that under mission teaching, Christianity and modernity came as a package. This set the terms for nationalist intellectuals, although their work involved undoing the package and remaking it on different terms (Personal correspondence).
6. Tim Couzens (1988) attributes this poem to Robert Grendon.

7. Zakes Mda tells me that he has heard this expression, which is still current. 'In Xhosa they say, "Uthetha ezika Nongqawuse." My understanding is that this statement is not questioning the credibility of the event, but Nongqawuse's own credibility. Ordinary people continue to believe that Nongqawuse was a liar. I have heard mothers yell at children they suspect to be telling lies: "Don't be a Nongqawuse here in my house"' (Personal correspondence).
8. These paradigms do not rise and fall in series – clearly, they co-exist over periods of time.
9. Isabel Hofmeyr suggests to me that the generic jostling in this passage is clearer in the original, where 'histori' (a school-derived notion of history) comes up against 'tshomo' (tale) and 'nnete' (truth, what happened) (Personal correspondence).

Chapter 3: Modernising tradition

1. As Nyembezi notes (1973, xix), R.R.R. (Rolfes) Dhlomo, the brother of H.I.E. (Herbert) was prominent, but he did not have the expansive vision of his brother, expressed in cultural criticism. Born Bambatha, Vilakazi was rechristened Benedict at the Catholic mission at Mariannhill in Pinetown.
2. The dispute is mentioned by several critics though not discussed in these terms: Albert Gérard (1971, 235–36); David Johnson (1996, 133–35); Michael Chapman (1996, 213–14); Bhekizizwe Peterson (1997, 103–30). Maria K. Mootry (1973) and Lewis Nkosi (1981) usefully compare the two poets.
3. See Lewis Nkosi (1998, 87).
4. It is not the case, as several writers assert, that after this criticism Vilakazi abandoned his efforts in rhyme in his second collection, *Amal'ezulu*. Adrian Koopman has pointed out to me the complex rhymes, *inter alia*, of the final poem, 'Sengiyakholwa'. Also, Vilakazi was not alone in experimenting with rhyme; J.J.R. Jolobe uses rhyming couplets in his Xhosa poetry in *Umyezo*, as Vilakazi himself shrewdly notices (Vilakazi 1946, 29n).
5. Gérard (1971) rightly remarks on the congruence between Dhlomo and the early négritudinists, at much the same time.
6. Aggrey's visit to South Africa under the auspices of the Phelps-Stokes Trust in 1921 had, according to Tim Couzens, 'caused a sensation'. Aggrey's message of interracial co-operation was warmly appreciated by the liberal intelligentsia of the day, both black and white (Couzens 1985, 82–85).
7. Insofar as Dhlomo and Vilakazi regarded orality as falling within the purview of literary history and criticism, they sought to extend the reach of what constituted 'literature' in a sense not current at the time. Overwhelmingly, studies of oral tradition were ethnographic rather than treated as 'art' in the post-Romantic

sense. Declining the ethnographic emphasis was therefore part of their achievement (see Vilakazi 1942, 270).

8. Vilakazi did read Richards, though there is more direct evidence of his other models, several of whom are unknown today: Elizabeth Drew, Philo M. Buck, John Middleton Murray, Charles Williams, and Charles Watts-Dunton. In one respect, Vilakazi may have been directly influenced by Richards's *Principles of Literary Criticism*, in using gestalt psychology to argue for the coherence of the *izibongo* which, he implies, is not always obvious from written transcriptions (Vilakazi 1993 [1938], 59; see Richards 1944 [1924], 83–91).
9. Tim Couzens, David Johnson, Leon de Kock, and Bhekizizwe Peterson document different aspects of this debate. Kwame Anthony Appiah traces the genealogy of the linkage of race and literature in *In My Father's House* (Appiah 1992, 74–78).
10. At the second of these conferences Vilakazi was appointed to a committee to explore the feasibility of a literature 'Bureau' under the auspices of the Inter-University Committee for African Studies and the Christian Council (Couzens 1985, 105).
11. In Vilakazi's memory the bell is named Angelus, but it would have been a particular peal rung as a call to prayer in the midst of the day's routines.
12. In his late, unpublished essay, 'Reflections on the Circle in Zulu Life and Thought' (planned as part of a monograph entitled *Zulu Life and Thought*) Dhlomo was wrestling with the same tension. The circle represents Africanity, the square, the European mind, but the emphasis is not on permanent difference, since each figure captures aspects of a complex and dynamic reality (Dhlomo papers, Killie Campbell Africana Library).
13. A parallel dilemma was being played out by liberal segregationists who debated the relative merits of 'adaptionist' and 'assimilationist' policies. With cultural relativism coming into prominence over earlier Victorian notions of spreading universal civilisation, segregationism could present itself as concerned with the survival of authentic identities. Beneath such sentiments lay anxieties about the aspirations of upwardly mobile middle-class Africans, and class-based mobilisation amongst proletarianised Africans, fears articulated by Heaton Nicholls: 'The adaptionist policy . . . assumes what is in effect the growth of a national consciousness amongst the Abantu themselves. . . . the opposite policy of assimilation substitutes class for race, and if continued on its present basis must lead to the evolution of a native proletariat, inspired by the usual antagonisms of class war' (in Peterson 1997, 112).
14. In the *English in Africa* collection of Dhlomo's essays, this point is elided from the original. I am quoting the original version from *The South African Outlook*.
15. While the line includes Es'kia Mphahlele and before him, Lewis Nkosi, Vilakazi,

interestingly, is one of Ndebele's precursors in questioning the epistemological and aesthetic limitations of journalistic prose. Castigating the political writers of his own generation (including D.D.T. Jabavu, Z.K. Matthews, A.G.W. Champion, Jordan Ngubane, and others), he said, 'Most of this is second-rate and negligible as literature, and its effect has been to delay the development of purely artistic expression. These writers . . . fail to universalise their particular political handicaps and to transform them into generalised suffering, expressed symbolically in poetic or prose forms' (Vilakazi 1946, 283). By way of contrast, he admires Langston Hughes's short fiction, citing the image of a young violinist, the victim of a lynching, his body 'like a violin for the wind to play' (Vilakazi 1946, 284). Vilakazi excluded Dhlomo from his accusations.

16. Couzens notes that the mythopoeic additions in the second edition, which were written into Dhlomo's own copy of the first edition, are drawn largely from Eileen Krige's *The Social System of the Zulus*, published in 1936 (Couzens 1985, 243). That Dhlomo's relation to his material should have been partly anthropological is not altogether surprising, given his overall stance. The following is also revealing: 'If I could know more about Zulu custom then I could write very well but I don't know it very much. If I get a chance I'll go around Zululand and see these old people. I think it's wrong because I haven't been to Zululand. I've been brought up in Johannesburg. Even if I've got inspiration to write sometimes I feel I cannot' (in Couzens 1985, 352).
17. It is in this respect that I differ slightly from Thengani Ngwenya's (1998) otherwise illuminating study of Vilakazi's inspirational poems. Ngwenya emphasises the fact that Vilakazi seeks traditional sanction, thus Africanising his dependence on the Romantics. In my reading, Vilakazi's uncertainties are never quite so repressed.
18. Unless indicated otherwise, translations of Vilakazi's poems are those done jointly by D. McK. Malcolm, J. Mandlenkosi Sikakana and Florence Louie Friedman, published as *Zulu Horizons* (1973). Adrian Koopman has pointed out how free these translations are, which renders some of them unreliable in an assessment of Vilakazi's own expression.
19. The anachronism of Shaka's subjugation of Langalibelele, who survived the former by two generations, cannot go unnoticed here.
20. A perceptive, unpublished essay by Sarah Hensey, a student of Adrian Koopman's, explores the tension between the verbs *thwala* (to carry) and *thwasa* (to become possessed), and their related nouns *umthwalo* (burden) and *ithwasa* (initiate), and how it illuminates Vilakazi's conception of his role as poet.
21. See also Dhlomo (1946). Dhlomo maintains this reading in his 'Masterpiece in Bronze' essay on Vilakazi in *Drum* of July 1952.

Chapter 4: Fugitive pieces

1. Mphahlele used the phrase in a letter to Guy Butler from Philadelphia, shortly before his return (see Butler 1989, 5).

Chapter 5: Lyric and epic

1. It would be years before this kind of direct engagement became politically possible, only after the waning of Black Consciousness and its displacement by the alliance politics of the United Democratic Front in the early 1980s. Njabulo Ndebele's critique of the English Academy in 1986, published in *Rediscovery of the Ordinary*, may represent such a delayed encounter.
2. Robert Young's argument concerning the Maghribian origins of post-structuralism is an elaboration of Jameson's point.
3. We should entertain the possibility that some of the force of the category, 'Soweto poetry', lay in its power to challenge Eurocentric elements in the literary academy. Whether this was the agenda of the poets themselves during their formation, and whether they were much concerned with supporting white critics in their efforts to reform the curriculum, is debatable. It should also be noted, however, that it is easier now to acknowledge the presence of the lyric in Soweto poetry than it was twenty years ago.
4. Nicholas Visser famously argued in relation to Serote's novel, *To Every Birth its Blood*, that 'in the very process of its composition, [it] was opened to the unfolding of history, to the unfolding of the momentous events as they occurred' (Visser 1987, 69). The events here are those of 1976. The argument was intended in the most literal sense: the novel became more mimetic of its times as its composition proceeded. If we modulate this literalism and directness, the observation is not unreasonable as a description of the situation of all the Soweto poets as the decade unfolded, except that, I would argue, it was not the pressures of *mimesis* that forced the shift, but the implicit demands of the rhetorical situation, the call to assume a position of authoritative witness.
5. Serote's metaphor is derived from the well-known saxophonist, Mankunku Ngozi, who released an album called *Yakhal'inkomo* in 1968, a lament on the death of John Coltrane. I am grateful to Michael Titlestad for referring me to Ngozi.
6. This raises the question of whether the poets were perhaps 'written into' the lyric tradition by their education. I would prefer to see this, however, as a case of the poets finding in that tradition a powerful discourse that answered to their situation.

7. As I have intimated, *To Every Birth its Blood* has produced a lively and continuing critical debate, which would be too extensive and digressive to enter into here, though it includes Visser (see Note 4 on page 212). Sole's account of the novel's structure and of the relationship between Serote's realist/historical and poetic/symbolic modes of narration is, in my view, more useful than discussions of the text that tend to force it into the prevailing categories of critical-theoretical debate between liberal humanism and materialism. The terms of this conflict are not easily mapped onto the categories of Black Consciousness, which as I have argued, borrowed loosely and eclectically from politicised psychoanalysis, existentialism, civil rights discourse, and Maoism. This mix facilitated an integration of individual and collective discourses that the academy, more influenced by the traditional liberal-Marxist divide, has not quite grasped or even tolerated.
8. Michael Green has developed the concept of 'future histories' as a way of accounting for a good deal of the fiction written in the early 1980s, by Serote in *To Every Birth its Blood* and others (see Green 1997, 235–87). My sense of Serote's poetry as offering an 'epic of futurity' accords with this description. Indeed, Green notes, citing Chapman, with whom I would agree in this respect, that Soweto poetry was essentially forward-looking, to a 'pre-Azanian' phase of history in which '"the people", including the participatory ideals of the black community, has increasingly begun to function as an inspirational myth' (Chapman 1982, 22; Green 1997, 253).
9. Kunene has mentioned this detail in personal communication.
10. Eileen Julien's treatment of the relationship between epic and novel in African fiction departs from Bakhtin in similar ways. In an analysis of Hampâté Bâ's *L'Etrange Destin de Wangrin* and Ousmane Sembène's *Les Bouts de bois de Dieu* she shows how African fiction re-appropriates epic, turning it to different uses. In Bâ, the epic hero is in decline as a result of degradation brought on by colonialism; in Sembène, the hero is reconstructed through collective action (Julien 1992, 51–84).
11. It should be noted, however, that in Ndebele's fiction the strong masculinity of the 'Soweto' period is tempered though the presence of women as agents of a deeper ethical consciousness.

Chapter 6: The experimental turn

1. In personal correspondence, Zakes Mda alerts me to the fact that colloquial speech has never abandoned the term 'location', which continues as 'lokasie', or 'kasie', 'lokeishining' (in Sesotho) and 'eLokshini' (Nguni). Alexandra in Johannesburg is unusual in that its residents will refer to it as 'tounship', while other

townships on the Rand are referred to as 'locations'. 'Location' continues in the slang of ostensibly global youth in the post-apartheid era, as in 'Lokshun' culture.

2. I must note here, however, that Angola, Mozambique and Zimbabwe have stronger 'experimental lines' than is the case in South Africa.
3. Muff Anderson tells me, however, that in the mid-1980s, *Life and Times of Michael K* was widely read and admired in Umkhonto we Sizwe (also known as 'MK').
4. Mda mentioned this in a discussion of his work at John Carroll University in Cleveland, Ohio, in January 2003.

Select bibliography

Abrams, M.H. 1981. *A Glossary of Literary Terms*. New York: Holt, Reinhart and Winston.

Anderson, B. 1991 [1983]. *Imagined Communities: Reflections on the Origin and Spread of Nationalism*. London and New York: Verso.

Andrzejewski, B.W., S. Pilaszewicz, and W. Tyloch (eds.). 1985. *Literatures in African Languages: Theoretical Issues and Sample Surveys*. Warsaw: Cambridge University Press and Wiedza Powszechna State Publishing House.

Appiah, K.A. 1992. *In My Father's House: Africa in the Philosophy of Culture*. London: Methuen.

Ashcroft, B., G. Griffiths, and H. Tiffin (eds.). 1989. *The Empire Writes Back: Theory and Practice in Post-Colonial Literatures*. London: Routledge.

———. 1995. *The Postcolonial Studies Reader*. London: Routledge.

Attridge, D. and R. Jolly (eds.). 1998. *Writing South Africa: Literature, Apartheid and Democracy 1948–1995*. Cambridge: Cambridge University Press.

Attwell, D. 1984. The British legacy in Anglophone African literary criticism. *English in Africa* 11.1 (May): 79–106.

———. 1987. Mofolo's 'Chaka' and the Bambatha Rebellion. *Research in African Literatures* 18.1 (Spring): 52–55.

———. 1993. *J.M. Coetzee: South Africa and the Politics of Writing*. Berkeley and London: University of California Press.

———. 1999. Reprisals of modernity in black South African 'Mission' writing. *Journal of Southern African Studies* 25.2 (June): 267–85.

———. 2004. South African literature in English. In *The Cambridge History of African Literature*, eds. A. Irele and S. Gikandi, 504–29. Cambridge: Cambridge University Press.

Ayivor, K. 1997. Thomas Mopoku Mofolo's 'Inverted Epic Hero': A reading of Mofolo's 'Chaka' as an African epic folktale. *Research in African Literatures* 28.1 (Spring): 54.

Bakhtin, M.M. 1985. *Epic and Novel.* Translated by C. Emerson and M. Holquist in *The Dialogic Imagination: Four Essays*, ed. M. Holquist, 3–40. Austin: University of Texas Press.

Barker, F., P. Hulme, and M. Iversen (eds.). 1992. *Postmodernism and the Re-reading of Modernity*. New York and Manchester: Manchester University Press.

Bartolovich, C. 2002. Introduction. In *Marxism, Modernity, and Postcolonial Studies*, eds. C. Bartolovich and N. Lazarus, 1–17. Cambridge: Cambridge University Press.

Bartolovich, C. and N. Lazarus. 2002. *Marxism, Modernity, and Postcolonial Studies.* Cambridge: Cambridge University Press.

Beckett, S. 1998. From 'Dante . . . Bruno . . . Vico . . . Joyce' 1929. In *Modernism: An Anthology of Sources and Documents*, eds. V. Kolocotroni, J. Goodman and O. Taxidou, 449–51. Chicago: University of Chicago Press.

Beier, U. 1979. *Introduction to African Literature: An Anthology of Critical Writing.* London: Harlow.

Bethlehem, L. 2001. 'A primary need as strong as hunger': The rhetoric of urgency in South African literary culture under apartheid. *Poetics Today* 22.2 (Summer): 365–89.

Bhabha, H. 1994. *The Location of Culture.* London: Routledge.

Bhabha, H. and J. Comaroff. 2002. Speaking of postcoloniality, in the continuous present: A conversation. In *Relocating Postcolonialism*, eds. D.T. Goldberg and A. Quayson, 15–46. Oxford: Blackwell.

Biko, B.S. 1972. *Black Viewpoint.* Durban: Spro-Cas.

———. 1978. *I Write What I Like.* Ed. C.R. Aelred Stubbs. London: Heinemann.

———. 1979. *The Testimony of Steve Biko.* Ed. A. Millard. London: Panther.

Boehmer, E., L. Chrisman, and K. Parker (eds.). 1994. *Altered State? Writing and South Africa.* Sydney: Dangaroo Press.

Boetie, Dugmore. 1969. *Familiarity is the Kingdom of the Lost.* London: Arena.

Bokwe, J.K. 1914 [1904]. *Ntsikana: The Story of an African Convert.* Alice: Lovedale Press.

Brown, D. 1997: Black consciousness, tradition and modernity: Ingoapele Madingoane's *black trial. Current Writing* 9.1: 1–26.

———. 2002. 'Structures of feeling' and constructions of history: Mazisi Kunene's 'Emperor Shaka the Great'. In *South and Southern African Literature: A Review*, ed. E. Durosimi Jones, 63–78. Oxford: James Currey; Trenton, NJ: Africa World Press.

Bunn, D. and J. Taylor (eds.). 1987. *From South Africa: New Writing, Photographs and Art.* Special issue of *TriQuarterly 69*. Chicago: Chicago University Press.

Bunyan, J. 1974 [1678]. *The Pilgrim's Progress.* Oxford: Oxford University Press.

Butler, G. 1989. Preface. In *Footprints Along the Way: A Tribute to Es'kia Mphahlele*, ed. P. Thuynsma, 5–6. Braamfontein: Skotaville; Yeoville: Justified Press.

Cary, J. 1947. *Mister Johnson.* London: Joseph.

Chalmers, J.A. 1864. The sowing begun. *Missionary Record of the United Presbyterian Church* 1 November: 198–200.

———. 1865a. Letter to Bryce Ross 30 January.

———. 1865b. Recreations of a missionary. *King Williamstown Gazette and Kaffrarian Banner* 3 April.

———. 1877. *Tiyo Soga: A Page of South African Mission Work.* Edinburgh: Andrew Elliot.

———. 1878. The native question. *The Christian Express* 1 March: 10–11.

———. 1879. The present state of the United Presbyterian Mission in Kafirland. Typescript, Cory Library, Rhodes University.

Chapman, M. (ed.). 1982. *Soweto Poetry*. Johannesburg: McGraw-Hill.

Chapman, M. 1984. *South African English Poetry: A Modern Perspective*. Johannesburg: AD Donker.

———. 1993. Red people and school people from Ntsikana to Mandela: The significance of 'Xhosa literature' in a general history of South African literature. *English Academy Review* 10: 36–44.

———. 1996. *Southern African Literatures*. London and New York: Longman.

———. 1997. Preface. In *Current Writing* 9.1: 1.

———. 2003. *Southern African Literatures*. Pietermaritzburg: University of Natal Press.

Chatterjee, P. 1986. *Nationalist Thought and the Colonial World: A Derivative Discourse?* London: Zed Books for the United Nations University.

Cochrane, J.R. 1987. *Servants of Power: The Role of English-Speaking Churches in South Africa, 1903–1930*. Johannesburg: Ravan Press.

Coetzee, J.M. 1973. Alex La Guma and the responsibility of the South African writer. In *New African Literature and the Arts: Vol. 3*, ed. J. Okpaku, 116–24. New York: Third World.

———. 1988. The novel today. *Upstream* 6.1 (Summer): 2–5.

———. 1993. Homage. *Threepenny Review* (Spring): 95–97.

———. n.d. Grubbing for the ideological implications: A clash (more or less) with J.M. Coetzee. Interview by A. Thorold and R. Wicksteed. *Sjambok*. Cape Town: University of Cape Town.

Comaroff, J. and J. Comaroff. 1991. *Of Revelation and Revolution: Christianity, Colonialism, and Consciousness in South Africa*. Chicago and London: University of Chicago Press.

———. 1992. *Ethnography and the Historical Imagination*. Boulder: Westview Press.

Constitution of the Republic of South Africa, Act no. 200 (1993). Statutes of the Republic of South Africa-Constitutional Law. Pretoria: The Government Printer.

Coronil, F. 1995. Introduction. In *Cuban Counterpoint: Tobacco and Sugar*, F. Ortiz, ix–lvi. Durham and London: Duke University Press.

Couzens, T. 1976. Black poetry in Africa. In *Poetry South Africa: Selected Papers from Poetry '74*, eds. P. Wilhelm and J. A. Polley, 47–59. Johannesburg: AD Donker.

———. 1981. 'The new African': Herbert Dhlomo and black South African literature in English, 1857–1956. Ph.D. diss., University of the Witwatersrand, Johannesburg.

———. 1984. Widening horizons of African literature: 1870–1900. In *Literature and Society*, eds. L. White and T. Couzens, 73. Cape Town: Maskew Miller Longman.

———. 1985. *The New African: A Study of the Life and Work of H.I.E. Dhlomo.* Johannesburg: Ravan Press.

———. 1988. Robert Grendon: Irish traders, cricket scores and Paul Kruger's dreams. *English in Africa* 15.2 (October): 78–80.

Crais, C. 1992. *White Supremacy and Black Resistance in Pre-Industrial South Africa: The Making of the Colonial Order in the Eastern Cape, 1770–1865.* Cambridge: Cambridge University Press.

Cronin, J. 1997. *Even the Dead: Poems, Parables and Jeremiad.* Bellville: Mayibuye.

Culler, J. 1985. Changes in the study of the lyric. In *Lyric Poetry: Beyond New Criticism*, eds. C. Hošek and P. Parker, 38–54. Ithaca and London: Cornell University Press.

Daymond, M.J., J.U. Jacobs, and M. Lenta (eds.). 1984. *Momentum: On Recent South African Writing.* Pietermaritzburg: University of Natal Press.

Daymond, M., D. Driver, S. Meintjies, L. Molema, C. Musengezi, M. Orford, and N. Rasebotsa (eds.). 2003. *Women Writing Africa: The Southern Region.* Johannesburg: Wits University Press; New York: Feminist Press.

De Kock, L. 1996. *Civilising Barbarians: Missionary Narrative and Textual Response in Nineteenth-Century South Africa.* Johannesburg: Wits University Press; Alice: Lovedale Press.

———. 2001. South Africa in the global imaginary: An introduction. *Poetics Today* 22.2 (Summer): 263–98.

De Man, P. 1983. Lyric and modernity. In *Blindness and Insight: Essays in the Rhetoric of Contemporary Criticism*, ed. W. Godzich, 166–86. Minneapolis: University of Minnesota Press.

Dell, S. 1996. Blackness and beyond: Black consciousness and the antinomies of identity negotiation in South Africa. MA thesis, University of Natal, Pietermaritzburg.

Derrida, J. and M. Tlili (eds.). 1987. *For Nelson Mandela.* New York: Henry Holt.

Deutsch, J-G., P. Probst, and H. Schmidt (eds.). 2002. *African Modernities: Entangled Meanings in Current Debate.* Portsmouth, NH : Heinemann; Oxford: James Currey.

Dhlomo, H.I.E. 1939. African drama and poetry. *The South African Outlook* 1 April: 88–90.

———. 1946. Three famous authors I knew – B.W. Vilakazi. *Inkundla YaBantu* 9.122 (August).

———. 1952. Masterpiece in bronze. *Drum* 2.7 (July).

———. 1977a. Language and national drama. *English in Africa* 4.2 (September): 9–11. Reprinted from *The New Outlook* March 1939: 8–11.

———. 1977b. Why study tribal dramatic forms? *English in Africa* 4.2 (September): 37–42. Reprinted from *Transvaal Native Education Quarterly* March 1939: 20–24.

———. 1985. *Collected Works.* Eds. N. Visser and T. Couzens. Johannesburg: Ravan Press.

———. 1993. Nature and variety of tribal drama. In *Foundations of Southern African Oral Literature*, ed. R. Kaschula, 187–202. Johannesburg: Wits University Press. Reprinted from Bantu Studies 13 (1939): 33–48.

———. n.d. *Zulu Life and Thought*. Unpublished manuscript. Killie Campbell Collection, University of KwaZulu-Natal: KCM 8266.

Dhlomo, R.R.R. 1930. *An African Tragedy*. Alice: Lovedale Press.

Dube, J.L. 1951 [1930]. *Jeqe: The Bodyservant of King Shaka*. Alice: Lovedale Press.

Fanon, F. 1963. *The Wretched of the Earth*. New York: Grove Press.

Farred, G. 2000. Mourning the post-apartheid state already? The poetics of loss in Zakes Mda's *Ways of Dying*. *Modern Fiction Studies* 46.1 (Spring): 183–206.

Frye, N. 1957. *Anatomy of Criticism*. Princeton: Princeton University Press.

Fuze, M. 1979 [1922]. *The Black People and Whence They Came: A Zulu View*. Translated by H.C. Lugg. Pietermaritzburg: University of Natal Press.

Gérard, A.S. 1971. *Four African Literatures: Xhosa, Sotho, Zulu, Amharic*. Berkeley and London: University of California Press.

———. 1986. *European-Language Writing in Sub-Saharan Africa*. Budapest: Akadémiai Kiadó.

Gibbons, R. 1989. *Writers from South Africa: Culture, Politics and Literary Activity in South Africa Today*. TriQuarterly Series on Criticism and Culture, No. 2. Evanston: TriQuarterly Books.

Giddens, A. 1991. *Modernity and Self-Identity: Self and Society in the Late Modern Age*. Cambridge: Polity Press.

Gikandi, S. 2002. Reason, modernity and the African crisis. In *African Modernities: Entangled Meanings in Current Debate*, eds. J-G. Deutsch, P. Probst, and H. Schmidt, 135–57. Portsmouth, NH: Heinemann; Oxford: James Currey.

Gilroy, P. 2004. A new cosmopolitanism. *The WISER Review* 1 (July): 3.

Goldberg, D.T. and A. Quayson (eds.). 2002. *Relocating Postcolonialism*. Oxford: Blackwell.

Gordimer, N. 1984. The idea of gardening. *New York Review of Books* 2 (February): 3, 6.

———. 1989. *The Essential Gesture: Writing, Politics and Places*. Ed. S. Clingman. London: Penguin.

Gray, S. 1989. Some problems of writing historiography in southern Africa. *Literator* 10.2: 16–24.

Green, M. 1997. *Novel Histories: Past, Present and Future in South African Fiction*. Johannesburg: Wits University Press.

Gunner, L. and Mafika G. (eds. and trans.). 1991. *Musho! Zulu Popular Praises*. East Lansing: Michigan State University Press.

Gwala, M.P. 1972. The black thing . . . is honest . . . is human. *SASO Newsletter* (January/February): 13–15.

———. 1975. Towards the practical manifestations of black consciousness. In *Black Renaissance: Papers from the Black Renaissance Convention*, ed. T. Thoahlane, 24–33. Johannesburg: Ravan Press.

———. 1977. *Jol'iinkomo*. Johannesburg: AD Donker.

———. 1981. Steve Bantu Biko. In *Reconstruction: 90 Years of Black Historical Literature*, ed. M. Mutloatse, 229–37. Johannesburg: Ravan Press.

———. 1982. *No More Lullabies*. Johannesburg: AD Donker.

———. 1984. Writing as a cultural weapon. In *Momentum: On Recent South African Writing*, eds. M.J. Daymond, J.U. Jacobs, and M. Lenta, 37–53. Pietermaritzburg: University of Natal Press.

———. 1988. Review of *Black Consciousness in South Africa: The Dialectics of Ideological Resistance to White Supremacy* by R. Fatton Jr. *Research in African Literatures* 19.1 (Spring): 89–94.

Haresnape, G. 1976. 'A question of black and white?' The contemporary situation in South African English poetry. In *Poetry South Africa: Selected Papers from Poetry '74*, eds. P. Wilhelm and J.A. Polley, 35–46. Johannesburg: AD Donker.

Hodgson, J. 1984. The genius of Ntsikana: Traditional images and the process of change in early Xhosa literature. In *Literature and Society* in South Africa, eds. L. White and T. Couzens, 24–27. Cape Town: Maskew Miller Longman.

Holquist, M. (ed.). 1985. *The Dialogic Imagination: Four Essays*. Austin: University of Texas Press.

Hošek, C. and P. Parker (eds.). 1985. *Lyric Poetry: Beyond New Criticism*. Ithaca and London: Cornell University Press.

Irele, A. 1981. *The African Experience in Literature and Ideology*. London: Heinemann.

Jabavu, D.D.T. 1921. *Bantu Literature: Classification and Reviews*. Alice: Lovedale Press.

———. 1943. *The Influence of English on Bantu Literature*. Alice: Lovedale Press.

Jacobson, D. 1994. The road to Griquatown. *Times Literary Supplement* 1 April: 3–4.

Jameson, F. 1988. *The Ideologies of Theory: Essays 1971–1986. Volume 2: The Syntax of History*. London: Routledge.

Johnson, D. 1996. *Shakespeare and South Africa*. Oxford: The Clarendon Press.

Jolobe, J.J.R. 1946. *Poems of an African*. Alice: Lovedale Press.

———. 1974 [1936]. Uthuthula. In *Umyezo*, Bantu Treasury Series No. 2, 1936: 85. Johannesburg: Wits University Press.

Jones, E.D. (ed.). 2002. *South and Southern African Literature: A Review*. Oxford: James Currey; Trenton, NJ: Africa World Press.

Jordan, A.C. 1940. *Ingqumbo yeminyana*. Alice: Lovedale Press.

———. 1973. *Towards an African Literature: The emergence of Literary Form in Xhosa*. Berkeley: University of California Press.

Julien, E. 1992. *African Novels and the Question of Orality*. Bloomington and Indianapolis: Indiana University Press.

Kaschula, R. (ed.). 1993. *Foundations of Southern African Oral Literature.* Johannesburg: Wits University Press.

Kirkwood, M. 1976. The colonizer: A critique of the English South African culture theory. In *Poetry South Africa: Selected Papers from Poetry '74*, eds. P. Wilhelm and J.A. Polley, 102–33. Johannesburg: AD Donker.

Kolocotroni, V., J. Goodman, and O. Taxidou (eds.). 1998. *Modernism: An Anthology of Sources and Documents.* Chicago: University of Chicago Press.

Koopman, A. 1980. Aspects of the *Isangoma* in the poetry of B.W. Vilakazi. *Theoria* 55 (October): 1–19.

Kunene, D.P. 1981. Introduction. In *Chaka*, T. Mofolo, trans. D.P. Kunene, xi–xxiii. 1925. London: Heinemann.

Kunene, M. 1979. *Emperor Shaka the Great: A Zulu Epic.* London: Heinemann.

———. 1981. *Anthem of the Decades.* London: Heinemann.

La Hausse de Lalouvière, P. 1992. Ethnicity and history in the careers of two Zulu nationalists: Petros Lamula (*c.*1881–1948) and Lymon Maling (*c.*1889–1936). Ph.D. diss., University of the Witwatersrand, Johannesburg.

Laband, J. 1995. *Rope of Sand: The Rise and Fall of the Zulu Kingdom in the Nineteenth Century.* Johannesburg: Jonathan Ball.

Lazarus, N. 1986. Modernism and modernity: T.W. Adorno and contemporary white South African literature. *Cultural Critique* 5: 131–55.

Legassick, M. 1993. The state, racism, and the rise of capitalism in the nineteenth century Cape Colony. *South African Historical Journal* 28 (May): 229–68.

Lestrade, G.P. 1935. Bantu praise-poems. *The Critic* 4.1 (October): 1–10.

Lindfors, B. (ed.). 1975. *South African Voices.* Occasional publication of the African and Afro-American Studies and Research Center in association with the Harry Ransom Center. Austin: University of Texas.

Lindfors, B. 2002 [1986]. Interview with Njabulo Ndebele. In *African Talks Back: Interviews with Anglophone African Authors*, ed. B. Lindfors, 226–48. Trenton: Africa World Press.

Majeke, N. (Dora Taylor). 1953. *The Role of the Missionaries in Conquest.* Johanesburg: Society of Young Africa.

Malan, R. 1994. Confessions of a white South African. *Style.* May 1994: 35–46.

Mamdani, M. 1996. *Citizen and Subject: Contemporary Africa and the Legacy of Late Colonialism.* Kampala: Fountain Publishers; Cape Town: David Philip; London: James Currey.

Manganyi, N.C. 1981. *Looking Through the Keyhole: Dissenting Essays on the Black Experience.* Johannesburg: Ravan Press.

———. 1983. *Exiles and Homecomings: A Biography of Es'kia Mphahlele.* Johannesburg: Ravan Press.

Marks, S. 1970. *Reluctant Rebellion: The 1906–08 Disturbances in Natal.* Oxford: The Clarendon Press.

———. 1986. *The Ambiguities of Dependence in South Africa: Class, Nationalism and the State in Twentieth-Century Natal.* Johannesburg: Ravan Press.

Mbembe, A. 2004. Faces of freedom: Jewish and black experiences. *The WISER Review* 1 (July): 4–5.

Mbembe, A. and D. Posel. 2004. A critical humanism. *The WISER Review* 1 (July): 2.

McClintock, A. 1987. 'Azikwelwa' (we will not ride): Politics and value in black South African poetry. *Critical Inquiry* 13.3 (Spring): 597–623.

Mda, Z. 1995a. *She Plays with the Darkness.* Florida Hills: Vivlia.

———. 1995b. *Ways of Dying.* Cape Town: Oxford University Press.

———. 2000. *The Heart of Redness.* Cape Town: Oxford University Press.

Merriman, N.J. 1957. *The Cape Journals of Archdeacon N.J. Merriman, 1848–1855.* Eds. D.H. Varley and H.M. Matthew. Cape Town: Van Riebeck Society.

Meyer, S. and T. Olver. 2002. Alternative modernities in African literatures and cultures. *Journal of Literary Studies* 18.1/2 (June): 1–23.

Mofolo, T. 1981 [1925]. *Chaka.* Translated by D.P. Kunene. London: Heinemann.

Moodie, D. (ed.). 1959 [1838]. *The Record: A Series of Official Papers Relative to the Condition and Treatment of the Native Tribes of South Africa.* Cape Town and Amsterdam: Balkema.

Moore, G. (ed.). 1962. *African Literature and the Universities.* Ibadan: Published for the Congress of Cultural Freedom by Ibadan University Press.

Mootry, M.K. 1973. Literature and resistance in South Africa: Two Zulu poets. In *African Literature Today No. 7: Poetry in Africa*, ed. E.D. Jones, 112–29. London: Heinemann.

Mostert, N. 1992. *Frontiers: The Epic of South Africa's Creation and the Tragedy of the Xhosa People.* London: Jonathan Cape.

Mphahlele, E. 1959. Negro culture in a multi-racial society in Africa. *Présence Africaine* 24–25 (February–May): 221–27.

———. 1960. Black and white. *New Statesman* 10 September: 342–46.

———. 1962a. *The African Image*. London: Faber and Faber.

———. 1962b. A reply. In *African Literature and the Universities*, ed. G. Moore, 22–26. Ibadan: Published for the Congress of Cultural Freedom by Ibadan University Press.

———. 1968. The wanderers: A novel of Africa. Ph.D. diss. University of Denver, Denver.

———. 1971 [1959]. *Down Second Avenue.* London: Faber and Faber.

———. 1972. *Voices in the Whirlwind and Other Essays.* New York: Hill and Wang.

———. 1974a. *The African Image.* London: Faber and Faber.

———. 1974b. Ezekiel Mphahlele's reply to Addison Gayle. *Black World* 23.3 (January): 5–21.

———. 1975. Death III: Variations on a theme by John Keats, or E.M. Scores 55,

Dec. 17th, 1974. In *South African Voices*, ed. B. Lindfors, 26–30. Occasional publication of the African and Afro-American Studies and Research Center in association with the Harry Ransom Center. Austin: University of Texas.

———. 1979. Exile, the tyranny of place and the literary compromise. *Unisa English Studies* 17.1 (April): 37–44.

———. 1984a. *Afrika My Music: An Autobiography, 1957–1983*. Johannesburg: Ravan Press.

———. 1984b. *The Wanderers*. Cape Town: David Philip, Africasouth Paperbacks.

———. 1986. Poetry and humanism: Oral beginnings. 22nd Raymond Dart Lecture, delivered 20 June 1984, University of the Witwatersrand. Johannesburg: Wits University Press.

Mqhayi, S.E.K. 1914. *Ityala lamawele*. Alice: Lovedale Press.

Msimang, C.T. 1982. Madingoane Ingoapele's 'black trial': A contemporary black epic. In *Soweto Poetry*, ed. M. Chapman, 204–12. Johannesburg: McGraw-Hill.

Mtshali, O. 1971. *Sounds of a Cowhide Drum*. Johannesburg: Renoster Books.

———. 1980. *Fireflames*. Pietermaritzburg: Shuter and Shooter.

Mudimbe, V.Y. 1988. *The Invention of Africa. Gnosis, Philosophy, and the Order of Knowledge*. Bloomington and Indianapolis: Indiana University Press.

Muller, C. 1997. 'Written' into the book of life: Nazarite women's performance inscribed as spiritual text in *Ibandla lamaNazaretha*. *Research in African Literatures* 28.1 (Spring): 4.

Mutloatse, M. (ed.). 1980. *Forced Landing: Africa South: Contemporary Writings*. Johannesburg: Ravan Press.

———. 1981. *Reconstruction: 90 Years of Black Historical Literature*. Johannesburg: Ravan Press.

Nandy, A. 1988. *The Intimate Enemy: Loss and Recovery of Self under Colonialism*. Delhi: Oxford University Press.

Ndebele, N. 1972. Black development. In *Black Viewpoint*, ed. B.S. Biko, 13–28. Durban: Spro-Cas.

———. 1980. The revolution of the aged. *Staffrider* 3.4: 2.

———. 1983. *Fools and Other Stories*. Johannesburg: Ravan Press.

———. 1994 [1991]. *South African Literature and Culture: Rediscovery of the Ordinary*. Manchester and New York: Manchester University Press.

Nelson, C. and L. Grossberg (eds.). 1988. *Marxism and the Interpretation of Culture*. London: Routledge.

Ngwenya, T. 1998. B.W. Vilakazi: The poet as inspired prophet. *Alternation* 5.2: 127–46.

Nkosi, L. 1979a [1967]. Fiction by black South Africans: Richard Rive, Bloke Modisane, Ezekiel Mphahlele, Alex La Guma. In *Introduction to African Literature: An Anthology of Critical Writing*, ed. U. Beier, 221–27. London: Harlow.

———. 1979b. *Mating Birds*. Johannesburg: Ravan Press.

———. 1981. *Tasks and Masks: Themes and Styles of African Literature*. Harlow: Longman.

———. 1983. *Home and Exile*. London: Longman.

———. 1998. Postmodernism and black writing in South Africa. In *Writing South Africa: Literature, Apartheid and Democracy 1948–1995*, eds. D. Attridge and R. Jolly, 75–90. Cambridge: Cambridge University Press.

Noyes, J. 2000. The place of the human. In *Senses of Culture: South African Culture Studies*, eds. S. Nuttall and C-A. Michael, 49–60. Cape Town: Oxford University Press.

Ntuli, D.B.Z. 1984. *The Poetry of B.W. Vilakazi*. Pretoria: Van Schaik.

Ntuli, D.B. and C.F. Swanepoel. 1993. *Southern African Literature in African Languages: A Concise Historical Perspective*. Pretoria: Acacia Books.

Nuttall, S. and C-A. Michael. 2000. *Senses of Culture: South African Culture Studies*. Cape Town: Oxford University Press.

Nyembezi, C.L.S. 1973. Benedict Wallet Vilakazi: A biographical note. In *Zulu Horizons*, B.W. Vilakazi, trans. F. Friedman from the literal translations of D. McK. Malcolm and J. Mandlenkosi Sikakana (*Inkondlo kaZulu* and *Amal'ezulu*), xvii–xx. Johannesburg: Wits University Press.

O'Brien, A. 2001. *Against Normalization: Writing radical democracy in South Africa*. Durham, NC: Duke University Press.

Okpaku, J. (ed.). 1973. *New African Literature and the Arts: Vol. 3*. New York: Third World.

Okpewho, I. 1979. *The Epic in Africa: Towards a Poetics of the Oral Performance*. New York: Columbia University Press.

Ortiz, F. 1995. *Cuban Counterpoint: Tobacco and Sugar*. Trans. H. de Onís. Durham and London: Duke University Press.

Osborne, P. 1992. Modernity is a qualitative, not chronological, category: Notes on the dialectics of differential historical time. In *Postmodernism and the Re-reading of Modernity*, eds. F. Barker, P. Hulme, and M. Iversen, 32–33. New York and Manchester: Manchester University Press.

Parker, P. 1985. Introduction. In *Lyric Poetry: Beyond New Criticism*, eds. C. Hošek and P. Parker, 11–28. Ithaca and London: Cornell University Press.

Parry, B. 1994. Some provisional speculations on the critique of 'Resistance' literature. In *Altered State? Writing and South Africa*, eds. E. Boehmer, L. Chrisman, and K. Parker, 11–24. Sydney: Dangaroo Press.

———. 2004. *Postcolonial Studies: A Materialist Critique*. London: Routledge.

Pechey, G. 1994. 'Cultural struggle' and the narratives of South African freedom. In *Altered State? Writing and South Africa*, eds. E. Boehmer, L. Chrisman, and K. Parker, 25–35. Sydney: Dangaroo Press.

———. 1998. Post-apartheid reason: Critical theory in South Africa. *Current Writing* 10.2: 3–18.

Peires, J. 1979. The Lovedale Press: Literature for the Bantu revisited. *History in Africa* 6: 155–75.

———. 1981. *The House of Phalo: A History of the Xhosa People in the Days of Their Independence.* Johannesburg: Ravan Press.

———. 1989. *The Dead Will Arise: Nongqawuse and the Great Xhosa Cattle-Killing Movement of 1856–7.* Johannesburg: Ravan Press.

Peterson, B. 1997. Monarchs, missionaries and African intellectuals: Redemption and revolution in South African theatre, 1900–1940. Ph.D. diss., University of the Witwatersrand, Johannesburg.

Plaatje, S.I. 1984 [1930]. *Mhudi: An Epic of South African Native Life a Hundred Years Ago.* London: Heinemann.

———. 1991 [1916]. *Native Life in South Africa.* Athens: Ohio University Press.

Polley, J.A. 1976. Foreword. In *Poetry South Africa: Selected Papers from Poetry '74*, eds. P. Wilhelm and J.A. Polley, 7–8. Johannesburg: AD Donker.

Pratt, M.L. 1992. *Imperial Eyes: Travel Writing and Transculturation.* London: Routledge.

Reyburn, H.A. 1932. Prologue. *The Critic* 1.1 (September): 1.

Richards, I.A. 1944 [1924]. *Principles of Literary Criticism.* London: Kegan Paul, Trench, Trubner & Co.

Ricoeur, P. 1984. *Time and Narrative* Vol. 1. Translated by K. McLaughlin and D. Pellauer. Chicago: University of Chicago Press.

Royston, R. 1973. *Black Poets in South Africa.* London: Heinemann.

Sachs, A. 1998. Preparing ourselves for freedom. In *Writing South Africa: Literature, Apartheid, and Democracy 1948–1995*, eds. D. Attridge and R. Jolly, 239–48. Cambridge: Cambridge University Press.

Said, E. 1979 [1978]. *Orientalism.* New York: Vintage Books.

———. 1993. *Culture and Imperialism.* London: Chatto and Windus.

Sanders, M. 2002. *Complicities: The Intellectual and Apartheid.* Pietermaritzburg: University of Natal Press.

Scheub, H. 1985. Zulu oral tradition and literature. In *Literatures in African Languages: Theoretical Issues and Sample Surveys*, eds. B.W. Andrzejewski, S. Pilaszewicz and W. Tyloch, 493–528. Warsaw: Cambridge University Press and Wiedza Powszechna State Publishing House.

Schlebusch, A.L. 1974. *Fourth Interim Report of the Commission of Inquiry into Certain Organizations.* Pretoria: The Government Printer.

Sepamla, S. 1983. *Children of the Earth.* Johannesburg: AD Donker.

———. 1984. *Selected Poems.* Ed. M.V. Mzamane. Johannesburg: AD Donker.

Serote, M.W. 1972. *Yakhal'inkomo.* Johannesburg: Renoster/Bateleur Press.

———. 1974. *Tsetlo.* Johannesburg: AD Donker.

———. 1977. Flight from Johannesburg: Feeling the waters. *First World: An International Journal of Black Thought* 1.2 (March/April): 22–25.

———. 1978. *Behold Mama, Flowers.* Johannesburg: AD Donker.

———. 1982. *Selected Poems.* Ed. M.V. Mzamane. Johannesburg: AD Donker.

———. 1987. *A Tough Tale.* London: Kliptown Books.

———. 1992. *Third World Express.* Cape Town: David Philip.

———. 1997. *Freedom Lament and Song.* Cape Town: Mayibuye Books and David Philip.

Shepherd, R.H.W. 1940. *Lovedale, South Africa: The Story of a Century, 1841–1941.* Alice: Lovedale Press.

Slemon, S. 1995. Unsettling the empire: Resistance theory for the second world. In *The Postcolonial Studies Reader*, eds. B. Ashcroft, G. Griffiths, and H. Tiffin, 104–10. London: Routledge.

Soga, T. 1865a. Defensor, reply to Chalmers. *King Williamstown Gazette and Kaffrarian Banner* 11 May.

———. 1865b. Letter to J.F. Cumming, 21 May. South African Library, Cumming Collection, MS box 1395 (138).

———. 1983. *The Journal and Selected Writings of the Reverend Tiyo Soga.* Ed. D. Williams. Cape Town: Balkema.

Sole, K. 1993. Authority, authenticity and the black writer. Ph.D. diss., University of the Witwatersrand, Johannesburg.

———. 1986. Oral performance and social struggle in contemporary black South African literature. In *From South Africa: New Writing, Photographs and Art*, eds. D. Bunn and J. Taylor, 254–71. Special issue of *TriQuarterly 69.* Chicago: Chicago University Press.

———. 1991. 'This Time Set Again': The temporal and political conceptions of Serote's *To Every Birth its Blood. English in Africa* 18.1: 51–80.

———. 1993. The role of the writer in a time of transition. *Staffrider* 11.1–4: 90–98.

Spivak, G.C. 1988. Can the subaltern speak? In *Marxism and the Interpretation of Culture*, eds. C. Nelson and L. Grossberg, 271–313. Urbana and Chicago: University of Illinois Press.

State Archives. Ezekiel Mphahlele, Ref. 1144/301.

Switzer, L. 1993. *Power and Resistance in an African Society: The Ciskei Xhosa and the Making of South Africa.* Pietermaritzburg: University of Natal Press.

Taylor, C. 1989. *Sources of the Self: The Making of the Modern Identity.* Cambridge: Cambridge University Press.

———. 1999. Two theories of modernity. *Public Culture* 11.1: 153–74.

Taylor, J.D. 1935. 'Inkondlo kaZulu' – An appreciation. *Bantu Studies* 9: 163–68.

Thoahlane, T. (ed.). 1975. *Black Renaissance: Papers from the Black Renaissance Convention.* Johannesburg: Ravan Press.

Thuynsma, P. 1989a. Introduction. In *Es'kia Mphahlele: A Bibliography*, eds. C. Woeber and J. Read, 1–3. NELM Bibliographic Series No. 2. Grahamstown: National English Literary Museum.

———. 1989b. *Footprints Along the Way: A Tribute to Es'kia Mphahlele*. Braamfontein: Skotaville; Yeoville: Justified Press.

Touraine, A. 1995. *Critique of Modernity*. Translated by D. Macey. Oxford: Blackwell.

Vail, L. and L. White. 1991. *Power and the Praise Poem*. Charlottesville: University of Virginia Press.

Van der Merwe, H. and D. Welsh (eds.). 1972. *Student Perspectives on South Africa*. Cape Town: David Philip.

Vaughan, M. 1990. Storytelling and politics in fiction. In *Rendering Things Visible: Essays on South African Literary Culture*, ed. M. Trump, 186–204. Johannesburg: Ravan Press.

Vilakazi, B.W. 1939. African drama and poetry. *The South African Outlook* 1 July: 166–67.

———. 1942. Some aspects of Zulu literature. *African Studies* 1: 270–74.

———. 1946. The oral and written literature in Nguni. Ph.D. diss., University of the Witwatersrand, Johannesburg.

———. 1973. *Zulu Horizons*. Translated by F. Friedman from the literal translations of D. McK. Malcolm and J. Mandlenkosi Sikakana (*Inkondlo kaZulu* and *Amal'ezulu)*. Johannesburg: Wits University Press.

———. 1980 [1945]. *Amal'ezulu*. Bantu Treasury Series No. 8. Johannesburg: Wits University Press.

———. 1982 [1935]. *Inkondlo kaZulu*. Bantu Treasury Series No. 1. Johannesburg: Wits University Press.

———. 1993. The conception and development of poetry in Zulu. In *Foundations of Southern African Oral Literature*, ed. R.H. Kaschula, 55–84. Johannesburg: Wits University Press. Reprinted from *Bantu Studies* 12 (1938): 105–34.

Visser, N. 1987. Fictional projects and the irruptions of history: Mongane Serote's *To Every Birth its Blood*. *English Academy Review* 4 (January): 67–76.

Voss, T. 1994. Sol Plaatje, the eighteenth century, and South African cultural memory. *English in Africa* 21.1 and 2 (July): 59–75.

Watt, I. 1957. *The Rise of the Novel: Studies in Defoe, Richardson and Fielding*. Harmondsworth: Penguin.

White, L. and T. Couzens (eds.). 1984. *Literature and Society in South Africa*. Cape Town: Maskew Miller Longman.

Wilhelm, P. and J.A. Polley. 1976. *Poetry South Africa: Selected Papers from Poetry '74*. Johannesburg: AD Donker.

Willan, B. 1984. *Sol Plaatje: South African Nationalist, 1876–1932*. Berkeley: University of California Press.

Williams, D. 1978. *Umfundisi: A Biography of Tiyo Soga, 1829–1871*. Alice: Lovedale Press.

———. 1983. Introduction A: Tiyo Soga (1829–1871). In *The Journal and Selected Writings of the Reverend Tiyo Soga*, ed. D. Williams, 1–8. Cape Town: Balkema.

Williams, P. and L. Chrisman (eds.). 1994. *Colonial Discourse and Post-Colonial Theory: A Reader*. New York: Harvester and Wheatsheaf.

Williams, R. 1963 [1958]. *Culture and Society: 1780–1950*. Harmondsworth: Penguin.

Woeber, C. and J. Read (eds.). 1989. *Es'kia Mphahlele: A Bibliography*. NELM Bibliographic Series No. 2. Grahamstown: National English Literary Museum.

Young, R. 2001. *Postcolonialism: An Historical Introduction*. Oxford: Blackwell.

Archival sources

African Studies Library, University of Cambridge
African Studies Library, University of Cape Town
Centre for African Literary Studies, University of KwaZulu-Natal
Cory Library, Rhodes University
Herskovits Library, Northwestern University
Howard Pim Library, University of Fort Hare
Killie Campbell Africana Library, University of KwaZulu-Natal
Natal Archives, Pietermaritzburg
Natal Society Library, Special Collections
National English Literary Museum, Grahamstown
State Archives, Pretoria
William Cullen Library and University Archives, University of the Witwatersrand

Index